Picking u Practical Guide for Surviving Economic Crashes, Internal Unrest and Military Suppression

By: Sorcha Faal
and
David Booth

First Printing: 2005

Printed in the United States of America

ISBN: 0-9753228-3-3

Long Trail Acres Publishing, LLC
848 N. Rainbow Blvd. #2098
Las Vegas, NV 89107

Table of Contents

Forward:

"You can no more win a war than you can win an earthquake."
Jeannette Rankin

Of all the definitions of war I have ever read, this is the best one that in my opinion, accurately describes what the effects of war are like to the average person.

Armies and Nations win and lose wars, people suffer through them, and have been doing so for thousands of years.

But war, like an earthquake, can be prepared for ahead of time, and that is why I have written this book, your concern about war affecting you and your loved ones is why you are reading it.

War is never the most pleasant of subjects to talk about, but it still remains a very real fact of life. Today we can see that the terrible specter of war is raising its head once more to confront the world. The lessons of past generations are never learned, so once again these horrors are being prepared to be inflicted upon an unsuspecting world.

As in the past, those who will be the most affected are those least prepared for it. The previous generations who have gone through the wars of the last century are seeing their numbers, and influence, slipping into the twilight of life. Their warnings no longer heeded, their advice no longer listened to.

3

Not to speak for them, but rather about them is the purpose of this book. For in their many stories you may personally find the guidance and wisdom to plan, not only for yourself but your family too, on what your course of action will be during this time of war.

If you live in an area that is prone to earthquakes you would diligently prepare yourself and your family to survive an earthquake should it occur. In a time of war, and especially with living in a country that is a party to an ongoing war, one should likewise diligently prepare.

The most important ally you'll have in the midst of the chaos of war is going to be your God and your Faith. This should always be your first preparation, your first priority. Do not wait until the war has approached your doorstep to do this, do it now.

This is the soundest advice I, or anyone else, can give you. You have no idea how important your faith is going to become in the coming years, do not neglect this advice.

I do not want you to enjoy this book either; I want you to think about every word and to contemplate within your souls everything that is written here. This is not a book meant for enjoyment, but rather is intended as a warning and for your instruction.

I wish you all the best,

Sorcha Faal
St. Petersburg, Russia
February, 2005

4

"Never, never, never believe any war will be smooth and easy, or that anyone who embarks on the strange voyage can measure the tides and hurricanes he will encounter. The statesman who yields to war fever must realize that once the signal is given, he is no longer the master of policy but the slave of unforeseeable and uncontrollable events."
Sir Winston Churchill

Introduction

The purpose of this book is intended to be a primer for those who have found themselves contemplating their nation being at war, and what their actions should be once this war appears across the borders of their homeland.

To the uninitiated and uninformed, and who are always the vast majority of a country's population, there is never seen in their mind's eye a reason for preparation.

After all, they have been told repeatedly by their leaders that their homeland is safe, the enemies to the homeland are outside of their borders and that no contemplation should even be considered that the war will be lost.

To speak in public, or amongst friends, even in church, speculation that the war could be upon your doorstep is likened to treason and unpatriotic actions by those who are unwilling to face the true reality of what war is.

And this reality of war has shown repeatedly throughout history that it is not a respecter of rules, patriotic feelings, national pride and least of all borders.

5

If your country is at war, your life will be changed, your country will be attacked and the possibility of your losing the war is very real.

History is littered with countless examples of those countries whose citizens failed to heed the knowledge of war. Hundreds of millions of lives now buried beneath the earth, on foreign battlefields, or just simply evaporated into dust and smoke, in the past century alone are testimonies to the arrogance of thought from those who believed in their righteous wars and their leaders' lies of protection.

Your reading of these very words shows that you are not like them and this book has been written for you.

But, this book is only the first step of what is a much longer journey that you're embarking upon. You will find within these pages the beginning of your serious thoughts towards war, its effects on yourself, your family and your possible ways of avoiding war's destructiveness.

By the time you have finished reading this book you will hopefully begin acquiring the much larger extensive information you'll need to know in order to survive. More importantly you'll have acquired within yourself the mindset, a new way of thinking, which will aid you in your further preparations.

War and its aftermath are survivable, even through the worst of them this has always been so, but they are only survived by those who have prepared themselves well to endure the many hardships it takes to do so.

So, Prepare Well.

6

*"You can't say that civilization don't advance,
however, for in every war they kill you in a new way."*
Will Rogers

Chapter 1: What Are the Signs

Throughout history great empires and nations have come and gone. From the Greek and Roman Empires of millenniums ago, to the great British, Ottoman and Austria-Hungarian Empires of the last century, history has shown us repeatedly that Empires do not last.

Not only do they not last, they end in violent upheavals and wars.

Yet as many times as human beings attempt to create new Empires they have yet to learn the harsh lessons of the past.

Today the world faces, once again, the spectacle of the falling and rising of Empires. Though their names are different now (United States Empire, Islamic Empire, Chinese Empire, and European Empire) the same harsh lessons learned by countless others throughout the centuries still apply.

We only have to go back less than a hundred years and see what the world was like in the years prior to, and during, the great wars of the 20th Century, and after which the entire structure of the world was changed.

Immediately prior the outbreak of World War I an American Military Colonel named E.M House, who was the chief advisor to President Woodrow Wilson, was sent to evaluate the European situation. Here is a part of the report he sent back to the United States:

"The situation is extraordinary. It is militarism run stark mad. Unless someone acting for you can bring about a different understanding, there is some day to be an awful cataclysm. No one in Europe can do it. There is too much hatred, too many jealousies. Whenever England consents, France and Russia will close in on Germany and Austria. England does not want Germany wholly crushed, for she would then have to reckon alone with her ancient enemy, Russia; but if Germany insists upon an ever increasing navy, then England will have no choice. The best chance for peace is an understanding between England and Germany in regard to naval armaments and yet there is some disadvantage to us by these two getting too close." [1]

The causes of World War II are no less militaristic, and follow me here as I do a comparison between pre-war Germany and the present day United States to see if they match up.

Anti-Communism/Islamic (outside threat and a common enemy); many of the forces which Hitler/Bush were able to bring under control in Germany/United States were actually opposed to Nazi/Republican rule, but accepted the rule, if only as temporary, for the greater goal of eliminating the spreading Bolshevism in Russia/Islamic Terror Networks. Hitler/Bush often expounded upon these ridiculous fears in his propaganda, promising an end to Bolshevism/Islamic militancy and the threat of communist/Islamic takeover.

Anti-Semitism/Islamic Hatred (outside threat and a common enemy); Anti-Semitist/Islamic policies of Nazi

Germany/United States were closely tied to Anti-Communism/Islamic Fears and the "Red Scare/Terror Scare" and the Jews/Muslims were blamed for Bolshevism/Terror and its spread. Anti-Semitism/Islamic Hatred, too, was magnified in German/United States Homelands by the use of subtle and not-so-subtle propaganda.

Adolph Hitler's/Bush's charisma (inspiration); when studying the causes of World War II/World War III, perhaps the most baffling aspect of the Nazi/Republican rise to power involves the leader himself. Hitler/Bush seemed to have a hold over his people by use of a steady and unwavering charisma. Even when the war was inevitably to be lost and the people of Germany/United States were disgusted with the entire war, many blamed the other Nazi/United States leaders, never removing Hitler/Bush from his pedestal. Furthermore, Hitler/Bush had a strongly developed understanding of the desires of the German/American people, and was always able to aim his promises in exactly the right directions.

The Propaganda used by the Nazi/Republican party (Mob mentality); again, Hitler/Bush and Goebbels/Cheney made explicit use of the mob mentality to rally the masses behind the Nazi/American flag. Hitler/Bush stated many times that the only way to use propaganda effectively was to aim it at the stupidity of the masses rather than the intellectuals. He used short slogans repeated again and again to drive ideas home into the minds of his followers. More importantly, however, Hitler/Bush staged massive Nazi/Republican support rallies such as the Nuremburg Rallies/Election Rallies in November each year, in which the people could look around and see how many "fellow countrymen" were upholding the ideals of the Nazis/Americans. This mass support Hitler/Bush used to demonstrate the power of the Nazi/American government, and to encourage continued support for the Third/Forth Reich.

The Lost Generation from World War I/Vietnam (Mob mentality); World War I/Vietnam had produced an entire generation of youth who had gone into a war of an extent which none could have guessed. This youth had no training in peace time careers, and, when the first Great/Vietnam War ended in 1918/1975, knew nothing but the art of war. Thus, the "Lost Generation" of German/American youth, displaced by its own society, played a major role in supporting Nazi/Republican rule and the onset of WWII/WWIII, as well as many of the brutalities which occurred under Nazi/American occupation of other countries.

The Great Depression/Stock Market Collapse (Inspiration -- in rebuilding Germany/America to its former glory); Hitler/Bush was able to add to the sense of pride which many felt at the acknowledgement of their "pure and superior Aryan/American blood" by claiming responsibility for the growing economy after the Great Depression/Stock Market Collapse. The inspiration of a new German/American nation rebuilding itself to its former glory, in addition to the security of finally having jobs and food, tempted many possible resistors of Nazi/American rule to ignore the regime.

Now with these two examples one can reasonably argue that the signs of war include the rise of both militarism and fascism, so let's take a look at what exactly they both are.

Fascism

The dictionary definition of fascism is: A system of government marked by centralization of authority under a dictator, stringent socioeconomic controls, suppression of the opposition through terror and censorship, and typically a policy of belligerent nationalism and racism; A political philosophy or movement based on or advocating such a system of government; Oppressive, dictatorial control.

From outside of the United States we can certainly see these types of forces at work from within that country, but let's look at how some of these Americans view this:

Laura Dawn Lewis is an American author and business woman who has worked for the Washington Post, Los Angeles Business Journal and CBS Radio Group. In an article of hers titled "What is Fascism?" she states:

"This may surprise most educated people. One of the more common government strategies today, especially in developing regions is fascism. Fascism is commonly confused with Nazism.

Nazism is a political party platform that embraces a combination of a military dictatorship, socialism and fascism. It is not a government structure. Fascism is a government structure.

The most notable characteristic of a fascist country is the separation and persecution or denial of equality to a specific segment of the population based upon superficial qualities or belief systems.

Simply stated, a fascist government always has one class of citizens that is considered superior (good) to another (bad) based upon race, creed or origin. It is possible to be both a republic and a fascist state. The preferred class lives in a republic while the oppressed class lives in a fascist state.

More than a class system, fascism specifically targets, dehumanizes and aims to destroy those it deems undesirable.

Until the Civil Rights act of 1964, many parts of the US were Republic for whites and could be considered fascist for non-Caucasian residents. Fascism promotes legal segregation in housing, national resource allocation and employment.

It provides legal justification for persecuting a specific segment of the population and operates behind a two tiered legal system. These two tiers can be overt as it was within Nazi Germany where Jews, Homosexuals, Catholics, Communists, Clergy and the handicap were held to one set of rules and courts, while the rest of Germany enjoyed different laws.

Or it can be implied and held up by consensual conspiracy, (people know it is wrong but do nothing to stop it or change it. Through lack of action, they give consent), as it was in the deep South for African Americans and others of color. In Fascism, one segment of society is always considered less desirable, sub-human or second class.

(Note: no single government is pure anything. Most have elements of several structures with one dominant structure). Below is the political definition and general characteristics of a fascist country.

General Characteristics of a Fascist Country:

1. Fascism is commonly defined as an open terror-based dictatorship which is:

Reactionary: makes policy based upon current circumstances rather than creating policies to prevent problems; piles lies and misnomers on top of more lies until the truth becomes indistinguishable, revised or forgotten.

Chauvinistic: Two or more tiered legal systems, varying rights based upon superficial characteristics such as race, creed and origin.

Imperialist elements of finance capital: Extending a nation's authority by territorial acquisition or by the establishment of economic and political domination of one state over its allies.

Though a dictatorship is the most common association with fascism, a democracy or republic can also be fascist when it strays away from its Tenets of sovereignty.

In the 20th Century, many Fascist countries started out as republics. Through the use of fear, societies gave up their rights under the guise of security. Ultimately these republics morphed into Fascist states.

2. Fascism is an extreme measure taken by the middle classes to forestall lower-working class revolution; it thrives on the weakness of the middle classes. It

accomplishes this by embracing the middle-class' love of the status-quo, its complacency and its fears of:

Generating a united struggle within the working class

Revolution

Losing its own power and position within society

In a more simplistic term the people currently in control fear that if they allow equal rights and equal consideration to those being oppressed, they will become oppressed and lose everything.

Generally those in power are of a smaller segment of society, but they hold the wealth and control of key systems like manufacturing, law, finance and government position, (i.e. the slave owners in the south prior to the civil war) and the oppressed vastly outnumber them, (the slaves during the same period).

In reality it is the oppressors' fear of retribution by the oppressed that perpetuates fascism; for justification they dehumanize, demonize, strip them of rights, add new laws, restrict movement and attempt to control them by whatever means possible to prevent an uprising.

It is very common in a fascist system to have the oppressed referred to as sub-human, animals, terrorists, savages, barbarians, vermin or any other term designed to create justification for the acts of terror and fascism perpetrated on the oppressed. Via dehumanization society can then accept that the oppressed are incapable of thinking or acting in a peaceful manner or taking

14

care of themselves, and thus society is exonerated from culpability in their own minds.

Propaganda, not persuasion, logic or law, is the tool of fascism, though at times very difficult to spot. It specifically rides the fact that negative behavior is innate, (born with) rather than a logical behavior in response to oppression. Propaganda also empowers the oppressors with elitism racially, socially, intellectually and/or spiritually.

The 7 conditions (Warning signs) that Foster & Fuel Fascism are:

Instability of capitalist relationships or markets
The existence of considerable declassed social elements

The stripping of rights and wealth focused upon a specific segment of the population, specifically the middle class and intellectuals within urban areas as this the group with the means, intelligence and ability to stop fascism if given the opportunity.

Discontent among the rural lower middle class (clerks, secretaries, white collar labor). Consistent discontent among the general middle and lower middle classes against the oppressing upper-classes (haves vs. have-nots).

Hate: Pronounced, perpetuated and accepted public disdain of a specific group defined by race, origin, theology or association.

Greed: The motivator of fascism, which is generally associated with land, space or scarce resources in the possession of those being oppressed.

Organized Propaganda: The creation of social mythology that venerates (creates saints of) one element of society while concurrently vilifying (dehumanizing) another element of the population through misinformation, misdirection and the obscuring of factual matter through removal, destruction or social humiliation, (name-calling, false accusations, belittling and threats).

The squelching of public debate not agreeing with the popular agenda via slander, libel, threats, theft, destruction, historical revisionism and social humiliation. Journalists in particular are terrorized if they attempt to publish stories contrary to the agenda.

Fascism dovetails business & government sectors into a single economic unit, while concurrently increasing in-fighting and distrust between the units fostering advancement towards war.

Fascism promotes chauvinist demagogy, (appealing to the prejudices and emotions of the populace) by fostering selective persecution and accepted public vilification of the target group. It then promotes this a "patriotic", "supportive" or "the party line" and disagreement with such as "anti-government", "anti-faith" or "anti-nation".

Fascism creates confusion through "facts". It relies on junk science, revisionism, the elimination of cultural records/treasures and obfuscations to create its case and gain acceptance. Fascism can also combine Marxist critiques of capitalism or faith based critics of the same to re-define middle class perceptions of democracy and to force its issues, confuse logic and create majority consensus between targeted groups. This is also

16

referred to as creating a state of Cognitive Dissonance, the mental state most human beings are easily manipulated within.

Both middle and upper-middle-class dictated democracy and fascism are class dictatorships that use organized violence (verbal or physical) to maintain the class rule of the oppressors over the oppressed.

The difference between the two is demonstrated by the policies towards non-lower-working class classes. Fascism attains power through the substitution of one state's form of class domination with another form, generally a middle class based republic segues into an open terrorist dictatorship, run by a few elite." [2]

The American political scientist Dr. Lawrence Britt has studied the fascist regimes Hitler (Germany), Mussolini (Italy), Franco (Spain), Suharto (Indonesia) and several Latin American regimes during his lifetime.

In perhaps one of the most clear warning signs of the impending Nazification of the United States Dr. Britt had prepared for his fellow countrymen a point by point critique showing how dangerous the times had become in American. It is worth your time in reading the words he wrote in his famous article;

"The 14 Defining Characteristics of Fascism"

1. Powerful and Continuing Nationalism -
Fascist regimes tend to make constant use of patriotic mottos, slogans, symbols, songs, and other paraphernalia. Flags are seen everywhere, as are flag symbols on clothing and in public displays.

2. Disdain for the Recognition of Human Rights - Because of fear of enemies and the need for security, the people in fascist regimes are persuaded that human rights can be ignored in certain cases because of "need." The people tend to look the other way or even approve of torture, summary executions, assassinations, long incarcerations of prisoners, etc.

3. Identification of Enemies/Scapegoats as a Unifying Cause - The people are rallied into a unifying patriotic frenzy over the need to eliminate a perceived common threat or foe: racial, ethnic or religious minorities; liberals; communists; socialists, terrorists, etc.

4. Supremacy of the Military - Even when there are widespread domestic problems, the military is given a disproportionate amount of government funding, and the domestic agenda is neglected. Soldiers and military service are glamorized.

5. Rampant Sexism - The governments of fascist nations tend to be almost exclusively male-dominated. Under fascist regimes, traditional gender roles are made more rigid. Divorce, abortion and homosexuality are suppressed and the state is represented as the ultimate guardian of the family institution.

6. Controlled Mass Media - Sometimes to media is directly controlled by the government, but in other cases, the media is indirectly controlled by government regulation, or sympathetic media spokespeople and executives. Censorship, especially in war time, is very common.

7. Obsession with National Security - Fear is used as a motivational tool by the government over the masses.

8. Religion and Government are Intertwined - Governments in fascist nations tend to use the most common religion in the nation as a tool to manipulate public opinion. Religious rhetoric and terminology is common from government leaders, even when the major tenets of the religion are diametrically opposed to the government's policies or actions.

9. Corporate Power is Protected - The industrial and business aristocracy of a fascist nation often are the ones who put the government leaders into power, creating a mutually beneficial business/government relationship and power elite.

10. Labor Power is Suppressed - Because the organizing power of labor is the only real threat to a fascist government, labor unions are either eliminated entirely, or are severely suppressed.

11. Disdain for Intellectuals and the Arts - Fascist nations tend to promote and tolerate open hostility to higher education, and academia. It is not uncommon for professors and other academics to be censored or even arrested. Free expression in the arts and letters is openly attacked.

12. Obsession with Crime and Punishment - Under fascist regimes, the police are given almost limitless power to enforce laws. The people are often willing to overlook police abuses and even forego civil liberties in the name of patriotism. There is often a national police force with virtually unlimited power in fascist nations.

13. Rampant Cronyism and Corruption - Fascist regimes almost always are governed by groups of friends and associates who appoint each other to government positions and use governmental power and authority to protect their friends from accountability. It is not uncommon in fascist regimes for national resources and even treasures to be appropriated or even outright stolen by government leaders.

14. Fraudulent Elections - Sometimes elections in fascist nations are a complete sham. Other times elections are manipulated by smear campaigns against or even assassination of opposition candidates, use of legislation to control voting numbers or political district boundaries, and manipulation of the media. Fascist nations also typically use their judiciaries to manipulate or control elections.

An interesting note to end this article: As of January 2004, the United States fulfills all fourteen points of fascism and all seven warning signs are present. But we're not alone. Israel also fulfills all fourteen points and all seven warning signs as well. Welcome to the new republic, redefined, revised and spun. It is not too late to reverse this in either country, but it will be soon. The first step is realizing it. The second step is getting involved. As the propaganda slogan disguising our current war goes, "Freedom isn't free." But our war for freedom isn't abroad; it's here at home." [3]

Militarism

The dictionary definition of Militarism is: "Glorification of the ideals of a professional military class; Predominance of the armed forces in the administration or policy of the state; A policy in which military preparedness is of primary importance to a state."

Just by this definition alone there can be no doubt as to the Militarization of the United States and its people. In the world we see today the sun doesn't set upon the Wehrmacht helmeted troops of the United States who are spread among every continent, and most nations, on the face of the earth.

From their smallest towns to their largest cities, the police forces, like their Nazi counterparts of last century, of the United States are but mirror images of their Military Forces. Frequently dressed all in black, combat boots laced high upon their legs, their machine guns in held in public view at all times, and like their Nazi police counterparts they are also proud wearers of the Wehrmacht helmets designed by Germany of Adolph Hitler himself.

Before continuing on to what these Americans are today it's very important to look back in time to see from where they have come from by listening anew to the founding men of their country.

"Before a standing army can rule, the people must be disarmed; as they are in almost every kingdom of Europe. The supreme power in America cannot enforce unjust laws by the sword; because the whole body of the people are armed, and constitute a force superior to any band of regular troops that can be, on any pretence, raised in the United States."

Noah Webster, <u>An Examination into the Leading Principles of the Federal Constitution</u>, 1787

"But the safety of the people of America against dangers from foreign force depends not only on their forbearing to give just causes of war to other nations, but also on their placing and continuing themselves in such a situation as not to invite hostility or insult; for it need not be observed that there are pretended as well as just causes of war."

John Jay, <u>Federalist No. 4</u>

"Guard with jealous attention the public liberty. Suspect every one who approaches that jewel. Unfortunately, nothing will preserve it but downright force. Whenever you give up that force, you are inevitably ruined."

Patrick Henry, speech in the Virginia Ratifying Convention, June 5, 1778

Now how far these Americans have come from these original ideals espoused by their founders, we can read in the words of the American author John Roberts in his article titled;

<u>United States Militarism</u>

"Unlike British, American militarism only dates back a couple of centuries. But as in other revolutionary regimes, there was, from its inception, an assumption that violence would be successful in the birth of the state.

Since that was allied to the practical and continuing subjection of a slave population, the hierarchical nature of US society was emphasized from the outset and the conquest of the indigenous native population over the next century merely confirmed the importance of the military in controlling and dominating the formative years of the republic.

The lesson of the civil war was that the republic could be very militaristic. After all, it achieved the first modern war, with railway transport as the key to final success and casualties on a truly industrial scale.

Even if successful generals might take care to retire, as Washington had done in an example praised and highly regarded, the military traditions were reborn and in the army and navy were treasured and eulogized.

The republic kept an honored place for its office class, already an elite that would wax through successive campaigns. By the time that overseas imperial expansion began in 1898 this was already clear.

However, the dynamic of democracy during years of peace was adequate to reduce the military to a subordinate position for the first two centuries.

Not until the Second World War did the tendency to rely upon military models and heroes as a guide to political choice become fully significant. The election of a pacific general - Eisenhower - as president was a sign of the changing times but the dismissal of another commanding general - MacArthur - by a civilian president had already quelled fears of a militaristic take-over.
And of course, the popular self-deception that imperialism was something for other nations and could only be abhorred by Americans, permitted the military to bask in democratic approval as being other than militaristic.

Bur the pattern of economic and military domination was laid down too clear to ignore or avoid. By 1951 the US had built up a nuclear weapon stock capable of destroying all civilization several times over and with a hundred military bases in dozens of countries, the influence of the military grew year by year.

The military-industrial-scientific-bureaucratic complex became steadily more important and the role of democratic politicians was correspondingly reduced and corrupted.

This occurred inexorably and was commented upon, but since its deep-rooted causes were being fed continuously by the expansion of American commerce and industry nothing could seriously challenge it.

The changes went hand in hand with the shift in social attitudes, from a democratic spirit that had been kept alive by the individualism of small communities and social groups to an acceptance of large-scale and hierarchical business and politics.

The susceptibility of the American public to the appeal of wealth and power became steadily more apparent. The old-style small-town model was replaced by the propaganda of giant corporations. Vast urban sprawls ensured also millionaire leaders (soon to be billionaires), chosen from a ruling class that either required great wealth to get on the ladder to the top, or who could enrich themselves on the way.

This changed pattern fitted much better with a hierarchical society that suited militaristic attitudes.

At the same time, the growing proportion of public wealth devoted to the military also ensured that the armaments industry, wrapped up with the nuclear and airplane corporations would become increasingly important.

The influence and overwhelming power of these groups ensured that they would play a greater and greater part in political life, perhaps culminating in the corrupt presidential election of 2000, when the oil industry and its Republican allies effected a take-over which led directly to a war both entered into mendaciously and illegal with a delusory "war on terrorism" that will be an excuse and a struggle that can last for decades.

Huey Long was reported as saying that fascism could come in the United States, but it 'will have to be called anti-Fascism' and the current militarism has be disguised as a drive to protect freedom, which is precisely what the present administration is about with its Patriot and other Acts.

The assault on Iraq to take over its oil-fields, slenderly disguised as an attack on the dictator who was a favored purchaser of American equipment until he failed to observe the entire US requirement, may be in trouble, but it is part of the American corporations' drive to take over more of the world.

That will require an intensification of the militarization of American society. The future of American democracy will be in as much peril as was the Iraqi dictator." [4]

But these are not warnings anymore about the likelihood of Fascism and Militarization, because they

25

are both now parts of the United States. History has also taught this hard lesson well, Fascism and Militarism are built only for war, and for no other reason.

And just by these two reasons alone, and the evidence for them, is the sign that citizens are given that war will soon be at their very doorstep.

You need no other signs than these to begin your preparations.

"What difference does it make to the dead, the orphans and the homeless, whether the mad destruction is wrought under the name of totalitarianism or the holy name of liberty or democracy?"
Mahatma Gandhi

Chapter 2: When to Leave

A decision to leave your homeland, the land of your birth, the land of your family, the land of your people and history, is perhaps one of the hardest decisions you will ever have to make in your life.

You can find comfort though, in knowing that you are not alone in the emotions you will go through as you contemplate this course of action.

Your decision on whether or not to leave should mostly, and firstly, be based upon you and your family's personal safety. The generally accepted rule throughout history has been to leave before an invasion and before your escape routes are cut off.

This isn't to say that you still can't escape under those circumstances, only that it is much easier for you if you do this ahead of those events.

This also applies to those circumstances where a totalitarian government is about to close its borders and increase the levels of police and military checkpoints prior to a total clampdown on a restless civilian population.

Whichever your particular circumstance may be, the decision to stay or to go, this is the FIRST one you must make. From that decision comes everything else, your planning, courses of action, your survival plans, everything!

In present day Iraq there is a young wife and mother named Rose who has recently gone through a similar circumstance and decision making process.

Listen to her words:

"A consequential decision

You might have noticed that I did not write anything valuable for the last couple of weeks. I'm going through a very hard time, it makes me unwilling to write or do anything. Today I decided to write maybe you will make me feel better.

My husband has a work opportunity in Dubai (United Arab Emirates), and the last couple of weeks we had to take the decision whether we should accept it or not. After deep thinking from both of us we decided that he will accept it, and that means we will leave to Dubai. I still can't believe it, I have always dreamed of traveling outside of Iraq but not for a long time, this time I don't know for how long.

My husband said till things in Iraq start to get better. But what if things never start to get better? I tried to put a list of negative and positive things and here they are:

The positive things:

He has a great job that he likes, a good opportunity to take his PhD from there, which I really want him to take.

I will see the world, and I might have the chance to work and put my daughter in a good school, without the fear of being killed or kidnapped for both of us.

If things start to get better in Iraq, we will return back and have good chance to find a good work again. And if things become worse than before, we took the right step from the beginning by having the chance to rebuild our future again.

The Negative things:

I will leave my parents alone, which is something that I don't know how I will handle. I cry every time I imagine myself leaving them alone in these terrible conditions. They have only me for them since my sister lives in Mosul. I blame myself for leaving them but at the same time I have to think about the future of my daughter too. They encourage us to leave, but I know from their deepest heart they wish we will stay. I also will lose all my friends here and of course IRAQ. My eyes are full of tears now.

I will lose all the nice memories in my house, I love my house and I can't take anything with me. We will leave in an airplane. I still can't imagine how I will close the house and move to the unknown.

These are not the only the bad things that bother me. There is another problem. Dubai refuse to give me a Visa because I'm an Iraqi that had never went to Dubai before the war. They will give my husband only because he had gone there several times and he has a work contract in Dubai. So he has to leave alone first and after he will have his residency he will take me as I'm his wife.

This procedure might take too long and we don't know how much it will take. Some said it took about a month and a half some said more some said less. But we don't know anyone who have made his residency after the war. (I meant for Iraqis). So we will take a chance. I don't know how I will stand to stay alone without him.

I depend completely on him in many things in the house, I can't go alone, I can't operate the generator alone, and so many problems we had that he used to take care for me.

I feel so depressed, we have never thought of leaving Iraq before, now we have to, we can't stand living here any more. My husband was so depressed the for the last few months till now, he said he needs to make a change we all need to make a change, even our way of thinking needs to change.

He will leave next month, and I will wait for him here. You will be my only way to relieve myself and be connected with the outside world. And after leaving Iraq I will give you some information about me and my family.

Thank you my friends

Thank you my friends for comforting me and giving me hope again. Your comments and emails calm me a lot. It's the hardest time I had in all my life. I have many things to think about, and my problem is that I think a lot and I want everything to run as scheduled.

This is my main problem, I think a lot, sometimes I hope to be cool for a short period, but this is me. My husband always says, I can't imagine you not thinking of a coming problem in your head.

Today my husband received his visa, and he will leave soon, I was so confused and I had mixed emotions. My mother in law cried as soon as she heard that he will leave soon, I cried with her and my husband tried to calm us.

Till now I can't accept the idea of leaving for a long time, and I can't stand it without my husband, I feel so weak without him, he gives me the power in everything.

About the generator, I can't operate it, because I have to pull a long string very hard and fast and it's too hard for me and I have a problem with my right shoulder because of it.

Anyway you will read many posts from me, when my husband is away, I will not have anything to do at the beginning till he will have his residency and start with my papers which is another problem I think about a lot, what if they do not allow me to enter Dubai?

Today we bought a few books, we have very few choices with books they are either political or religious ones. For me I don't like any of them. But today we found a book shop in a second floor of a building without a show room, but it was great, it contains many good books and they have a catalogue of their books, I wonder how many people know about it? The prices of books are rather high in Iraq, that's why very few people are reading books now.

These books will help me to kill the time when I will sit alone. I'm not going to read them now.

New update

Well, if you want to know my new update, nothing has changed till now, except that I was wrong with my husband's visa, my husband friend told him that his visa had finished so I wrote the past post according to that, then it turned out that there was a mistake and we are still waiting for it till now, nobody knows why it took so long. All we know is that everything might happen with Iraqis, we are so welcomed in all over the world!!!.

Thank you very much to those who offered me books, but I think it is impossible to have a way to receive them from you. For me I like books that make me understand the behavior of people and understand people very much, some family medical books and I also read for Agatha Christy .

The last books I bought I found a very interested book named body language by Allan Peez (I'm not sure about the spelling because the book is translated to Arabic) it teaches you how to understand people from the way of moving and sitting and talking. I also bought a novel named The House On Hope Street by Danielle Steel.

I know nothing about that novel or the writer but it said on the cover that the writer hits No. one in selling its novel according to the New York times.

The problem with our books as I said besides of being either political or religious is that when they translate some books to Arabic they lose most of their interest and they become like a lecture after reading few lines you fall asleep.

For me my best book I had read for several times and unfortunately I lost it somewhere, it belong to my father and it is very old, named how to stop worrying and start living. I used to read this every time I feel worried about something and it really works with me, I had two copies one in English which I lost and the other in Arabic, but as I said the Arabic makes it lose its value. I read it when I'm having exams or being under lot of stress.

As for things in Baghdad and for us, nothing new, I even stopped watching the news now, I don't need more stress than the one I have now.

The journey has started

Probably, when you read this post my husband will be on his way to Dubai, he will leave on Sunday afternoon. Don't ask me how I feel, because I don't know.

I cry a little and then smile because we will start our journey. Yesterday we heard two kidnapping cases and the reason is taking a ransom. Both cases took about $30,000 for each in order to free them. After hearing that I felt happy to leave Iraq. They hit one of them so hard that he was unable to walk or talk.

I'm worried now about the safety of my husband on his way to the airport and the airplane. It's private company and we don't know how good is their airplane.

It's still weird that it cost much less than the trip to Jordan, but this is the only way to Dubai now or going by ship which is another risk. If you go by ship you have to leave to Basra first. The trip in boat takes about 3 days. The plane takes about two hours and a half only. Typical me isn't it? Worried about everything.

I'm still here

My husband finally reached Dubai a couple of days ago. His journey was so long, it took about 12 hours till he finally reached Dubai. He started with his residency papers and he said things are doing fine.

As for me, I feel lonely but I hope I can travel sooner than I thought. As for my daughter she misses her daddy a lot and yesterday she cried in her room asking for her father to come back. He is so close to her even sometimes I think she loves him more than me, but I think this is natural.

My PC refuses to work on the local generator, I don't know why. So I open it only when we have national electricity and usually make a chat with my husband during that limited time. He started his work already. He sent me pictures about the view from his office and some gardens; it looks very nice and very clean.

I think I will visit my parents on Thursday and stay there for a few days, I hate that process but if I don't do that my parents will get upset and think that I don't like to stay in their home. I still did not arrange anything from what I'm going to take or leave here, I want my husband to start with my papers and then start to pack things.

I will be 28 years this month I hope he could mange to come before my Birthday. We have been married for almost seven years and we celebrated my birthday and his only a few times (there are only 21 days between my Birthday and his).

Anyway I have nothing to say since I did not go out the last couple of days or see people. Some of my friends promised to visit me next week.

Quick update

I have not made any post because the land line is not working and hence I cannot get an internet connection at home. I've also spent a few days at my parents' house where there is not computer. So this is only to say that I am still hanging there.

By the way, my husband got his residency and is working on my papers now.

Leaving soon

My husband finished my papers and he came back on Sunday. We shall leave within a couple of weeks after we finish packing our things. I will be busy in the next couple of weeks but I will write you a post when I reach Dubai. I have many things I want you to know about me and family that I decided to talk about when I am out of Iraq.

I also will make a comparison between Iraq and Dubai when I reach there. The last week was a so horrible week for me. We had very heavy rain and it affected almost everything in our lives. The telephone lines of most people I know were damaged including mine.

They fix my line after few days but they made a mistake and gave us another No. and I still have the wrong no..

The second bad damage I had is in our local power transformer it fell from its pillar and blown up. This made the power transformer drag three of the pillars and the result we still don't have elect. for more than 8 days and guess what, till now the only thing the maintenance did is that they came and took the old transformer and left without doing anything. Now we are depending completely on generator.
I am very busy and tired now. I want to leave ASAP because everyone is under stress now. I still feel guilty for leaving my parents and every time I see them I spend the whole day depressed. I never have the chance to leave Iraq and I am afraid of missing my family and friends and getting home sick.

The last time I traveled was when I was 3 years old, of course I don't remember anything from it. I went to Germany and Denmark at that time with my parents. After that I was unable to travel because of the wars we had.

So see you in Dubai. Wish me luck."[5]

It doesn't matter from what country you're from, what language you speak, your religion or your politics either....when it comes to leaving to avoid a war and its consequences the decisions all condense down into those concerns and thoughts of family.

It has always been this way throughout history.

Rose and her husband's decision was based upon their need to sacrifice their homeland, their families and their home for the future of their daughter, and who will hopefully grow up in a place far away from the troubles and agony of war.

It is called the prioritization of both Love and Duty. Which is stronger? Only each and every single individual can answer that question based upon their own unique circumstances, which is not mine, or anyone other's place to make this decision for you.

"It is well that war is so terrible, or we should grow too fond of it."
Robert E. Lee

Chapter 3: Planning to Go

Once your decision has been made, and it's been decided that you are going to leave, the next decision is where are you going to go to?

The first possible choice is to stay within the borders of your homeland, but if living in a potentially unsafe area it would be wise to relocate.

Cities and large urban areas are the worst places to be in during times of war. Aside from their value as military targets by enemy forces they are also likely to have large concentrations of police, military forces, war equipment and all of the security issues associated with them.

These areas will also have the largest concentrations of criminals, black marketers and have the highest potential for outbreaks of disease.

War conditions in large cities and urban areas are also prone to prolonged outages of electrical, water, sewage and medical services. These areas will also be chronically short of food, medicines and all basic human needs services.

The primary duties of both the police and military forces will be towards warfare and security concerns, and towards the caring for of protection of their citizens' wellbeing and welfare.

Due to the large concentrations of criminals in these areas you can also expect incidents of rape, murder and theft to rise, and again without normal responses from either the police or military forces.

Counter insurgency forces will also frequently target police, military and civilian concentrations, as will conversely police and military forces target the civilian population.

Frequent raids and sweeps by these police and military forces are indiscriminant and have no respect for either rights or human life. Their missions are to subdue all of their enemies, and all of their enemies are identified as anyone not being one of them.

Fathers coming home from work, mothers washing their clothes, children walking to school, all of these civilians are targets to both sides fighting in a war, and you must always remember this.

The ongoing conflict between the Palestinians and the Israelis provide numerous and graphic examples of the cost of living in cities and urban areas during times of war.

Here is one first hand story:

Settlers killed in bypass road attack, News of the attack

"While sitting with friends in my house in Ramallah at around 8:30 pm after a day's work at the university, I hear voices outside calling, "Nigel...Najeeb...Nigel!" It's the shebab ('guys') from the Computer Center, trapped by a yet another checkpoint at the settler bypass road near Surda, the setting for many previous diary entries.

In fact there are two checkpoints, a Palestinian Police checkpoint just before it inside the northern Area "A" border of Ramallah and an Israeli checkpoint just outside. The shebab live on the other side of both, in Birzeit village, so they are likely to be spending tonight with friends in Ramallah.

They reported hearing sirens earlier, and the combination of Israeli and Palestinian checkpoints suggests that there has been an amaleeyyah ("operation") near Beit El settlement. In fact, the last time we saw joint checkpoints there enforcing a closure was in May, when a settler was killed while standing at a bus stop outside Beit El.

It was therefore pretty safe to assume that something similar had happened. This was confirmed later, when we heard that a car had been ambushed on the settler road, just over one year after a similar incident near the same spot.

No surprise
We had been expecting it. Each time we pass the glistening black slice out of the valley floor, I have been prophesying to anyone unfortunate enough to be in the same car as me that blood will be spilled on that settler road.

For starters, the road is a security nightmare. Built by an Israeli settler community obsessed with their security, one wonders at the glaring stupidity inherent in the construction of a road on confiscated Palestinian land that runs along the bottom of a valley with rolling hills on either side of it. A perfect place for snipers to anonymously pick off the settlers cars below, never mind drive-by shootings on the long, dark winding road, far from earshot.

The settlement at Beit El ("Bethel" from the Bible, the site where Jacob had his dream) has attracted high numbers of religious settlers, who have established a yeshiva (Jewish religious school) and a unpleasantly right-wing radio station called Arutz Sheva ("Channel Seven").

This brand of settlers are cut from a whole different mould than those, say, in secular Ariel (west of Nablus) which is advertised as a dormitory suburb of Tel Aviv. These settlers manifest the profound arrogance common to religious extremists, and regularly and openly express a disturbing contempt for the humanity of the Palestinian population, discussed in a previous entry written after a visit to Beit El during the December 1995 Israeli redeployment from Ramallah.

This environment produces the kind of people who, rather than using the new redeployment-inspired bypass road that halved their travelling time to Tel Aviv, continued for several days to drive through Ramallah, Israeli flags hanging out of their cars, all to communicate to the Palestinian population that God gave the Jews - not them - all of the land including Ramallah.

In Arabic, "Ramallah", actually "Ram Allah" as it is two words, means "Hills of God", and it would seem obvious from the amount of Palestinians happily living in its city limits who God has given it to. The handful of Israeli settler cars that actually use the bypass road since redeployment often choose to do without an Israeli military escort, as if unaware that the Palestinian population are not avid supporters of their land expropriation and racist arrogance towards them.

Racial hatred

Settlement security chief Nahum Korman is from Hader Betar, another Jewish residential installation situated to the west of Beit Jala, near Bethlehem. On October 27th, Korman kicked and, with his gun butt, beat to death 11-year-old Hilmi Shoushi, a Palestinian child from inside the Green Line on his way home from school. In an initial statement by 'Judea and Samaria' police spokesman Boaz Goldenberg, one of the first and most telling questions that arose was whether there had been "any Jewish witnesses".

As Korman killed Hilmi in front of several Palestinian villagers, there was no shortage of Palestinian witnesses. They reported that the boy was simply walking along with two friends when Korman's four-wheel drive vehicle sped into the village of Husan and he jumped out to chase after them on foot. Earlier, stones had been thrown at settlers' cars and Korman seemed to be out for retribution, as he certainly had not seen Hilmi or anyone else throw a stone.

An article in the Friday 1 November 1996 edition of the Israeli Yediot Aharnot newspaper quoted Korman as saying, "Not only didn't I kill the boy, but I did the utmost to save his life." His lawyers denied he hit the boy at all. His brother, Ya'acov, stated that Nahum's own children had been stoned as if that was somehow relevant and that he "believed in [his] brother's goodness."

Korman was later remanded and charged with manslaughter. He'll be out of jail before any Palestinian currently serving time for a comparable crime, that's for sure. Israeli women protestors outside the 1 November hearing carried placards quoting from Bialik: "The devil has not created a revenge for the blood of a small child."

Crossing paths
A few weeks ago as I was passing the Ramallah bypass road, a settler car waited to cross the Ramallah-Birzeit road. There were no military vehicles, no checkpoints at this strategic node whose introduction the Palestinian Authority unthinkingly agreed to in the Oslo 2 negotiations.

The car's sole occupant, a 30-something Jewish woman wearing a broad-rimmed red hat styled more suitably for watching the horse races at Ascot, seemed dressed to underline her privilege as one of the West Bank's first class citizens.

As she accelerated unconcerned across the road and down the valley bypass road towards Tel Aviv, she clearly did not feel it important to consider the resentment felt by those whose path she had just crossed."[6]

From World War II and Nazi Occupied France we can understand this too by knowing the story of Jacques Lusseyran.

"Blinded in an accident when he was eight years old, Lusseyran was a brilliant student and courageous leader who led a double life as resistance fighter and brilliant student until his arrest by the Gestapo and internment at the Buchenwald concentration camp.

Jacques and his family were living in Toulouse when the German army marched up the Champs Elysee took over the center of the city and threw Paris into chaos.

Thousands of people crowded the roads trying to leave and those who remained were relieved that there was no destruction, bombing or shooting. Jacques' father, an engineer, was ordered to return to Paris in September 1940.

The family settled in an apartment on the Boulevard Port-Royal in the Latin Quarter, a part of the city known for centuries as the place where poets, writers, and artists lived, worked and met with one another in the cafes that lined the streets. After the Nazi occupation, the city was wrapped in a silence, broken only by the ringing of the church bells. The familiar sounds of automobiles, buses and trucks had vanished along with the lively chatter that made the streets of Paris so lively. The silence made the streets seem wider and the houses taller.

Ever since he lost his sight in an accident when he was eight years old, Jacques relied on sounds to bring him information and create images in his mind.

Without sight, Jacques learned to concentrate his attention to sounds, touch and smell. His family encouraged his independence and never isolated him. He mastered Braille reading and writing in six weeks and returned to his school his friends.

When his family lived in Toulouse, he was as much at home on country roads and mountain hikes as he was on the streets of Paris.

Life in Paris in the autumn of 1940 had become a struggle; food shortages forced housewives to stand in lines for hours waiting to purchase their share of the meager food supplies.

The fuel shortage caused constant cold and Paris clocks were turned to Berlin time. Logic seemed to have vanished along with the hustle and bustle of the streets.

No one was talking about the occupation. People turned away from one another when the words "Nazi" "Gestapo", "torture" or "killings" were mentioned. Jacques wondered if people were simply afraid to talk or afraid to face the reality of the occupation.

But like other boys, he was eager to get on with his life. Blind students were required to take a special exam to prove they could keep up with their studies

A good student and well prepared, Jacques passed the exam and was accepted to the Louis Le Grand Lycee, a well known secondary school in the Latin Quarter.

Impatient to begin his studies he had to wait a month before the lycee opened. The new fascist government had closed all the schools in Paris.

Jacques spent his time rediscovering the Paris streets with his friends, Jean and Francois. His parents gave him the two small rooms in the back of their apartment.

A long corridor separated the rooms and this gave Jacques the privacy he needed to study and meet with his friends. Jacques arranged his furniture and stacked his Braille books neatly against the walls.

The school opened in October and school life resumed in a normal fashion, in spite of the new rules imposed by a government eager to conform to Nazi ideology. The principal read announcements from Marshall Petain and other government officials over the loudspeaker.

Jacques walked to the lycee with Jean and Francois every morning, and could never understand why he attracted so much attention.

Groups of other boys seemed always to be trailing behind him and when he reached the school, the concierge greeted Jacques by shouting, "It's the Lusseyran parade".

Enrolled in philosophy, psychology and history classes, Jacques found his history class to be the most interesting. His history teacher commanded Jacques' attention with his rapid speech and warm resonant voice.

He told class about the war and Hitler's ambitions. One by one, the Germans occupied Austria, France, Holland, Denmark and Norway.

Hitler's plan was to make all of Europe subservient to Germany and 85% of the agricultural and industrial production of France was being sent to Germany.

Incidents of Nazi brutality were becoming more and more obvious and they were happening to people Jacques knew. Francois was almost in tears as he told Jacques of Mr. Weissberg's arrest.

Weissberg was Francois' good friend and tutor and when he arrived for his weekly biology lesson, Weissberg's rooms were empty. The concierge told Francois that the Gestapo had arrested Weissberg that morning. Weissberg was Jewish. Soon after Jacques heard about other Jewish friends who were taken away by the Gestapo.

The French police were acting like Nazis, there were book burnings, arrests and racial laws. Paris newspapers were censored and carried only German news.

Some boys at Louis Le Grand joined Nazi youth clubs and boasted that the Nazis were good for France. Jacques' school was closed for a month after a demonstration by university and lycee students. Twenty students were shot and killed.

It was freezing cold in his little room; Jacques felt his fingers stiffening and had to stop reading. The frightening events that were happening around him dominated his thoughts; something had to be done to arouse the conscience of the French people.

The idea of forming a resistance group of young students took shape in his mind.

Knowing his friends as well as he did, Jacques was not surprised that Jean and Francois readily agreed and they began to organize a resistance group made up students from Louis le Grand and the university. In school the next day, they spoke with trusted classmates.

A few days later, ten boys crowded into Jacques' room, and the next week 52 boys showed up. The student resistance group called the "Volunteers of Liberty" became a reality.

From now on there was to be no turning back and no giving in to fear. Jacques warned the boys to say nothing about the meeting, even to their families. Gossip was dangerous and would give them away.

No more than three boys would meet with one another at any one time. A Central Committee was formed to keep the students in touch with one another. Their task was to inform the French people about the brutality of Gestapo arrests, the persecutions and torture of captured resistance fighters and the arrests of Jewish people.

News of the War was to be gathered by listening to forbidden radio broadcasts from England and Switzerland. The "Volunteers of Liberty" planned to write and circulate a secret paper that they called "Le Tigres". Before they could begin, more students had to be recruited.

Jacques was elected to the Central Committee and went to the first secret meeting with Francois. The meeting was held in an old apartment house in a working class section of the city, the old building was chosen because there were always people coming in and going out and the arrival of strangers was not likely to arouse suspicion.

Jacques was to be responsible for interviewing everyone who wanted to become a "Volunteer". The other boys trusted his ability to judge people.

The "Volunteers" sent word out about the secret resistance group to the lycees and university. Students who wanted to join were watched for several days or sometimes weeks by one of the original 52 members. Those who were considered trustworthy were told "to visit the blind man."

Jacques conducted the interviews in his rooms. Two short rings and one long ring of the doorbell told him that a perspective volunteer had arrived. The rules were strict. No one was interviewed if he was not expected or did not appear within five minutes of the specified time.

No one was given Jacques' name. Forced to rely on his instincts, Jacques knew he was not infallible and was constantly on guard. It was too easy to be trapped by an informer or spy.

He planned the interviews carefully and discussed nothing of importance for the first 10 minutes. Sometimes he conducted the interview in the dark because he forgot to turn on the light.

Taking his time, Jacques listened intently to the words and the silences. Elaborate explanations and well-rehearsed speeches aroused his suspicions. He knew they covered lies and deceit.

He also knew that anger was a difficult emotion to disguise. If Jacques considered a boy trustworthy, he gave his name to the Central Committee and he was admitted to the "Volunteers of Liberty". At first, only young students between 17 and 19 appeared, but after a few weeks, older students from the university began coming. Jacques interviewed 600 young men in less than a year

The Volunteers did not think of themselves as a professional group, they were simply young students eager to liberate their country from the terror of Nazism.

They wrote, mimeographed and distributed their bulletin, "Le Tigres", to houses all over Paris. One boy watched the exits while the other went from floor to floor, carrying his shoes in his hands and slipping the paper under doors.

The French government no less than the German characterized the Resistance as a gang of terrorists. Denouncing them was seen as a civic duty, for which informers received money. Jacques and the other leaders were aware of the dangers; resistors who were caught were arrested and punished severely.

It was also disappointing that so few of Jacques' classmates were willing to join the Volunteers, only 6 boys of the 90 enrolled in the elite classes at Louis Le Grand joined. In every class, there were 2 or 3 boys willing to report them to the police.
Some of the teachers were also Nazi collaborators and they had to be careful never to talk about their activities at school. There were many narrow escapes.

Surveys, discussions, choosing articles for the bulletin and frequent Central Committee meetings kept Jacques busy. Meetings were never held in the same place.

Always by Francois or Jean, Jacques traveled on the routes set up for safety. Schoolwork occupied his daytime hours, but at 5 PM, Jacques became a resistance fighter and sometimes did not return home until 11 PM.

Keeping up his grades while devoting so much time to the "Volunteers" took all his energy, but he succeeded and graduated from Louis Le Grand in the Spring of 1941. He enrolled at the University and planned to take the special exam to qualify for "Ecole Normale Superieur", the highest institution in the French educational system.

The Vichy government and its Nazi racial laws, declaring students with disabilities to be ineligible, dashed his hopes. Disappointed and angry, Jacques wanted to fight the ruling, but he knew that he would put the "Volunteers" in jeopardy by calling attention to himself, so he put his ambitions aside and decided not to appeal the ruling.

In 1943, the work of the "Volunteers of Liberty" caught the attention of the "Defense de la France"; an official Resistance group connected with Charles deGaulle and the Free French forces.

The "Defense de la France" had more funds, its own print shop, trucks disguised as delivery wagons, an organized editorial board, a radio transmitter and a channel to the deGaulle government in London. The "Defense de la France" had everything the Volunteers lacked.

When Jacques was contacted by a leader of Defense de la France, he agreed to meet with him. Accompanied by

Georges, they met Phillipe, the leader in the back room of a small restaurant.

Jacques immediately liked the relaxed manner of the big man with the warm friendly voice, calm manner and keen sense of humor. Phillipe had solutions to difficult problems and talked of the advantages of merging the "Volunteers of Liberty" with the "Defense de la France".

Their main task would continue to be the distribution of a secret newspaper. "Le Tigres" was to become a real newspaper called "Defense de la France".

The "Volunteers" merged with the "Defense" and for the next six months, Jacques and Georges met with Philippe every day.

They planned a complicated system of drop-offs, mailboxes and hidden communication and both Jacques and Georges became members of the executive committee.

As part of a major group, Jacques no longer felt alone or isolated, but he found the work to be harder and more demanding, One hundred thousand copies of "Defense de la France" a two page newspaper were to be printed and distributed all over France.

Every article was carefully reviewed for its power to impress readers and make them aware that there was an active French resistance. The paper was filled with articles telling people of the brutal treatment and torture of arrested resistors, the slaughter of Jews in the death camps and appealing for passive resistance to Nazi orders.

On February 16, 1942 the Nazi government issued the order, demanding that all young Frenchmen over 21 years be sent to Germany as forced labor. Thousands of young men were sent to Germany, the only exceptions were students and heads of families.

The order strengthened the Resistance movement and the "Defense de la France" grew. Eighty young people, including Georges became professional underground operators. Francois was placed in charge of resistance in Brittany.

The members of the "Defense de la France" were young men and women who carried the secret to all parts of France at the risk of their lives. Georges and Jacques were responsible for the distribution of the newspaper in Paris. The two friends agreed that if one were arrested, the other would carry on the work.

The office where the newspaper was printed came under Gestapo suspicion and for three days, everyone who came out of the office was followed. The young people working with Jacques learned how to avoid being followed; they would go into a bakery and leave by the back door, board a subway train and exit at the next stop.

They led the spies down false trails, while the equipment was packed up in small trucks with signs, "fragile", "meteorological" or "optical equipment" were pasted on the outside of the trucks and a new print shop was prepared and the distribution of "Defense de la France" was resumed.

The government of Free France, established in Algiers, asked resistance groups to coordinate their efforts as much as possible. Jacques met with leaders of other groups including the famous writer, Albert Camus, who worked for the group called "Combat".

The work was dangerous; the students could be betrayed at any time. Still in charge of recruitment, Jacques was taken by surprise a young man named Elio, who came to his home without prior notification.

The group was looking for someone to coordinate the distribution of the newspaper to the industrial and mining communities in the north and Elio, a native of the north was willing to give up his studies to devote himself full time to the resistance movement.

Elio had good recommendations, but something about him aroused Jacques' suspicions. His heavy handshake and low voice lacked honesty and conviction and Jacques did not trust him.

Phillipe said they could not afford to be too cautious and against his better judgment, Jacques reluctantly agreed and Elio joined "Defense de la France", went to the city of Lille in the north and established a network for the distribution of the newspaper.

Thousands copies of "Defense de la France" were being distributed throughout France. Jacques and Georges were busy with distribution activities in Paris until the morning in July 1943 when two officers and four armed soldiers knocked on the door of the apartment in the Boulevard Port Royal.

Heading straight for Jacques' rooms, they sent his Braille papers flying. Jacques worried that his parents would be arrested too. They knew of his activities and never did anything to discourage him. He felt relieved that he was the only one arrested.

At Gestapo headquarters, Jacques discovered that the Nazis had a record of every one of his activities from the day Elio joined "Defense de la France". When they took him to the Fresnes prison, his suspicions were confirmed. It was a mass betrayal; every one of his friends except Philippe had been arrested.

He was taken from Fresnes to Gestapo headquarters 38 times, he was threatened with death, beaten, and questioned from 7 o'clock in the morning to 7 o'clock, but he was resolute and determined not to give them any information.

In July, he was sent to Buchenwald. Starved and sickly, Jacques tried to keep up his spirits and those of his friends. Knowing German and Italian, he even translated for other prisoners.

The United States Third Army liberated Buchenwald in April 1945. Jacques was one of thirty survivors of the 2,000 people who were arrested at the same time he was.

He and Phillipe were the only leaders of the "Defense de la France" to survive the war. The newspaper of the "Defense de la France became the "France Soir", one of the most important daily newspapers in France.

Jacques returned to the university and his studies and his fight to be admitted to the Ecole Normale Superieur. Finally admitted to the elite school, graduated and took a teaching position in Paris.

In the 1950's he moved to the United States and taught Literature at Western Reserve University and the University of Hawaii. He was tragically killed in a tragic automobile accident when he was only 47 years of age." [7]

With careful planning you can keep your own story from someday in the future being read by those wondering, "Why didn't they leave when they had the chance?"

If you believe that the war will be less likely to affect you and your family in the countryside of your own country, you should immediately plan to go there.

If you believe that there will be no safe places from war, and its consequences, in your own homeland, then now is the time to make your plans to leave.

"The art of war is simple enough. Find out where your enemy is. Get at him as soon as you can. Strike him as hard as you can, and keep moving."
Ulysses S. Grant

Chapter 4: Conversion of Wealth

You have determined that the war conditions in your country are such that a decision has been made to leave, and that the time to make your plans to accomplish this is right now.

But before this plan can be made and put into action you first must know how much money you are able to put together, and in what time frame you are able to do it in.

You do not make a plan and then try to find a way to pay for it, you instead accumulate all the available cash resources you have and once this amount is known then, and only then, can you realistically look at all of the options available to you.

The timing of this is one of the most crucial actions on anyone's part seeking to escape from war.

The longest possible time frame available between when you see war coming and when you escape from its dangers is also that which guarantees your success.

The shortest time frame is when you find yourself in a line of refugees, a suitcase, or two, in your hands and you are broke and penniless and are at the mercy of whatever terrible forces await you at your journey's end.

With a lot of time available to you, your plans would be not only for your escape but also for your resettlement in another country of your choosing.

The longer the war goes on the less likely you'll be able to either convert your present wealth into usable cash or to choose the country you wish to flee to.

Remember this, the closer war comes to your doorstep the narrower are your chances of escaping its ravages.

Governments at war and their military leaders, also know the likelihood of their citizens fleeing, especially the richest, the most skilled and the most educated of them.

That is why these governments begin the step by step process of tightening border controls, increasing police and military presences in the population centers, restricting travel, increasing banking laws and restricting the ability of their citizens to overcome debt.

The present day United States is the perfect example of this in that every week new laws and security measures are being put into place to insure them that their most valued citizens, and those needed for their continuing war efforts, will not be able to leave.

It must also always be remembered that none of these actions are taking in the span of weeks or months, but in years. The historical time period from last century between free societies going from total freedom to total lockdown has averaged 8 years.

In the United States their clock started ticking in 1999, which leaves them very little time to accomplish any of the goals outlined in this book, though certainly not impossible.

What is Money

The dictionary definition of Money is: A medium that can be exchanged for goods and services and is used as a measure of their values on the market, including among its forms a commodity such as gold, an officially issued coin or note, or a deposit in a checking account or other readily liquefiable account.

At this point in time there is something you have to understand, the money you have in your pocket, whether it be in Rubles, Dollars, Pounds or Euros, is NOT money.

During times of war there is one form of money, and no other, and that is gold.

If you have paper bills in your pocket you have exactly that, paper. If you have gold, you have real money.

From the United States to Europe to the deepest and darkest corners of Asia or Africa, if you have gold you have money. Never forget this, your government hasn't.

One of the first actions of the American Roosevelt administration in their preparations for World War II was to confiscate the gold of all of their citizens. And likewise did the communists in Russia. And likewise did the Nazis do in Germany. And likewise did the Fascists do in Italy.

No country at war will willing allow its citizens to have access to gold money so that they may escape.

Over the past 25 years the Central Banks of the United States and Europe have been selling off their vast hoardings of gold for the only reason of keeping its true value down, and therefore not an attractive option for investment.

This is the same thing they did during the last century too in their run-up to their two World Wars. But, once their economies began to crash, they then re-confiscated all of the gold they had originally sold.

The wisest citizens of these countries however refused to turn their gold over, even though it turned them into criminals, and the wisest of those wise citizens used their gold, their real money, to leave their homelands and re-locate to safer countries.

Therefore, the first action that should be taken by anyone converting their wealth into money is to buy as much gold as possible. These purchases of gold should also be spread out between various denominations and issuing countries. (I will go more into depth about the reasons for this in later chapters.)

In a fascist country destined for global war their military leaders will first destroy the investment vehicles for their economy, stocks, bonds and other like monetary investments.

They will begin by creating an atmosphere of never ending good times, everyman can be wealthy, everyone will be set for their entire lives, there will never be an ending to the rising of these investments, the old rules no longer apply, we are a new generation.

The only thing more absurd than them saying these things is that time after time, century after century; the average citizens actually believe them.

These people actually become blinded by greed to the point that all common sense has left them. They never learn that the only wealth they accumulate in this type of manner is that which can be wiped away in an instant by their fascist government leaders and bankers.

One moment, one year, these citizens are giddy with wealth, the next moment, the next year, the find themselves virtual paupers to the State, nothing more than economic slaves to the war ambitions of their military masters.

But if these same citizens had instead put all of their wealth into gold, a real thing, not an ink notation on a piece of paper, then they would be truly wealthy. And, like all of those people from history who have survived, they would also be able to escape the ravages of war.

The conversion of your wealth to real money therefore becomes your priority. Remember too that you are converting your assets into wealth so as to be able to escape war. Therefore, the sooner you act the more real money you'll have.

Keep in mind too, you are not converting your wealth in order to pay your debts, you are leaving your homeland. Even if you have to purchase gold using your instruments of debt (credit cards, mortgage loans, personal loans, etc.) this is what you must do.

No mind should be paid either to the things that you own, except those most personal to you (pictures, movies, jewelry, hand carried family heirlooms, etc.). Your goal is escaping and building a new life all over again someplace else, and in another country, everything of value to your old life must be sold.

Your one and only objective is to accumulate as much gold as possible in the shortest amount of time as possible. Once you are safely out of the way of war then, and only then, should your thoughts turn back to the accumulation of those things that make your life comfortable.

"You cannot simultaneously prevent and prepare for war."
Albert Einstein

Chapter 5: Where to Go

You've seen the signs that war is inevitable and could soon be on your very doorstep. You've also made the decision to go, are completing your plan for leaving and are in the process of converting your wealth into usable money.

So now you have to decide where to go to.

Your primary consideration is to put as much distance between yourself, war and the effects of war. It wouldn't make much sense to find your self in a country that though they may not be directly at war, they could still suffer the effects of it.

This consideration alone eliminates for you many of the world's smaller island nations, and they should not be considered.

In the world today there exists between 189 to 266 nations, depending upon who you ask.

The United Nations has 190 members, but this doesn't include some nations, like Taiwan and the Vatican. The CIA World Fact Book lists the most nations but some of these are territories and colonies, like Bermuda and Puerto Rico which are governed by other nations.

Even though you may not have any racist feelings, this is an issue that cannot be overlooked as many of the world's nations are racist and living in them could present future problems for you, especially if you find yourself being a minority in that country's population mix.

Religion is another very serious consideration as there are those countries that do not have religious freedoms and there are those that also have frequent violent clashes between opposing religions groups and factions.

Language isn't a major factor of consideration but should not be ignored either. You should include in your preparations the learning of the local language of whichever country you choose to relocate to.

During your time of transition in learning the language of your new host country you will find available English language resources in most any country of your choosing.

A country's compatibility with your skills and education level should also be considered. In a country short of skilled carpenters, doctors, nurses, heavy equipment operators, etc. you will find your opportunities greatly enhanced should you have those skill sets most needed by them.

Availability of housing and services should also be considered, but not to the point of duplicating your present lifestyle. You should be prepared for living standards below those currently enjoyed in many Western nations.

The social and political stability of a country is another consideration; you wouldn't want to move to a country, especially after leaving one at war, only to find yourself embroiled in another war.

Now there are a countless number of questions, concerns and investigations that are going to have to be asked and answered. The vast majority of these are also going to be ones relating to your own unique circumstances, and no one book, including this one, could possibly answer.

But to the most general of these questions most of them are also common sense.

So let's take a look around the world now and explore some possible options that may be available to you. Remember though, this is far from a complete list and is meant only as a beginning guide for consideration.

As I had previously said, your main choice will be based upon those circumstances and necessities of life unique to you, and you alone.

Canada

To the English speaking people of the world Canada would appear at first glance to be a viable choice of countries to relocate to. This would especially hold true for Americans as these countries border each other.

Canada and the United States have traditionally held close ties between them but over the past 8 years there are growing divisions between them relating to the United States as growing threat to world peace.

Canada has also recently denied their airspace to United States missiles, but in all practicality, and if needed, it is highly unlikely that the United States would abide by this decision of the Canadian government.

The country of Canada itself is one of the two largest landmass countries in the world, however a large portion of this land is uninhabited and undeveloped and in the Arctic Regions of the far north.

Canada also an immigration quota that have seen over the past 15 years has seen a high of 256,759 immigrants allowed (1993), a low of 152,001 (1987). [8]

Canada has frequently dissented with the United States in the United Nations but on the larger issues of common security in their border regions they frequently agree on many issues and Canada has also enacted laws to return to the United States various categories of citizens that the United States deems a threat.

Where in previous wars United States draft resisters and military forces deserters found safe haven in Canada, this is presently not the case, and as recent Canadian Court cases have found in ruling against American soldiers seeking refuge there.

Should a land invasion of the North American continent occur it should be expected that Canada would move to defend the United States, though is not for certain and would depend upon various and current International circumstances.

It is also a possibility that Canada in a few years could actually designate itself a Neutral country, such as

Sweden, Switzerland, Spain and Portugal did on the European Continent during World War II.

Declaring one's country Neutral however is only valid depending upon the wishes, and actions, of the larger aggressors to the conflict. Should the United States need for their war effort the vast raw materials possessed by Canada, there should be no illusions to the fact that they would take them, and by force if necessary.

Likewise, a major invasion of Canada by forces from Europe and/or Asia would be a likely scenario by those forces opposed to the United States for the purpose of keeping on the North American Continent large contingents of American military forces.

It should also be expected that when major conflicts erupt within the United States, either through invasion or civil war, Canada will close its borders to Americans and expel those American refugees that do manage to cross its borders.

In just these few considerations Canada would not be the best of choices for re-location, with the slim exception being their large and vast interior sections. But, these areas are only for the most hardy and self sufficient people as there would be no way to duplicate a Western life style in these regions.

Let's look now at what the current requirements are for immigration to Canada as provided by the Canadian Government:

Moving to a new country offers exciting opportunities and new beginnings!

"This information will help you get ready to leave your home country and make a new life in Canada. It tells you what documents you will need to bring, what to expect in the first few days and weeks, how to find a place to live, get a Social Insurance Number and a health-care card, and find a job.

It also explains what services you can expect to receive from the immigrant-serving organizations across Canada. You will also find useful information about Canada's geography, history, government and way of life, and about how to become a Canadian citizen.

GETTING READY BEFORE YOU LEAVE FOR CANADA

Essential documents

When you travel to Canada, you will need to have the following documents with you:

A Canadian immigrant visa and Confirmation of Permanent Residence for each family member traveling with you;

A valid passport or other travel document for each family member traveling with you;
Two copies of a detailed list of all the personal or household items you are bringing with you; and two copies of a list of items that are arriving later.

Note: The lists should state how much your personal and household items are worth.

You must also bring with you enough money to cover living expenses such as rent, food, clothing and transportation for a six-month period. You may be asked to show proof of your funds.

Do not pack your documents in a suitcase. You will need to have them available to show to immigration and customs officials.

Important documents

Depending on your personal situation, you should bring the following important documents with you to Canada:

Birth certificates or baptismal certificates;

Marriage certificates;

Adoption, separation or divorce papers;
School records, diplomas or degrees for each family member travelling with you;

Trade or professional certificates and licenses;

Letters of reference from former employers;

A list of your educational and professional qualifications and job experience (this is also called a résumé);

Immunization, vaccination, dental and other health records for each family member;

Driver's license, including an International Driver's Permit, and a reference from your insurance company;

Photocopies of all essential and important documents, in case the originals get lost (be sure to keep the photocopies in a separate place from the originals); and car registration documents (if you are importing a motor vehicle into Canada).

What you should know about health care:

Canada has a public health-care system known as "medicare." It provides insurance coverage for health-care services to all Canadian citizens and permanent residents. (You will be a "permanent resident.") The federal government sets health-care standards for the whole country, but the programs are run by the provincial ministries of health. More information on the health-care system can be found in your first few days in Canada.

Apply for provincial health-care coverage as soon as possible after you arrive in the province where you plan to live.

Note: British Columbia, Ontario, Quebec and New Brunswick have a three-month waiting period before you become eligible for medicare coverage. If you are planning to settle in any of these provinces, you should buy private health insurance coverage for the first three months. Insurance companies are listed in the Yellow Pages of all Canadian telephone books, under "Insurance."

What you can bring into Canada:

There are strict laws about what you can bring into Canada.

Cars must meet Canadian safety and pollution control standards. Many cars are not allowed into the country.

Contact Transport Canada for more information before you ship your car.

Transport Canada, Vehicle Importation
330 Sparks Street, Tower C
Ottawa, Ontario K1A 0N5
Telephone: 1 (613) 998-8616
(when calling from outside Canada)
1 800 333-0371
(toll-free, from inside Canada)
Web site: www.tc.gc.ca
(follow the link to Vehicle Importation)

The following items cannot be brought into Canada:

Unauthorized firearms, explosives, fireworks and ammunition;

Narcotics, other than prescription drugs;

Meat, dairy products, fresh fruits and vegetables;

Plants, flowers and soil;

Endangered species of animals or products made from animal parts, such as the skin, feathers, fur, bones and ivory;

Cultural property, including antique and cultural objects considered to have historical significance in their country of origin (you may, however, bring family heirlooms);

More than 200 cigarettes (you must pay tax on the excess amount) per person over 18 years of age if you are immigrating to Quebec, Alberta, Saskatchewan or

Manitoba, or per person over 19 if you are immigrating to Ontario or any of the other provinces; and more than 1.5 liters of wine or 1.14 liters of commercial alcohol (you must pay tax on the excess amount) per person over 19 years of age.

Getting ready to look for work:

If possible, have your documents translated into English or French before you leave for Canada. Essential documents for looking for work include:

A résumé of your education, work and volunteer experience, and your skills and qualifications;

Diplomas, degrees, certificates and other qualifications;

Letters of recommendation; and school records or transcripts.

Research the labor market in the part of Canada where you plan to settle. The following federally funded Web sites will be helpful:
www.workinfonet.ca

This is a national Web site for career and labor market information. It contains job information for each province and territory. It also contains information on self-employment, education and training.
www.workdestinations.org

This Web site offers labor market information, which can help you search for work and make general employment, training and career decisions.
www.theworkplace.ca

Getting ready if you are a business immigrant

If you are coming to Canada as a business immigrant, use the Internet to find out about sources of financing, business opportunities, export and investment services, self-employment assistance and information for small businesses.

There are many rules for starting a business in Canada. The following Government of Canada Web sites will help you get a head start in your planning:

www.cbsc.org: The Canada Business Service Centre's Web site is your single point of contact for information on government services, programs and rules for business.

www.strategis.gc.ca: This Industry Canada Web site has business information to help you find partners, do market research, find new technologies, and learn about financing opportunities and growth areas in the Canadian economy.

www.bdc.ca: This is the Web site of the Business Development Bank of Canada. It provides financial and consulting services to Canadian small businesses, especially those in the technology and export sectors of the economy. It also offers information on how to start a business and make it succeed.

www.strategis.gc.ca/sc_mangb/smallbus/engdoc/sbla.ht ml: This is the Web site of the Canada Small Business Financing Program. The program can help you finance your own business.

www.contractscanada.gc.ca: This Web site has information on how and what the Government of Canada buys (both goods and services).

www.cic.gc.ca: This is the Web site of Citizenship and Immigration Canada. It describes the Business Immigration Program. You will find many answers to your questions at this site.

Communities across Canada:

Most newcomers to Canada tend to settle in the three biggest cities -- Toronto, Montréal and Vancouver. But many newcomers and many Canadians choose to live in the medium-sized cities, which they feel have as much to offer as the larger cities with a better quality of life.

Among the medium-sized cities are Halifax, Québec City, Ottawa, London, Windsor, Sudbury, Winnipeg, Saskatoon, Regina, Calgary, Edmonton and Victoria. All of the medium-sized cities have diverse, multi-ethnic populations ranging in size from approximately 100,000 to one million people, and all have the variety of public and private institutions and services found in the largest cities.

Some newcomers like the idea of living in smaller cities or towns like Moncton, Fredericton, Red Deer and Kelowna, or prefer to live in a rural area. Depending on your skills or professional qualifications, some regions may have better job opportunities than others.

Visit the Web sites of each province and territory to see what each has to offer.

To find these Web sites, visit
http://canada.gc.ca/othergov/prov_e.html.

Each Web site has a list of government departments and agencies. In the bigger provinces, some government departments may have their own Web sites, with more detailed information.

You may also find a directory of on-line services, a link to educational institutions, and a link to major cities and towns. Most of the Web sites also have a tourism section, where you can discover the special attractions of each province and territory.

The Web site www.workdestinations.org has links to information on the labour market and the housing market of communities across Canada. It also has useful tips and information about moving within Canada.

You can also visit a Web site called Canadian Government Information on the Internet at http://cgii.gc.ca/muni-e.html. It is another useful link to federal, provincial and municipal government information.

Francophone communities -- French is the mother tongue of 6.6 million Canadians. Most Francophones live in Quebec, but almost one million live in Canada's other provinces and territories.

The Atlas de la francophonie at
http://franco.ca/atlas/francophonie/english/index.cfm
has information on the francophone communities in each of Canada's provinces and territories. Or check

out interesting links to official language organizations at www.ocol-clo.gc.ca/links_liens.asp?Lang=English.

The Canadian climate: What to expect and what clothes to bring

Most of Canada has four distinct seasons: spring, summer, autumn and winter. The temperatures and weather in each season can be different from one part of the country to another. Here is what you can expect:

Spring: Spring is a rainy season in most parts of Canada. Daytime temperatures rise steadily, but the nights remain cool. Average daytime temperatures are about 12°C in March, April and early May.

Summer: Summer officially begins on June 21, but July and August are summer for most Canadians. In summer, the weather is very warm in most parts of the country. In southern Canada, daytime temperatures are normally above 20°C and can sometimes rise above 30°C.

Autumn: The autumn season, or fall, as it's often called, begins in September. The weather cools and the leaves on many trees change colour and fall to the ground. It can also be very rainy at this time of year. In some parts of Canada, especially northern or mountain regions, snow may begin to fall by late October. Average daytime temperatures are about 10°C to 12°C in most of the country. The autumn months are September, October and November.

Winter: During the winter months (December, January and February), the temperature in most of the country usually stays below 0°C, day and night. Temperatures in some parts of the country periodically drop below -25°C, while along the West Coast, the temperature rarely drops below 0°C. In most of Canada, snow will be on the ground from mid-December to the middle of March. The higher in elevation and the farther north you go, the longer and colder winter becomes.

Schools and universities:

There is no national school system in Canada. Schools and universities are run by the provinces; therefore, education varies somewhat from province to province. Most elementary and secondary schooling is public, meaning it is free and open to everyone.

Depending on the individual province, primary education starts at pre-kindergarten and continues to the end of grade 6 or 8. This is followed by secondary education or high school. In some provinces this may be divided into junior high (grades 7 to 9) and senior high (grades 10 to 12). Normally, students must complete the required academic courses in high school in order to be admitted to university or college.

The regular school year runs from late August or early September until mid- to late June. New students can usually be registered throughout the school year. Most schools are closed on national holidays. Also, all schools are closed between Christmas Eve and New Year's Day, and most are closed for a week in March for spring break. The longest school holiday occurs over the summer months of July and August.

Universities and community colleges hold their regular classes from late August or early September until April, although some courses are offered from January to

April and a smaller number are available over the summer months. University and community college courses are not free and the costs vary among the provinces.

When you register your children at the local school or school board office, you must take with you:

Canadian immigrant visa (Record of Landing);

Birth certificate or baptismal certificate;

Vaccination certificate; any previous school records.

Your children's language and mathematical skills will be assessed, if necessary, and they will be placed in the program the school thinks is best for them.

Immigrating to Canada as a Skilled Worker:

Skilled workers have education, work experience, knowledge of English and/or French and other abilities that will help them to establish themselves successfully as permanent residents in Canada.

Applying to come to Canada as a Skilled Worker is not difficult.

Will You Qualify as a Skilled Worker?

Skilled workers are people who may become permanent residents because they are able to become economically established in Canada.

To be accepted as a Skilled Worker, applicants must:

Meet the minimum work experience requirements;

Prove that they have the funds required for settlement; and earn enough points in the six selection factors to meet the pass mark.

Minimum Work Experience Requirements:

Skilled workers are people who may become permanent residents because they have the ability to become economically established in Canada.

You must meet the following minimum work experience requirements to allow you to apply as a skilled worker:

You must have at least one year of full-time work experience. You must have been paid for this work.

Your work experience must be in the category of Skill Type 0, or Skill Level A or B on the Canadian National Occupational Classification (NOC).

You must have had this experience within the last 10 years.

National Occupation Classification (NOC)

The NOC is a classification system for jobs in the Canadian economy. It describes duties, skills, talents and work settings for occupations.

National Occupation Classification list.
http://www.cic.gc.ca/english/skilled/qual-2-1.html

National Occupational Classification
http://www23.hrdc-
drhc.gc.ca/2001/e/generic/welcome.shtml
Skilled Worker Self-Assessment Test
http://www.cic.gc.ca/english/skilled/assess/index.html

Proof of Funds

The Government of Canada does not provide financial
support to new skilled worker immigrants.

You must show that you have enough money to support
yourself and your dependants after you arrive in
Canada. You cannot borrow this money from another
person. You must be able to use this money to support
your family.

You will need to provide proof of your funds when you
submit your application for immigration.

The amount of money that you need to have to support
your family is determined by the size of your family.

Number of Family Members Funds required (in
Canadian dollars)

1 $9,897
2 $12,372
3 $15,387
4 $18,626
5 $20,821
6 $23,015
7 or more $25,210

You do not have to show that you have these funds if
you have arranged employment in Canada.

How Much Money should you bring?

Find out how much it costs to live where you are planning to settle in Canada.

Bring as much money as possible to make moving and finding a home in Canada easier.

Disclosure of funds:

If you are carrying more than CDN $10,000, tell a Canadian official when you arrive in Canada. If you do not tell an official you may be fined or put in prison. These funds could be in the form of:

Cash;
Securities in bearer form (for example: stocks, bonds, debentures, treasury bills);

Or negotiable instruments in bearer form (for example: bankers' drafts, cheques, travellers' cheques, money orders.)" [9]

As you can see from this example of the procedures needed to immigrate to Canada, there is a tremendous amount of information that will have to be acquired by you beforehand.

This will equally apply to any other country you might be considering to both a larger and smaller extent, but this information is more than sufficient for you to begin your preparations.

Let's look at some other countries you might consider, but not to the depth we've gone into with Canada.

Switzerland

Though Switzerland has finally relented in its decade's long hold out from becoming a member state of the United Nations and joined the organization in 2002.

It still remains a Neutral nation and there are very few scenarios one could envision that would drag this European country into a war.

It is also unlikely that Switzerland would be considered a military target by any warring faction for a number of reasons, the first being the huge number of military forces that would be needed to conquer it.

With a population of just over 7.5 million citizens, Switzerland has one of the world's largest military forces with a standing army of over 1.5 million soldiers.

But, as one of the most secure countries in the world it is also one of the hardest to immigrate too due the high costs associated with living there. It is also one of the few countries in the world you would consider where your Western lifestyle would not be that greatly changed.

The decision to immigrate to Switzerland would have to be based upon your amount of worth. The greater this amount, the greater your chances will be of successfully immigrating to this country.

To live and work in Switzerland you would need a work and residence permit, which is actually one document that entitles you to live and work in a particular area and work for a specific employer.

For those having the resources to invest in businesses these permits are frequently granted, and language will not be a problem as many Swiss citizens also speak English.

One permit is Permit B, and is a one year residence permit for employment with some minor restrictions. Another is Permit C which is a permanent residence permit available after 5 years of continuous residence in Switzerland and has very few restrictions and allows you to purchase land, live in other areas of the country and allows you to be self-employed.

It is strongly suggested that if Switzerland is your country of choice that you contact a Swiss Immigration service, which are private companies, who will assist you with all the information and procedures you will need to make this move a successful one.

Belize

Belize, which is the former British Honduras, is located in Central America in the Eastern Caribbean and is bordered by Mexico to the west and north and Guatemala to the remainder of the west.

It is an English speaking nation with a stable government and small economy. What is attractive about Belize are the open immigration laws they have that invites retirees and entrepreneurs alike, and after 5 years allows them to apply for citizenship.

You do not need a visa to enter Belize if you are a citizen of the United States or the EU. After one year of continuous residence you can then apply for Permanent Residence permit and pay a fee of $100US.

A deposit may also be required and ranges from $100US to $1,200US but is refunded after 3 years, and at which time your residency is granted.

After being a Permanent Resident for 5 years you can than acquire citizenship.

The laws in Belize also allow you to import your car and household items duty-free, along with light aircraft, boats and other forms of transportation.

Any income you derive from outside of Belize is also non-taxable, but you are not excluded from joining the local economy.

But there are a couple of important considerations too, very important ones; You must be able to show that you have at least $2,000US in monthly income or have on deposit $524,000US and be at least 45 years of age. Your children are excluded from this requirement.

The physical infrastructure of Belize would also allow you to maintain a Western lifestyle, and actually allow you more luxuries than either the United States or the EU due to its low cost of living and low priced housing.

There is also a yearly quota of around 20,000 immigrants per year that you could logically assume would be filled rather quickly as war approaches.

Ireland

Ireland can be considered because of its Neutrality, but on the other hand its close proximity to both England and the European continent would tend to make me think that it could be drawn into a much larger war involving its neighbors.

Being an island nation, and though able to support an agricultural industry, it could definitely be affected by both air and sea blockades and other war type actions.

Paraguay

For those of you looking for one of the easiest countries to enter, Paraguay should be considered.

Located in the heart of South America Paraguay has for many years been the choice for those fleeing the effects of wars. And in some cases, those being sought by International authorities for war crimes.

Your language skills would be needed for this country as their two official languages are Spanish and a local dialect called Guaraní.

With a population of around 5 million this country has many expatriate communities, including Russian, American, Canadian, Korean, Japanese and Italian, just to name a few.

Their main industry is agriculture so during times of global war they are self sufficient and could hardly be considered as anyone's target during a global war. (With one exception being for their hydro-power producing facilities for Brazil, but if attacked would not effect the country as a whole.)

Their immigration procedures are also pretty simple and straight forward:

Documents Required to Apply for Residence in Paraguay

1. Identification document (passport, etc.);

2. Police or court records from the applicant's country of origin; *

3. Birth certificate; *

4. Civil state certificate (marriage, divorce, separation, widowhood); *

5. Health certificate from the country of origin, or country of last residence; *

6. Consular tourist visa for the countries that require it;

7. Proof of economic solvency that must be demonstrated by one of the following:

a. Deposit to a checking or savings account at a Paraguayan bank in the amount of at least five thousand dollars US ($5000.00 USD) or its equivalent value in local or foreign currency. The bank account must be in the name of the applicant; or

b. Real estate property deed of a property located in Paraguay; or

c. University diploma attached to an offer of employment or work contract in Paraguay with the indication of the amount to be received in fees or salary. A commercial license will not be accepted.

- The documents stated in 2, 3, 4 and 5 must be legalized at the Paraguayan consulate in the country of origin. The identification document does not require legalization. For more information, please view the procedures for legalizations.

Additional Required Documents to Obtain in Paraguay

1. Certificate issued by the National Police, Identifications Department of Paraguay;

2. Interpol certificate, issued by the regional office in Asuncion, Paraguay;

3. Life and residence certificate, issued by the jurisdictional police station;

4. Proof of legal entrance to the country (visa or sealed passport), issued by the immigration authorities at the control posts (airports and border);

5. Six 3 x 3 identification colour photographs; and,

6. Affidavit stating that the applicant will abide by the laws of the country signed by a notary public.[10]

I want to remind you again that this chapter is not meant to be either a complete list of those countries you may choose or a complete list of all of those things that you'll need to consider in choosing a country to re-locate to.

But what you should realize by now is that there are many things you'll have to think about, plan for and acclimate yourself to, with the important goal of knowing as much as you can about where you are going before you go there.

Keep in mind too that as war draws ever closer to you, more and more countries will be closing their doors and not allowing any immigrant into their countries. Therefore, it is always better to act sooner than later when it comes to these matters.

"One is left with the horrible feeling now that war settles nothing; that to win a war is as disastrous as to lose one."
Agatha Christie

Chapter 6: What is a Refugee

The dictionary definition of the word Refugee is: One who flees in search of refuge.

If you ever find this word being used to describe you and your family it means that war has not only caught up with you, but has overrun you, and you now have become homeless and are moving towards where you hope you can find peace, safety, food and shelter.

Like all contingencies of war though being a Refugee is something you can plan in advance for, and believe me, you REALLY want to plan in advance for this!

There can be many reasons for finding yourself being a Refugee during times of war; including enemy troops advancing towards your town or city, your own soldiers occupying your home and lands, aerial bombing attacks, gas/biological/nuclear attacks….the reasons can be many, the end result is the same…you and your family are heading towards a destination you do not know and away from a life that will never be again.

And that is the first place to begin in being a Refugee, setting your mind to survival for yourself and your family. There are countless hundreds of millions of your fellow human beings that have walked the same roads you'll be walking down and they survived, you can too.

Your first and most important battle in being a refugee is the one you have in your mind. Terror has to be conquered so that you'll continue to be an effective leader to those around you. The ability to think fast, extremely fast, on your feet is going to be the difference between death and survival in many instances, so prepare yourself for that.

Personal health is next on your priority list, if you are not in good physical shape, able to walk many miles in a single day, and at times have to run at full speed for short distances, your journey as a refugee will be over before it has started.

You must further be prepared for experiences that actually can't be prepared for, and this is not a contradiction but a statement of fact.

How do you in fact prepare to watch as your wife, daughter or mother is raped? How do you prepare to watch the sudden deaths by bombs and gunfire of those closest to you, yet still continue on?

How do you walk away from one child lying dead beside the road with no burial or time to mourn while holding the hand of your other child?

Not only are these the things you will most have to contemplate before becoming a Refugee, these are those things that you will also be experiencing while you take this journey. You must be prepared.

Three Stories

The Story of Salihovic Hata and Sajit

"Salihovic Hata was born in 1947 in the village of Tegare in the municipality of Bratunac. Her father died when she 3 years old and since then her mother had to take care of 5 children from the money received from her father's pension.

Hata married Sajit when she was sixteen and moved to the village of Skelanie near Srebrenica, on the border with Serbia. They had two children: a daughter, Munevera born in 1966 and a son, Abid born in 1969.

Her husband worked as a carpenter for a company from Belgrade until 1992. During this time they built a house in Skelani.

The aggression of the Serbs towards the Bosniaks began on May 8, 1992. Her husband had to stop working for the Serb company.

On May 11, 1992 Hata was arrested by Serbian forces in Skelanie. She was taken with all the other women to a gymnasium where they were kept as prisoners for 5 days.

After 5 days of negotiating with the Serbs they were set free but were not allowed to return to their houses again. The Serbs transported them to Bajina Basta, a town across the Skelane River in Serbia where they spent one night in a warehouse.

After that sleepless night, the Serbs came with buses and transported them all to Macedonia. In Macedonia they were accommodated with host families and they stayed there for 3 months.

The women could not seek employment in Macedonia because they were refugees and so they decided to go to Austria on their own. In Austria they stayed in a refugee camp in Batkrojice.

After 3 and a half months they went to Germany, because the heard the conditions were better there for refugees. On December 12, 1992 they went to Germany, and stayed there until May 25, 1998.

However, the living conditions in the German refugee camp were just as bad as in Austria. After a couple of months though the German government gave the women some social assistance and the women were able to get their own flat.

On June 26, 1992, her 22-year-old son Abid was killed somewhere near Tuzla where he was serving as a soldier in the BiH army. Before joining the army he was studying medicine, but he decided to join the army to defend his country from the Serbian aggressors.

Hata and Sajit heard about the death of their son on December 31, 1992.

Hata and Sajit fell into a deep depression after losing their son. They didn't care about their movements and problems anymore; the only thing that mattered to them was the death of their son.

Because of all the pain in her soul and the depression, Hata became very ill with diabetes. They both lost their will to live.

Hata and Sajit continued to receive horrible news.

They found out that 60 of their closest relatives were killed in Skelanie. Hata's mother, who was 81 years old, was shot in her house in Skelani. During this time Hata didn't hear any news about her daughter Munevera, her son in law or her grandchild.

Later, in 1993, she heard that her daughter and grandchild were fine, they had escaped Skelani and were in Srebrenica but Serbian forces killed her son- in-law.

The problems for her daughter did not end in Srebrenica, she gave birth to a baby girl 2 months before the massacre in Srebrenica. Srebrenica had been declared a UN Safe Haven but was captured anyway by the Serbian army in July 1995.

The Serbs separated the women from the men. Munevera almost lost her 9-year-old son. She spent 3 days and 2 nights hiding with her son and her 2-month-old baby under a truck.

She managed to hide her son and baby and go to Tuzla. After that she went to Germany and was reunited with her mother and father.

Hata and Sajit returned to Bosnia on May 25, 1998. They moved into an abandoned Serb house in Ilijas. Their daughter and grandchildren are still in Germany."
[11]

The Story of Hasancevic Safeta

"Hasancevic Safeta was born on August 19, 1958, in Tuzla Municipality, in the village of Lukavac. She finished secondary school in Tuzla and then married Huso in Doboj.

Her husband was born in the village of Grapska on January 26, 1954. He currently works in Croatia as a carpenter and a ceiling installer.

They have two sons; Elder Alen was born in 1978 and Amir in 1980.

Safeta and Huso built a house in Grapska and lived there for 15 years.

On May 10, 1992, Grapska fell to the Serbs and they, together with 4,000 others, were forced to escape in many different directions. Many of them were imprisoned, especially the men -- 245 men were taken to concentration camps in Manjaca and Batkovici.

The Hasancevic lost four of their closest family members and two brothers-in-law were imprisoned in the Manjaca concentration camp for one and a half years. The Hasancevic family fled to Split.

They experienced many difficulties during their journey; they passed through Serb barricades in Brcko, Modrica and Pelagici.

Safeta traveled alone with four children, her own two and her neighbor's children. They did not know whether they would ever reach a free territory; they experienced a fear they will never forget.

94

When they finally reached Split they found a private accommodation that cost 500 DM a month to rent. They were one of the very few families who were able to rent the flat thanks to Safeta's husband who worked in Croatia before the war.

The neighbor's children lived with them for five years. Safeta's son, Alen, finished at the top of his class at the technical secondary school. Amir, Alen's brother, finished the first two years of his secondary education in Split and then continued his studies in Sarajevo.

After living in Split for five years the Hasancevic family decided to return to Bosnia. They could not return to Doboj so they decided to go to Ljubni, where most of the other people from Doboj had fled.

On December 1,1997, after living in Ljubnici for two months a tragic event occurred; Alen suddenly died. He seemed completely healthy but then his heart just stopped -- he was only 20 years old.

This tragic event changed Safeta completely. Her world collapsed and she fell into a very deep depression. She was constantly haunted by these questions: "Why did I lose him? Why after all these years of trauma from the war? Why?"

Safeta explained: "So many times we needed to adapt to a new environment; in Split, we had to make new friends, to find everything we needed ourselves."

After living through all the tragedies of the war Alen had finally succeeded in finding himself and had developed a strong character -- it seemed so unfair that he died after all this. Safeta simply could not accept this destiny: "The biggest sorrow is your own sorrow", she added.

Safeta tried to find some comfort by talking with her female friends and with her neighbors who were experiencing similar problems, but she could not find any consolation.

The only thing that that forced her to step out of her depression was her love and commitment toward her younger son Amir. She knew how much he needed her in his life: as a mother and as a friend. She knew that because he was still growing up he needed her guidance and support.

The necessity to have to care for her younger son motivated her to keep going and with tremendous effort she partially succeeded in recovering from her depression." [11]

Muharrem's Long Road to Freedom

"When I was seven I saw an army tank run over a man – on purpose. The communists were fighting the democrats for control of the government.

I lived in Tirana, the capital of Albania, one block from the embassy compound. There were a lot of demonstrations, a lot of fighting. I left in 1991 with my parents when I was eight years old. They wanted a better life for me.

For the next two years we lived in Hanover, Germany. I went to school; my parents worked, it was a good life, but then our refugee visa ran out and we had to leave.

So, we went to Greece, where one of my two older, married sisters had settled with her husband when our family left Albania. With both parents working, I was left alone all day; I could not go to school because we had no visa to be in the country.

When I wasn't at the beach, I watched TV – in Greek, which is how I learned the language. Then in 1995 my mother's best friend informed us that she had been able to get us a warranty (sponsorship) that would allow us to return to Germany, so we had to return to Albania to pick it up; the warranty turned out to be no good.

Eventually my dad did manage to get "papers" (warranty) to go to Germany – but only for himself. After he had been gone a month, my mom and I moved to Czechoslovakia because my dad had been able to arrange "papers" (warranty) for us through a friend to go there.

After being there two months, we simply walked across the border into Germany where it had been arranged for a friend of the family to meet us and drive us to Dad, six hours away.

But, after only three months in a German refugee camp, Mom and I had to escape. Since three years had not yet elapsed from our first "visit" to Germany, we were not entitled to legal "papers".

The officials were after us; we saw my father get "detained" one day as he was returning to the refugee camp. Three months later they sent him back to Albania, but in the meantime, Mom and I "escaped" to Holland; she had "connections" there.

We spent the next four months in a Holland refugee camp that we were allowed to enter because we had passed ourselves off as Kosovars, and that made us refugees. (Kosov at one time belonged to Albania, which is predominately Muslim, but it had been "sold" many years ago to Serbia, which is predominately Catholic; the Kosovars were fighting for the right to reunite with Albania.)

It was while we were in the camp that my second, older sister (married and also living in Greece with her husband and son) notified us that my mother had won the LOTTO. No, it wasn't like the Connecticut LOTTO where you win millions; ours was worth much more – freedom! In Albania there is a lottery system to determine who will be allowed to legally go to the United States. My mother had entered the lottery one-and-a-half years ago. Finally, her name had been picked. (The LOTTO winner may take his/her family.)

First, we had to return to Albania for one year to get all of the paperwork complete that would give us a green card, a visa, a passport.

Our first stop in the United States was New York City. That was a bad stop. There I got involved in an Albanian gang; I had to get "involved" in order to protect myself from the other four ethnic gangs.

While I did finish eighth grade, our first year there, my freshman year found me in increasing trouble. That is why my parents moved to Bristol – to find a better life for me. We think we have found freedom – finally."
[12]

Having read these three stories you can begin to understand how terrifying and hard to both body and spirit being a Refugee can be.

Though there are numerous International Treaties and Laws that govern the treatment of Refugees, you must always remember that you are not going to be cared for or looked after to any extent greater than you are prepared to help yourself, and your family.

"The greatest discovery of my generation is that a human being can alter his life by altering his attitudes of mind."
William James

Chapter 7: Left Behind

The quotation I am opening this chapter with speaks to what is going to be your most important asset if you find yourself left behind, your mental attitude.

Whatever the reasons may be that you have found yourself unable to leave an area about to consumed by war do not matter, and have no bearing on what your actions will be.

You have been left behind, you are on your own, there is no fast viable escape, all you have left to do is prepare, and that is what this chapter is about, preparing.

The first rule of safety and survival in war zones can be summarized in three words…location, location and location.

The further you are away from the prime areas of targeting by military forces the greater will be your chances to survive.

The places to avoid at all costs are: Large cities and urban areas, Airports of any kind, Large Interstate and International roadways of all kinds, Coastal areas, Government buildings of all kinds, Railways and Sports stadiums.

Large cities and urban areas, especially in America, are specifically designed to able to closed off in a short amount of time by the fewest available military forces. This is generally due to many of them being completely circled by large highway systems.

Airports are utilized during war for both the transportation of troops and equipment and will be heavily restricted areas and constantly patrolled.

Interstate and International roadways will be the primary routes for large troop and equipment movements and will likewise be heavily patrolled and security measures will also include aerial patrols by combat planes and helicopters.

All types of Government buildings will have tight security and constant patrols of military forces.

Railways will be constantly patrolled by both land and air forces to protect these vital transportation routes for the movement of heavy battle equipment and larger troop movements.

Sports stadiums of all kinds will be utilized by the military forces as holding areas for large concentrations of dissidents, captured prisoners and those awaiting classification.

So the first part of your planning should include a way that you will be as far away from these types of areas as possible. Even if you're presently living in one of these large cities, preparation is possible, and affordable.

Your immediate needs of preparation therefore are to find yourself a location away from these areas as soon as possible. This doesn't require you to purchase a rural property, but rather to know how to get to a rural area, and in the shortest amount of time.

You should not just choose one location but two at the least, three or four would be better. You are not going to know ahead of time which routes to safety are going to be open to you, so it would be very unfortunate to find yourself having to head in a southerly direction when all of your plans have been made for a northern route.

Your plans must assume that you will have no access to food, water or shelter for an extended period of time also.

If you live in a city or a large urban area you would first prepare a backpack with food, water, clothing and only those personal supplies that will keep this backpack comfortably on your back for walks of at least 20 miles a day.

Those with younger children that will to be carried will have to rely on one person's ability to shoulder this load for the entire family for long stretches at a time.

If you have planned ahead you will only be carrying those supplies you will need for a one days journey, because beforehand you will have designated those locations in which you have buried, or otherwise concealed, those supplies needed for each subsequent day after the first one.

Remember too, all of your plans should be centered on your having to walk. This isn't to say that you won't be able to drive a car, motorcycle or bicycle, but rather that in times of war your most reliable form of transportation will be your own two feet.

It is much easier to go around roadblocks, mob actions, troop concentrations, etc., by walking instead of by driving or being driven.

The essence of your plan is for survival, and survival entails escape, evasion, concealment and foraging. And none of these can be accomplished without planning.

Planning and preparation are two important attitudes to start adjusting your mind set to. There is nothing greater than a well executed plan that has been diligently planned for.

I remember reading an article once that said, "Survival Planning Begins at Home", and thinking how wrong that statement was. Not at 'home' does survival planning begin, but in your MIND. Never forget this.
Other considerations for being left behind to face the onslaught of war would include:

Personal Safety: Do you own a weapon? If not, can you acquire one? How much ammunition should have? What are the basics in knowing how to use a weapon, your weapon, in a combat atmosphere? Where and how can you store a weapon so it remains hidden from military forces actively searching for it?

Personal Health: What types of medications do you need for your health and survival? (This goes also for those family members with you.) Do you know first aid? Can you stitch your own, or someone else's wound? Do you have, or know how to acquire the medicines and medical equipment you may need?

Money: If you had to leave your home right this minute how much money would you have? If all banking activities have been halted, how could you acquire more money in the shortest amount of time? If you are put onto a restrictive list by the authorities how could you access your banking reserves, safety deposit boxes, investments or other like assets?

Personal Possessions: If you had to leave your home right now, and with the prospect that you would never return, what would happen to your most cherished possessions, your photographs, documents and other important papers?

Security: If you are on a list to be taken into custody, and after you have left your residence, who would know about your plans of escape? What would your neighbors know? What would your relatives know? What clues to your escape plan would they be able to be found at your home or at your work?

These of just a very few of the questions you have to ask yourself, and the plans you are going to have to make if you either plan on being left behind, or you are not able to escape in time.

Do not by any means take this information as all you need to know either. For that you will need much more information, and there are a number of good resources available to you, including books and Internet resources.

As I have previously pointed out, being left behind should never be your first option, escaping before war comes to your doorstep should always be your first priority.

104

"I know not with what weapons World War III will be fought, but World War IV will be fought with sticks and stones."
Albert Einstein

Chapter 8: Invasion

There are a number of dictionary definitions that apply to the word Invasion, but this is the most important one to remember: A large-scale onset of something injurious or harmful.

Merely by the fact that your country is presently at war, either directly or indirectly (such as being an ally to a warring party or a supplier of materials to one side or the other) Invasion will remain a fact of life you not only have to consider, but also plan for.

History is littered with countless examples of those Nations who believed themselves impervious to invasion but then found themselves grossly unprepared as they were overran.

Likewise there have been those countries that were not direct parties to a war but because of geographic position, oil, or mineral resources or for any numbers of reasons have found themselves overran by invading armies.

Invasions can take many forms also, from massive land invasions, aerial assaults or sea invasions.

Invasions are seldom ever announced in advance and rather come as a surprise to the country that is being invaded. Other scenarios will show massive terrorist activities by underground organizations or Special Forces of an invading army that are meant to disrupt a countries military response to an invading force.

These disruptions can take many forms including; blowing up of rail lines and bridges, disrupting communication sources and the use of poison gas, biological and/or nuclear weapons.

It is also to the advantage of an invading army to strike terror among the civilian population as mass movements of people away from an invasion area also inhibits the movement of counter attacking forces heading towards the invasion area
.

The intelligence organizations of an invading army will also have pre-knowledge of the civilian population in their area of operations and plans to subdue them.

This will include the immediate imprisonment of all men of fighting age, in some countries (Like the United States and Israel where women are allowed to fight in their military forces.) this will also include women.

Extreme tactics of terror will also be used against the civilian population in order to shock them into inaction. This frequently takes the form of the indiscriminant killing of civilians, and is a tactic well known, and well used, by military forces, especially the United States.

But more than anything else I, or anyone else, could write about invasions, the most important thing to remember is that your life, and those of your family, will be changed forever.

Three Stories

The Story of Eva Galler

"The last thing my father told me as he pushed me from the train was 'You run. I know you will stay alive, you have the Belzer Rebbe's blessing.' He was very religious and he believed this.

I was born in a little city in Poland named Oleszyce. Our community consisted of 7,000 families, half of them were Jews. My father, Israel Vogel, was the head of the Jewish community, the head of the Kehillah.

In our part of Poland there was a famous Rabbi, the Belzer Rebbe. When I was born there was a big fire in the Rebbe's house. He had many invitations to stay with people while his house in Belz was being rebuilt. His personal secretary, his Gabbai, went to look at all these places and chose ours.

Our house was big enough to accommodate the Rebbe's household. This was a great honor. He lived with us for three years.

At this time I was an infant in the cradle. My mother had lost four children. We were supposed to go live in a house we owned next door. My mother refused to move me out of our main house until the Belzer Rabbi blessed me. It was said that he gave me a special blessing. The whole city knew about this.

My father had a business of distributing religious articles. The occupation of a majority of the older Jews in our community was to make these articles, like Torahs and tefillin. I was interested in how they were made. They would stretch animal skins on a frame to make the parchment.

The parchment would be cut into sheets. Sofers or scribes would then write the letters on the parchment. It took a scribe an entire year to write a Torah. They sewed the parchment sheets together into the scrolls with threads made of animal sinews.

My father could recognize the handwriting of all of his scribes. Every week they brought their work to my father to get paid. He would then distribute the religious articles to buyers in Germany, Austria, Czechoslovakia, Hungary, Rumania and later, after my brother emigrated, to the United States.

My mother, Ita Prince, was an orphan. The family she lived with was too poor to afford a dowry, and in those days it was hard to get married without one. My father was a widower with six children. My mother was 18 and my father was 34.

They matched my mother up with my father because he was rich and because he promised to take in all her sisters and provide dowries for them. She did not want to marry him, but she had no choice.

Her foster family said, "If you do not marry him you will have to provide for yourself and your three sisters." It was a business proposition. My mother had eight children. I was the oldest child. I felt sorry for my mother because she was always pregnant.

At that time it was considered unimportant for a girl to have an education. The government gave you only a basic education, and after that you had to pay. My father educated the boys.

After I completed seventh grade my father did not think I should go to high school. I went on a hunger strike. I did not eat and I locked myself in the room until my father agreed that I could go to high school. I had also gone to cheder to get a religious education.

In our city everybody was observant. Everyone went to synagogue and everyone ate kosher. On Shabbos the men wore streimels. When it was time to go to synagogue on Friday night, the shammes would holler in the street or knock on the doors.

The Jews and the non-Jews in our town did not mix socially, only in business. The anti-Semitism was very strong; we felt it all over. The gentile children did not want to associate with us, and they called us names.

The Jewish children were not permitted to take part in school plays. The Christians were told that the Jews killed Christ. On Easter they would throw stones at us. However, there were no pogroms at this time, before the Germans came into Poland.

We were aware of the Nazis and events in Germany from the newspapers. I remember the incident at Zbaszyn when the Polish citizens were expelled from Germany and were forced to return to Poland. This led up to Kristallnacht, which happened in Germany.

I remember that one refugee family did not have a place to live, and my father gave them a room.

Somehow we did not believe Hitler would come to Poland. Until the last minute people did not believe that the Germans would invade us. The Polish soldiers used to sing patriotic songs. They would not give up an inch of our Polish soil to the last drop of their blood. They sang songs about fighting for the port of Danzig.

People did not believe that the Germans would come until they saw the airplanes. It was so sudden. In a couple of days the Germans occupied the whole of Poland. Then there was not anything one could do.

It was too late. The Germans and the Russians had a treaty, the German-Soviet Non-Aggression Pact, which divided Poland at the River San. Because our town was on the Russian side, the Germans occupied our part of Poland for just two weeks. Then, according to the Treaty, the Russians came in. Until 1941 the Russians were in charge.

I still had a year left to finish high school. But my father could not continue his business because the Russians did not permit the practice of religion. As the oldest child I had to take a job to support the family. Jobs were hard to get.

The Russians gave the first jobs to poor people and to working people. Because my father was considered a rich businessman, he was called a capitalist. As the daughter of a "capitalist" I could not get a job.

So I wrote a letter to Stalin. I wrote him that we were a large family and my father was too old to work. I received a reply from his office, and I was given a job. They wrote it up in the local newspaper. I started out as a secretary and advanced to assistant assessor in the local internal revenue office.

We did not expect anything to happen. One Saturday evening in June 1941 we went to sleep. About 6 o'clock Sunday morning we heard gunshots and went out to see what was happening. German motorcycles were going down the main street. Soldiers were shooting right and left. Whoever was on the street was killed right away. This is when our problems began.

The Jews were not permitted to keep a job. People started to trade their belongings with the farmers for food. Potatoes and flour were more important than money.

If someone had savings in the bank, all the money was confiscated. If someone had cash at the house, it did not last too long. Best off were the people who had stores and who could hide the merchandise.

The first thing they did was to make a Judenrat. A few Jews became responsible for the entire Jewish community. To these people they gave orders which they had to pass on to us. Every day there was a different decree. We had to put on armbands so we would be recognized as Jews.

Our armbands were white with blue Stars of David sewn on. Every day orders came for people to go to work at hard labor or to do work like cleaning toilets. The Judenrat had to deliver the number of people they required.

Already it was a fight for survival. We had to do what they wanted. If we did not, we would be killed immediately. We did not have a newspaper or a radio so we did not know what was going on in the outside world. We just hoped to stay alive and that the war would end before they would do something to us.

We were not allowed to walk down the sidewalks, but had to walk down the middle of the street. The street in our town was not paved. When it rained it became a street of mud. Once my mother forgot and walked on the sidewalk.

A young man walked by, a Ukrainian man who was a teacher. He had helped my brothers with their homework and had come to our house. He went and hit my mother when he saw her walking on the sidewalk. My mother came in and cried. She said, "If a German had done it, I would have said nothing. But this man should have been an intelligent person: he came into my house and I fed him."

Even your friends could turn against you. It was as if anyone could pick on the underdog. I did not understand. I felt degraded. There were times when I envied a dog. A dog has his master who takes care of him and feeds him. We were outside the law. Anyone could do with us as they wanted.

I was luckier than most people under the Germans. I understood the tax books. For almost a year I was sitting in city hall with the armband working on the tax books. I worked for them until they could train somebody else. I did not receive any pay. I got bread, which was better than getting money.

When I brought the bread home, I gave everyone a piece. My little brother looked for crumbs on the floor because he was hungry and wanted more, but nobody could have more. Now I feel so guilty. I hit him because he took the crumbs from the dirty floor.

In those days the way they delivered messages was by a city drummer. He beat his drum calling out "Ja wam tu oglaszam"" I have an announcement for you." In our town the drummer's name was Pan Czurlewicz. He wore a uniform like a policeman.

He came to our street drumming and calling until everyone came out of their houses. "All the Jews must assemble in the city square," he said, "If they find someone missing they will be shot."

When we arrived at the city square, we saw a fire in the middle of it. The whole inventory from the synagogue was burning, the prayer books, the torah scrolls, everything was burning.

The German soldiers pushed the young girls up to the old men and made them dance around the bonfire. When we looked up we saw that each of our town's three synagogues was on fire.

All around us our neighbors and friends were watching and laughing at us like they were at a show. This hurt us more that what the Germans did. After the fire burned down they told us to line up and parade through the whole town so everyone could see us. This I will never forget.

We were living in conditions of hunger and fear, but we were still in our own homes. People made hiding places in their houses to hide from the Germans.

Our hiding place was in the attic behind a double wall. Whenever we saw the Germans, we would run to the attic and hide. Even the little children understood that if they made noise it was a matter of life and death.

This continued until September 1942. One day the drummer came. He announced that all the Jews had to take what they could carry and walk the seven kilometers to the next town of Lubaczow. There was a ghetto there.

All the Jews of Oleszyce and the neighboring villages were moved to the ghetto in Lubaczow. The ghetto was the size of one city block for 7,000 people. We slept 28 people in a room that was about 12 by 15 feet. It was like a sardine box. People lived in attics, in basements, in the streets--all over. We were lucky to have a roof over our heads; not everyone did.

It was cold. In one corner there was a little iron stove but no fuel. We were not given enough to eat. The children looked through the garbage for food. There was not enough water to drink.

There was one well in the backyard, but it would not produce enough water for everybody. To be sure to get water you had to get up in the middle of the night. Once I had a little water to wash myself, and my sister later washed herself in the same water.

Some people started to eat grass. They would swell up and die. Because of the unsanitary conditions people got lice and typhus. My brother Pinchas got night blindness from lack of vitamins. Every day a lot of people died. It was a terrible situation. People were depressed. There was nothing to do. They waited and hoped and prayed.

Then, beginning on January 4, 1943, the Gestapo and the Polish and Ukrainian police started to chase all the Jews out from their houses. The deportation took several days. People ran and hid. The Jewish police helped to find the people in hiding. They had been promised that they would stay alive if they cooperated.

We knew where we were going. A boy from our town had been deported to Belzec camp. He escaped and came back to our town. He told us that Belzec had a crematorium. Deportation trains from other cities had passed by our city and people had thrown out notes.

These notes were picked up by the men forced to work there. The notes said, "Don't take anything with you, just water."

They took us to a cattle train. People started to run away from the train, but they were shot. Once on the train we had to stand because there was no room to sit down. A boy tore the barbed wires from the train window. The young people started to jump out of the window.

Many jumped. The SS on the rooftop of the train shot at them with rifles. My father told us, the oldest three, "Run, run--maybe you will stay alive. We will stay here with the small children because even if they get out, they will not be able to survive." To me he said, "You run, I know you will stay alive. You have the Belzer Rebbe's blessing." He was very religious and he believed this.

115

My brother Berele jumped out, then my sister Hannah, and then I jumped out. The SS men shot at us. I landed in a snowbank. The bullets did not hit me. When I did not hear anything anymore, I went back to find my brother and my sister. I found them dead. My brother Berele was 15. My sister Hannah was 16. I was 17.

I took off my star and I promised myself that never again would I ever wear a star. I ran back to the city where we lived. We had a Gentile friend there, a lady to whom we gave a lot of our belongings. She was scared to keep me. Gentile families who were found to be hiding Jews would be killed. She hid me behind a cedar-robe in the corner.

I was standing there listening to people come in. They were discussing how they were killing the Jews, how the Jews were running away, who had been shot. It was a small city. They felt sorry for the Jews. It was a sensation, a thing to talk about. They felt sorry but they forgot right away.

In the evening when it became dark she gave me half a loaf of bread and 25 Polish zlotys. She told me to go. I went to another family's house that I knew who lived close to the woods. He was a forester.

When I worked with the taxes, I had helped them. They were afraid to let me in. It was already dark. I could not walk. It was freezing cold. There was snow. I was not well dressed.

I went in the barn where they had a newborn calf, and I lay down with it to keep me warm. About twelve o'clock the wife came to look at the calf. She saw me and felt sorry for me. She let me come and sleep in the house, but in the morning she told me to go.

I wanted to go to the train station, but I was afraid to go in our city because everybody knew me. So I went to the woods and walked to the next station 32 kilometers away.

At that time it was thought that there were partisans in the woods. People were afraid to go in the woods, but I was not afraid. I was walking in the deep snow, and in the evening I came to the station in Jaroslaw.

At the Jaroslaw station I bought a ticket for Cracow. I figured that Cracow was a big city with a big Jewish community. Maybe the ghetto would still be there. In the train station I saw the person who took over my job at the internal revenue.

I was frightened that she might recognize me. I kept walking around the block until the train came. Then I got on the train. This was another situation. I did not have any documents. The lady that gave me the bread had given me some papers from her daughter, but they were not good enough. There were identification checks on the train. Every station I would move to another wagon.

In Cracow I spent two days and two nights living in the train station. There was a curfew at night because of the war. People who came into the city late had to stay in the train station until morning, so there were always a lot of people there. I moved around a lot so people would not recognize me, from one bench to another, from one room to another.

It was a big station. But I did not have any money, and I did not have any bread. I had never been to Cracow before. I did not know where the ghetto was. I did not see anybody with an armband, and I was scared to ask someone where the ghetto was.

I walked and walked. I was hungry. I figured the only thing to do was to jump in the river. I came to a market place, a farmers' market. I could hear running. They closed up the market place and took all the young people aside. I could hear the girls and boys talking.

They were catching boys and girls and sending them to work in Germany. Nobody would go work freely in Germany; they had to use force. This was how they rounded up the people. I was very glad that I was caught with those people. I was caught as a Gentile and not as a Jew.

They took us to an old school at Number 4 Wolska street. First they sent us to take baths, and they disinfected our clothes. A lady inspected our hair; because I had been in the ghetto, I had lice. She cut my hair short and put something in it. Next they sent us to doctors. If you had certain kinds of sicknesses, you would be relieved.

I prayed to God that they should not find anything wrong with me--after such a long time in the ghetto, after the malnutrition. Thank God, I passed the physical. If I had been a boy, I could not have passed. None of the Polish boys were circumcised, but the Jewish boys were.

A Jewish boy would have been recognized by the doctors right away. I assumed the identity of a Polish girl, Katarzyna Czuchowska, a name I made up. I took a different birthday, May 12th.

We were put on a train and taken from Cracow to Vienna. They sent us to a place where the German farmers came to pick up workers. It was something like a slave market. One family liked me and took me to their farm, which was on the border with Czechoslovakia in the Sudetenland.

The farm was a bad place because the husband was at home and he was a very mean person. The neighbors said that he avoided the draft by bribing someone. He made anti-Semitic remarks, even though he did not know I was Jewish.

After a year I got sick. They transferred me to a smaller farm where there were nice people. There were no males there, and I had to carry sacks of grain. At Christmas, when the husband came home on leave, they made homemade wine from their vineyards.

The husband got drunk and he began to curse Hitler, "Hitler, you so-and-so! If it were not for Hitler, I would be home with my family." I was scared someone would hear him, so I closed the door so nobody would come into the house.

I was scared that they would find out I was Jewish. I was not afraid of the Germans because I was not different looking from anyone else. But I was afraid of my friends, the Poles. I was scared that one of them would recognize me. They were country girls, and I was afraid that they would figure out how much more educated I was.

I was the letter writer for everybody. If someone needed to write a love letter, they came to me. The Poles got letters from their families and packages of clothes. My letters were returned. I made up the excuse that my family was resettled and they did not know where I was. After a time when I saw that nobody recognized me, I felt secure.

Then a terrible thing happened. Before Easter, Marie, the farm lady I worked for, told me that I had to go to confession. I was a religious Jewish girl, and I did not know what Catholic girls did at confession. I lay awake nights worrying what I would do until I came up with a solution.

My Polish friends did not speak German, which I had picked up easily because I knew Yiddish. My friends were going to go to confession at the Slovakian church, where they spoke a language close to Polish.

I asked Marie to let me take confession at her church in the German language. She showed me the prayer book where I had to confess my sins. I figured if I did not say the words exactly right, the German priest would not be suspicious because I was just a Polish girl.

So I made up some sins and went to confession. My heart was pounding; I was so scared. I saw what other people were doing, and I imitated them. I went up to the German priest, and he put something on my tongue. Somehow I blacked out; it must have been the fear. When I came to, Marie asked me why I was so pale. I made up the excuse that I was weak from fasting. Later on everything went smoothly.

The worst part was when I tried to go to sleep. In the daytime I did not have time to think. I got up at five o'clock in the morning, milked ten cows, then went into the fields. But at night I was afraid to sleep. I dreamed about my family and my friends.

I had horrible nightmares: I dreamed I saw my whole family with the Germans running after us. I hid but I could not escape from them. I wondered if my family were dead or alive. I dreamed I saw my dead sister and brother on the cattle train to Belzec. I woke up shaking in a cold sweat. At that time I prayed to God.

I promised myself, "If I will survive, I will return to the religion of my parents. I will observe." And that's how I survived.

They brought sixty Jews to a big farm to work. There were guarded by the SS. One day I passed three of them, and I felt such an urge to talk to them. I saw that other boys and girls were talking to them, but I was scared that if I talked to them, I would get emotional or reveal something, and they would recognize me.

I do not know what happened to those people.

In May 1945 the Germans started to draw back, and one day the Russians came in. I was still scared to tell anyone I was Jewish. I looked at the Russian soldiers to see if I could recognize anyone who was Jewish, but I didn't.

Now came the time that I could help my people, the German farmers. The Russians started to rape the German women. When they came to our door, I spoke to them in Russian. They stationed a Russian captain in our house. He saw to it that nothing happened to our family.

I wanted to go back to Poland. I figured that maybe I would still find somebody alive. It was a long journey back to Poland. The mail started up. I had a brother and sister from my father's first marriage who were alive.

He had immigrated to the United States in 1933, and she had gone to Russia. He wired her and she came and got me and took me to Breslau (Wroclaw). We could not go back to our city because Russia had taken that part of Poland.

I had written to a friend and not one Jew went back to our city. I learned later that from my whole city of about 3,000 Jewish families, just 12 people survived.

The Red Cross had lists of people who had survived, but we could not find anybody from our family. My half-brother attempted to get me a visa to the United States, but there were quotas. I got a transit visa to Sweden. Meanwhile, from the Red Cross lists I found a friend from Oleszyce who had been in Auschwitz.

She was the only other person who jumped from the same train as I did and lived. Her fiancee had met my future husband at the train station in Cracow. My husband was in the Polish army.

He and I were childhood friends from Oleszyce. Her fiancée invited my husband to come to their wedding, which was two weeks before I was supposed to go to Sweden, but they did not tell me anything about him.

At the wedding Henry walked in--He did not know that I had survived--I did not know that he had survived. I almost dropped from the chair. I thought I was seeing a ghost. Henry right away asked me to marry him.

I said, "No, Henry, I have to wait; I am going to Sweden." Henry went with me to Warsaw to catch the first airplane that was going from Warsaw to Stockholm after the war. Henry said, "I will come to Sweden." Four weeks later Henry came illegally on a coal boat to Sweden. He paid a sailor who smuggled him onto the boat.

At that time most of the survivors were single. People married people that they did not know just to get somebody, just to have a family. When Henry and I were young children in school, he would come to our house under my window and talk to me. We were friends. Not boyfriend and girlfriend. I was too young. But we were attracted to one another.

When the Swedes let Henry out of quarantine, he asked for political asylum. He did not want to be in Poland, a communist country, in a communist army. A Rabbi married us three weeks later on Christmas Eve. I did not even have a coat. I had to borrow a coat from the girl next door to go to Synagogue.

We took a furnished room and went to work in a restaurant. We were dishwashers. Henry washed the big pots and I washed the glasses. We lived on one salary and with the other we bought things that we would need for the house.

After three months I got a job in a factory making blouses, and Henry got a job in a tailoring factory. No one gave us anything; we started out from nothing. We worked our way up with our ten fingers. Henry learned tailoring in no time.

They sent him to a school to learn to be a foreman. He got a high school degree; he took correspondence courses; he learned English. After three years my eldest daughter was born.

We came to the United States on May 2, 1954, when our quota came. After eight years in Sweden it was difficult to adjust to life in New York City. It was difficult for me not knowing the language.

When I came to the United States I spoke Yiddish, Hebrew, Polish, Russian, German, and Swedish, but not English. I was pregnant and stayed at home. My oldest daughter came home with her school books—"See Dick run". I learned English by helping my daughter with her homework. I tested her on spelling, and she tested me.

As soon as I learned the English language, I adjusted. After seven years in New York, we thought we would like it better in a smaller community.

We came to New Orleans in 1962. Eventually, my husband started his own tailoring business. I had two other children, both girls.

There are times when I ask myself, "Where was God when my parents were taken away from me? When my youngest brother shouted, which I still hear him screaming, I want to live too!"

When they took us away, he shouted, "I want to live, I want to live!" This picture will never, never in my life

124

disappear from my eyes. A lot of times when I lie down, I still hear that voice. He was 3 years old.

Even though they were that small, the little children knew what was happening to them. And I ask myself a lot of times, "Where was God? Where is God?" I don't try to search any deeper because I think without religion it would be harder for me to live.

If you lose your parents at any age, it hurts. To lose your parents in that way, at that age, and to be alone in the world... If you cannot grieve right away, it stays with you for your whole life.

You need compassion to be able to talk out your grief. Time is the best doctor. As the days and weeks and years go, it grows weaker and weaker. But you never forget. I tell my students that they should cherish their parents and obey them. A parent is always at your side.

In Poland, after the war I was sick emotionally and physically. I had to go to a doctor to get shots to gain weight. In Sweden I went to a psychiatrist because I could not get over those terrible nightmares.

Today I see that when there is a disaster, they send people to a psychiatrist or a psychologist. We had to work out our own problems. As parents we were overprotective to our children. My eldest daughter was accepted at an Ivy League college, but I was afraid to let her go away from home to school. We were afraid to let our children know too much about our past.

I taught Hebrew and prepared children for their Bar Mitzvahs. A friend encouraged me to go to college. In 1985 I graduated from the University of New Orleans.

It was my children that made me talk. In the beginning I did not talk to anybody. I did not tell anything. My daughter had to write a paper for school, and she got me to talk. Now, Henry and I go to schools to talk with students about the Holocaust. That is how life goes on." [13]

The Story of Jeannine Burk

"I was a hidden child. I hid in this woman's house from ages three to five. I am grateful to her, but I do not know her name. I will never be able to thank her in a public way.

Belgium was supposed to be neutral during the war but Hitler paid no attention to treaties. Unfortunately, the King of Belgium helped him.

Rumors began to circulate in Brussels that things were going to get very uncomfortable for the Jews. There must have been a network of underground resources where you could inquire about hiding Jews.

My father had found a place for my brother to go. He had a place for my sister to go. He found this place for me to go.

My father took me on a streetcar. This memory is etched in my mind because it is the last time I ever saw my father. We rode to the end of the line. I remember getting off with him.

I remember walking what appeared to me to be a long distance. He knocked on a door and a woman answered. I went inside. That was the last time I ever saw my father.

I lived inside this house for two years. Occasionally, I was allowed to go out in the back yard. I was never allowed to go out front. I was never mistreated. Ever! But I was never loved. I lost a great part of my childhood simply because I was a Jew.

The Nazis used to love to parade. When they used to parade, everybody on the street had to open their doors to watch. The lady I was staying with had to open her door and watch too. She would hide me in the outhouse. I was petrified.

I did not know exactly what I was afraid of, but I remember being absolutely petrified. An outhouse is small, and I would retreat to the farthest little corner. There was a crack in the front of the outhouse. I thought that if I could see them parading outside they would be able to see me.

I remember one time pushing open the outhouse door and crawling on my hands and knees after this pussy cat. I grabbed the kitty and pulled it inside with me. I wanted partly to protect it and partly to hold onto something because I was so alone and so scared.

My life as a hidden child was...how can I say it...I had no toys. The only fresh air I got was when I was allowed to go in the backyard. I made up imaginary friends because I had no one to play with. I do not remember being hugged and kissed. That was my life for two years.

The rest of the story was told to me afterwards by my sister. My brother was twelve years older than I was. He had already been hidden in a Christian home for boys. My older sister was eight years older than I was.

She could not be easily moved because she had a bone disease, osteomyelitis.

Some neighbors snitched on us. One morning at 5:00 o'clock the Gestapo went through the neighbor's house, jumped over the brick wall and pounded on the room where my parents were sleeping.

They broke down the door. The Gestapo took my father and threw him in the truck. They wanted to take my mother, but she wouldn't go. My mother told them, "You can shoot me here, but I will not leave my daughter."

The Gestapo pulled the blankets off my sister and saw that she was in a body cast. The officer said that they would be back later for them. And that is what they did.

By some miracle my mother made one last phone call to a Catholic hospital, and they agreed to take my sister. An ambulance came to get her. The Germans used to take over hospitals for their own use. However, the one place they would not go was the isolation ward.

The nuns felt that it would be better for my sister to risk contracting a disease rather than to risk letting the Germans find a Jewish child. My sister lay in bed in the isolation ward for two years.

Once my sister was hidden, my mother went to hide in a pre-arranged location. It was a nursing home out in the country. There was a stereotype about Jews, that they had dark hair and hooked noses.

My mother was blonde and blue-eyed. She did not fit the picture that they were looking for, so she was safe working as a practical nurse in the country.

In the fall of 1944 I remember my mother coming to get me. Then we went to get my sister. She had to learn to walk all over again. My brother found his way back to the house where we had lived.

One day we saw soldiers on the street. Every family took in a couple of soldiers. I remember them giving me chocolate, and I also remember starting school.

We were waiting for my father to come back. Periodically there were groups of survivors and prisoners of war who would march home. They must have been reunited in one particular place. I remember standing outside with my mother, sister and brother and waiting and waiting for my father to come home. We kept waiting and waiting.

Later we found out from an agency that my father had been exterminated. He had been gassed in Auschwitz. If I had been home when they took my father, I would be dead too. They would have gassed me instantly. That is what they did to little children.

I was never allowed to have a father. I don't have a picture of my family except for one little picture of me and my father. I have no idea of what the five of us looked like together. None.

And all because he was a Jew. He never killed anyone. He never robbed anyone, yet they murdered him. They exterminated him simply because he was a Jew.

After the war my mother struggled to take care of us. We had nothing. We were poor. My mother contracted breast cancer. They removed a breast, but it was too late. The cancer had spread all over her.

She knew she was going to die because the night before she had all of us come to the hospital room. She said to me, "You gotta be a good girl." My sister-in-law took me back to her house while my brother and sister stayed overnight at the hospital.

The next day they came back to get me. She had died during the night. My mother was only forty-five when she died. God gave her too little time. I still cry for her.

My mother died in February 1950, when I was ten. In March 1950 the International Ladies' Garment Workers' Union was having a 50th anniversary celebration in Atlantic City.

The Union had sent money to help the children. They invited two kids from France, two kids from Italy and one from Belgium. The director of my school knew us and asked my sister.

The first little girl had either gotten sick or chickened out. Having had nothing for most of my life, I thought the trip was like heaven. We were treated like royalty.

We landed in New York and visited the Union headquarters. They were so good to us. They gave me a new watch and one for my sister. There was this wonderful man, Mr. Rubin. Also, this journalist and his wife really took a liking to me.

They took me to Klein's Department Store, to the Toy Department. They said, "You can pick out any doll you want and anything to go with her." I guess I have always been a certain way. I picked out just one doll and nothing else. Oh, I loved that doll. She really was beautiful. The trip was the most incredible six weeks.

A month after I got back to Belgium, we got a letter from the Savage family. In America there had been a news article about our trip in the Forward Yiddish Newspaper. Some of my father's sisters had gone to America before the war. The Savages were related to them.

My brother had gotten married and had two kids. My sister was engaged to be married. The Savages offered to bring me to America. My sister thought I had a chance to be adopted and to have a better life.

Leaving Belgium was the most traumatic thing that had ever happened to me. I was close to my brother and my sister. To me it looked as if they did not want me anymore now that they were married.

The Savages had gone to a lot of trouble. They had obtained special permission from the governor of New York to get me a visa outside of the immigration quotas.

The Sabena flight took eighteen hours. I had never been on an airplane before. At the stopover in Greenland I ate an ice cream cone. I got sick on the plane. When we landed in New York my only thought was where can I hide so I can go back with the plane.

The day I landed was my twelfth birthday. I did not speak any English. I did not know what the people looked like who would be coming to get me.

When they saw me, the Savages were mortified because I was so skinny. I weighed 62 pounds. When they gave me a bath they said my skin was grey. It would have been better if they had not adopted me. I guess they did the best they could.

I was young when I got married. I had two boys, and later I got divorced. I was alone for a long time. Then I met Maurice. In 1970 my ex-husband's family introduced us.

Maurice was a widower with four children. When we met he was singing in a barbershop quartet in Atlantic City. Maurice is the most wonderful person in the whole world. It is like God finally said, "OK, you deserve him". We have six wonderful children and nine grandchildren.

I did not start to speak about the Holocaust until after I joined the New Americans Social Club. I think it was partly from denial and partly from guilt. Can you imagine? I was a grown mother with six kids and I would be driving in City Park and I would imagine that my father would show up.

In 1985 I went to the World Gathering of Holocaust Survivors held in Philadelphia. It was an incredible experience. Several of us from the New Americans went together. Elie Wiesel spoke. I was with a lot of people who had experienced harder things than I had. But we were all survivors.

At the Gathering there was a book of German records. The Germans were meticulous record keepers. This book contained the names of people who had been deported to the concentration camps. This was the first time that I saw my father's name as being deported.

For years I really had the fantasy that he would find us, but in Philadelphia I saw his name. They had added the dates when the person came back from the camps. Next to his name there was nothing. This was the first time it sank in. He was not coming back. I was glad my sister and brother-in-law were there.

At the Philadelphia gathering there was a stage. Survivors would get up on the stage and say, "Is anybody here from this town" or "I survived this camp." They were hoping to meet someone. It was heartbreaking to see that after so many years people were still searching. People were still hopeful.

I think that my parents may have paid the woman I was hidden with. If it were not for her, I would not be here. I don't know where she lived. My sister doesn't know, and my brother doesn't know.

My father was killed, and my mother died when I was ten. My parents were the only two people who knew where I had been hidden. I would like so much to do something for that woman.

I am sure she is not alive, but maybe her daughters are. I would like to thank her, and I can't because I don't know who she was. I don't have a clue. What seemed a far distance to a three-year-old may not be so far away to an adult, but I don't know. I have no idea.

I did not observe anything for the longest time. I did not believe in God. I think a lot of survivors feel guilty about surviving: "Why am I alive and why is my father dead?

Maybe God chose me because I am able to make a little contribution by telling this now."

People ask me, can I forgive? I can't. I cannot forgive. I blame the German people a great deal because I feel they were passive.
They turned away. They may have the audacity to say they did not know. That is unacceptable. Until they can own up to it, I can't forgive." [14]

The Story of Solomon Radasky

How did I survive? When a person is in trouble he wants to live. He fights for his life...Some people say, "Eh -- What will be, will be." No! You have to fight for yourself day by day.

Some people did not care. They said, "I do not want to live. What is the difference? I don't give a damn." I was thinking day by day. I want to live. A person has to hold on to his own will, hold on to that to the last minute.

I am from Warsaw. I lived in Praga, which is the part of the city across the Vistula river. I had a nice life there; I had my own shop where I used to make fur coats.

In Warsaw when a Jewish holiday came we used to know it was a holiday. All the stores were closed, and the people were in the synagogues.

Out of the 78 people in my family, I am the only one to survive. My parents had 3 boys and 3 girls: My parents were Jacob and Toby; my brothers were Moishe and Baruch, and my sisters were Sarah, Rivka and Leah. They were all killed.

My mother and my older sister were killed in the last week of January 1941. The year 1941 was a cold winter with a lot of snow.

One morning the SD and the Jewish police caught me in the street. I was forced to work with a lot of other people clearing snow from the railroad tracks. Our job was to keep the trains running.

When I returned to the ghetto I found out that my mother and older sister had been killed. The Germans demanded that the Judenrat collect gold and furs from the people in the ghetto.

When they asked my mother for jewelry and furs, she said she had none. So they shot her and my older sister too.

My father was killed in April 1942. He went to buy bread from the children who were smuggling food into the ghetto. The children brought bread, potatoes and cabbages across the wall into the Warsaw ghetto.

A Jewish policeman pointed out my father to a German and told him that he saw my father take bread from a boy at the wall. The German shot my father in the back.

The deportations started on July 22, 1942. My other 2 sisters and 2 brothers went to Treblinka. After that I never saw anybody from my family again.

I am a furrier. In the ghetto I worked at Tobbens' shop. We made lambs' wool jackets for the German army. These were short jackets; today we would call them Eisenhower jackets.

For lunch they gave us bread and soup. In the evening we got another bread and coffee. When Poles came to the shop, we could trade with them for extra food. We gave them a few shirts for a piece of salami and some bread or potatoes to make a soup. But how long could our situation last?

One day there was a selection and I was pulled from the shop. However, I was lucky because a Volksdeutscher told them I was a good worker. So I was allowed to go back to the shop, and someone else was put in my place.

A friend told me that he saw one of my sisters working at Shultz's shop. I wanted to see her, but I was 3 kilometers away and I did not know how to get there.

A Jewish policeman told me that he could get a German soldier to go with me and bring me back. It would cost 500 zlotys, which was a lot of money, but I said OK.

The soldier put me in handcuffs, and he walked behind me with a rifle like I was his prisoner. When I got to Shultz's shop, I could not find my sister. Then I found that I was stuck there.

I could not go back because the ghetto had been surrounded by German soldiers. The next morning was April 19, 1943, which was the day the Warsaw Ghetto Uprising began.

On May 1, 1943, I was shot in the right ankle. The bullet went through the meat and not the bone, so I did not lose my leg. I was taken to the Umschlagplatz. The Treblinka extermination camp could only take 10,000 people a day. In our group we were 20,000. They cut off half of our train and sent it to Majdanek concentration camp. Majdanek was another death camp.

At Majdanek they took our clothes and gave us striped shirts, pants and wooden shoes. I was sent to Barracks 21. As I lay in my bed, an older man asked me how I was. He said, "I can help you." He had been a doctor in Paris. He took a little pocket knife and operated on me.

To this day I do not understand how he could have kept a knife in the camp. There were no medicines or bandages. He said, "I have no medication, you have to help yourself. When you urinate use some of the urine as an antiseptic on your wound."

We had to walk 3 kilometers to work. I had to hold myself up straight without limping and walk out of the gate of the camp. I was scared. If I limped, they would take me out of line. At Majdanek they hung you for any little thing. I did not know how I would make it. God must have helped me and, I was lucky.

We stood at the appell in our wooden shoes. Then when we got out of the gate we had to take off our wooden shoes and tie them over our shoulders with a piece of string.

We had to walk to work barefoot. There were little stones on the road that cut into your skin and blood was running from the feet of many people. The work was dirty field work. After a few days some people could not take it anymore, and they fell down in the road.

If they could not get up, they were shot where they lay. After work we had to carry the bodies back. If 1,000 went out to work, a 1,000 had to come back.

One day as we were standing at appell, a man in the back of the line smoked a cigarette. Heavy smokers would find a piece of paper and light it just to feel like they were smoking something. A German, the Lagerfuhrer, came up riding a tall, black horse.

The horse had a white patch on his head and its legs were white too. It was a beautiful horse. The Lagerfuhrer held a whip in his hand. This man was a monster. It was late in the day and the sun was going down. He saw the smoke from the cigarette.

The Lagerfurhrer looked down at us and demanded to know who had smoked a cigarette. No one answered. "I am going to hang 10 dogs," he said. "I will give you 3 minutes."

They called us dogs because we had tags with our numbers on them; my number was 993. We looked from one to the other, but no one answered.

The Lagerfurhrer did not wait 3 minutes; he did not wait 2 minutes. He took his whip and he cut off 2 rows of 5 prisoners. I was in the group of 10.

He asked, "Who wants to go up first on the bench?" You had to go stand on the bench and put the rope around your neck. I was in the first three to go up on the bench. I climbed up and put the rope around my neck.

He started beating us. He beat me so much the blood was running down my head.

Before this happened, a soldier had come to Majdanek for the purpose of selecting three groups of 750 people to take to another camp.

I had been selected to be in the second group of 750. This soldier had been in Lublin at the main office processing our papers. While I was standing on the bench, the soldier came back to the gallows area.

When he saw what was happening, he started hollering, "Halt, Halt! What is happening here?"

The Lagerfurhrer said, "A dog smoked a cigarette. They won't say which one, so I am going to hang 10 dogs."

"Whose dogs?" the soldier asked. "I have papers to transfer these people, and I cannot bring in dead dogs. I have to bring them alive."

The soldier took off the rope that had been around my neck. All it would have taken was a few seconds more and I would have been dead. He just had to kick out the bench. The soldier beat us until we jumped down from the bench and got back into the line.

The soldier took us to the railroad tracks, he put us on a train and the next morning we left Majdanek. I had been there 9 weeks. We were on this train for two nights and a day with no food or water. In my 9 weeks at Majdanek I had not changed my shirt or washed myself. We were eaten up with lice, and many of us were swollen from hunger.

When we got off the train, we saw that we had arrived at Auschwitz. There was a selection and some of us were machine gunned in a field there. They did not take them to the gas chambers.

I was taken to get a number tattooed on my arm. I got Number 128232. The separate numbers add up to 18. In the Hebrew language the letters of the alphabet stand for numbers. The letters which stand for the number eighteen spell out the Hebrew word "Chai", which means life. After I was tattooed, I was given a potato.

I was first sent to the camp at Buna. After I got out of quarantine, I was put to work building railroad tracks. The Capo there was a murderer. I am short, and he would put a short man together with a tall man to carry twenty-foot lengths of iron. The tall man I worked with had to bend his knees.

One time I fell down and could not get up. The Capo started screaming and beating me, and he pulled me aside. There was a selection, and we had to take off our clothes and stand naked the whole night.

The next morning a truck with a red cross came, and they pushed us into it, one on top of the other. We thought that they were going to take us to the gas chambers.

Instead, we were taken to the Auschwitz I camp. A Polish man came out of a building, and he asked us to call out our numbers. I said, "128232". He looked at a paper and asked my name? I said, "Szlama Radosinski", which is my name in Polish and doesn't sound like a Jewish name. He asked me where I was from? "Warsaw", I said. How long was I there? "I was raised there", I said.

He started to cuss me like I never heard before in my life. He pulled me out of the line and put me in a corner. He said, "Stay here". He brought me a piece of blanket to cover myself with. I was freezing, so he brought me inside the barracks.

I lay down. I did not know what was happening or what to think. A young guy came up to me and said, "I know you". I asked him, "Who are you?" He said his name was Erlich and that he knew me from Majdanek.

I asked him what this place was. He said it was the hospital barracks, Block 20. He told me, "It is very bad here. Dr. Mengele comes two times a week to make selections.

But this is Tuesday and he will not come again this week. I will let you know what is going to happen." I had not eaten since Monday. He gave me a bread.

Erlich had been there 5 weeks. He had come from Majdanek to Auschwitz the same day as I did. Two of the doctors at the hospital knew his grandfather, who had been their rabbi in Cracow.

They had hidden him from Dr. Mengele. Those doctors had tried to help hide Jewish people in Cracow. When the SS came, they killed the Jews they hid and took the doctors to Auschwitz.

On Thursday Erlich came to me and said, "You have to get out of here." I said, "What am I going to do--jump from the second floor window?" In the afternoon he

141

came again and said, "You have to get out of here, or after tomorrow you are going to be dead."

About an hour later a man came in and sat at a table. He asked, "Who wants to go to work?" The Poles in the hospital were not worried about going to work. Why should they go work when they were getting packages from the Red Cross and having enough to eat?

I had to get this work. The man at the table asked me my number and then he cussed me out. I begged him, "I want to go out. I have friends outside. Please let me out." He gave me a piece of paper that said Block 6.

I walked to Block 6, and I showed the paper. The man there said, "I cannot let you in until 9 o'clock at night." I stayed there until the men returned from work. One man asked me, "You are new here; where are you from and what did you do?"

I said, "I am from Warsaw and I was a furrier." He asked me where I lived, and I told him. He asked me if I knew a certain man's name and I said, "Yes, he is a furrier too, and he lives in such and such street."

One of the men said, "I don't believe you; what is this man called? He has a nickname." I said, "This man has a little piece of skin hanging down by his left ear, and they call him 'tsutsik' (Yiddish=nipple)." When I said this, they started to help me. They brought me a big piece of bread and some cold soup.

They asked me where I was going to work, and I showed them the piece of paper. They said, "Oh, No! You will not make it over 8 or 10 days in that job." The job was to work in a coal mine.

"The longest anyone lives in that job is two weeks. After that they go to the crematorium." I was scared. My number was registered as working there. I said, "If I do not go there, then I am going to be hanged next to the kitchen, and the prisoners are going to walk by me."

They said, "Don't worry." One guy calls another guy and says, "Go fix this!" They went to the Capo with the piece of paper. This Capo was a murderer. He had a green triangle. The Germans opened up the jails and they made the prisoners our bosses.

Some of the boys worked in Canada. When the transports came they separated the valuables. They risked their lives to smuggle out gold and other things. Every day they brought this Capo cigarettes or salami, so he said, "Yes."

The next morning they woke me up and they took me with them. They put me in the middle of the line and we walked together out of the gate. They told me that as soon as we get out of the gate, I would be safe because over 6,000 prisoners walk out of the gate every day and nobody knows who is who.

There was a beautiful orchestra playing by the gate. They would not let me go to the other job. I stayed with them until the last minute when Auschwitz was liquidated. They helped me out with little pieces of bread and a little soup.

One day the boys asked me if I could make a cap for the Capo, and they brought me some striped material. I took a piece of string to take a measurement. I asked them for some thread and a needle, and I made the cap in about 2 hours.

For stiffness I took some paper from a cement bag and doubled the material at the top. The Capo liked the cap. I was his guy from then on, and he never beat me the whole time.

I was working for over a year with the boys at the same job, digging sand. Ten of us worked in the sand mine. There was a little guy from Breslau that we made our supervisor. He stood on top, and we were 20 feet down below. Every day we loaded up a wagon with the sand and pushed it 16 kilometers. That was 2 trips of 4 kilometers one way and 4 kilometers coming back-- over 10 miles a day.

Twice a day we carried sand to Birkenau to cover the ashes of the dead. The sand was to cover the ashes that came from the crematoria. I did this for more than a year.

The ovens were on one side of the crematoria, and the ashes came out this side. The other side was where the gas chamber was. The Sonderkommando, took the ashes out of the ovens. There were big holes for the ashes and we covered the ashes with sand.

I saw when the transports came. I saw the people who were going in, who to the right and who to the left. I saw who was going to the gas chambers. I saw the people going to the real showers, and I saw the people going to the gas.

In August and September of 1944 I saw them throw living children into the crematorium. They would grab them by an arm and a leg and throw them in.

One Saturday, when we were working, we turned around and saw a soldier with a rifle, so we started to speed up. The soldier said, "Slow down; today is your Sabbath." He was a Hungarian, and he said, "Come to my barracks at 4 o'clock, and I will have something for you.

I will put out a bucket with trash in it. Look under the trash, and you will find eleven pieces of bread." For two or three weeks he put out bread for us. He asked us to bring him money from Canada, which we did. He used to tell us the names of the Jewish holidays. One day he disappeared.

The Russians were pushing back the Germans at Stalingrad. Transports were coming from the Lodz ghetto. That is when we saw them grab the little children by the head and the leg and throw them into the crematoria alive. Then the Hungarian people were coming.

There was this group of young people who wanted to destroy the crematoria. There were four crematoria in Birkenau. The young girls worked at an ammunition factory, and they smuggled in explosives. One crematorium was destroyed. They hung 2 of the girls in front of us when we came back from work.

Life was going on. Everyday was a different problem until January 18, 1945, when they began liquidating Auschwitz. On the 18th I left Auschwitz, and 9 days later the Russians liberated it. Those 7 days cost me 5 months.

When we left, everybody had to get out of the barracks. I was walking the whole night with a rabbi from

Sosnowiec. The Rabbi had come from Block 2, which was the tailor shop. I saw that the soldiers behind us were shooting the people who fell down.

The Rabbi fell down in the road and this boy from Belgium and I held up the Rabbi between us and kept walking. We saw a sled pulled by a soldier, and we asked him if we could pull the sled with the Rabbi in it until morning.

The guys who lived in Block 2, the tailors' barracks, could get some of the gold and the diamonds that people had sewn into the linings of their clothes. They gave their block leader some gold and diamonds to let them hide the Rabbi in the barracks. They hid him in a closet that they had built in the wall.

They put the Rabbi in the closet when they went out to roll call at 6 o'clock in the morning and took him out when they came back in the evening. Many times I went there at 5 o'clock in the morning to say Kaddish for my parents with the Rabbi.

At daylight we came to a small town and the farmers let us stay in the stables. In the evening we had to get out. We walked to a railroad station. In two days the train brought us to Gross-Rosen camp. I never saw the Rabbi again.

Gross-Rosen was murder. The guards walked around with iron pipes in their hands. They said, "We are going to help you; we are going to get you out of here." We were put in a shed with two thousand men. In the daytime we had to stand up, and at night we slept head to foot.

The only food we got was a slice of bread and a cup of coffee at night. I thought I was going to die there.

They walked us to the railroad station, and in 3 days we came to Dachau. The train ride was terrible; the train pulled up and pulled back, up and back. We ate snow for water.

A man was in there with his son who went crazy. The son grabbed the father by the neck and choked him to death. At Dachau there was a selection for the typhus blocks. I had a friend from Radom who was strong. He could have made it, but they put him in the typhus block.

I left Dachau on the 26th or the 27th of April, 1945. I was liberated on May 1st. During this time we were traveling on trains. We were in Tutzing and in Feldafing and in Garmisch.

There were big mountains there. One day they had us get out of the train, and we had to go up twenty feet to the other side of the mountain. Then the Germans set up machine guns and started to fire at us. A few hundred were killed as we ran back to the train.

The next day we heard planes dropping bombs. A few hours later the soldiers opened the door to the train. They said they needed a few people to work cleaning up from the bombs, but we were scared to go.

So they said "You, you and you out," and they caught me. I said to myself, "I think this is the end. After all these years in the ghetto and losing everybody, now this is the end. Who is going to be left to say Kaddish for my family?"

We went to this small town on the other side of the mountain where the train station had been bombed. To one man they gave a shovel, to another a broom and to me they gave a pick. I saw a counter in the station where they were selling little black breads.

I said to myself that I would like to eat a piece of bread before they kill me. I was ready for Kiddush Hashem. I grabbed a little dark bread into my jacket and started eating it. A soldier saw me and he howled, "Go to work." I stayed until I had eaten the bread. I did not move, even though he beat me.

I fell down and he kicked me and I got up. I had to finish eating that little bread. Blood was running down my head. When I finished, I went to work. I had gotten my wish. Then I knew that I was going to survive.

Early at 4 a.m. the next morning near Tutzing we heard heavy traffic on the highway. We pushed to look out of the two little windows of the train. We expected to see the Russians coming but it was the Americans. We hollered.

A jeep drove up with two soldiers. One was a short man, an MP. He spoke good German. He asked who we were. We said we were from the concentration camps. Everybody started hollering and crying. The American soldiers said we were free. They arrested the Germans and the Germans got scared. It was May 1, 1945.

The Americans cooked rice for us. The MP saw me take some rice and he said, "Don't eat that. If you do, you will die. There is too much fat in that for you to eat now. Because your stomach has shrunk, if you eat that you will get diarrhea. I will give you a piece of bread, and you should toast it."

"What is toast," I asked. He said, "Toast is when you make the bread hard." They brought us to Feldafing. I sat in the sun. I boiled a little water and sugar. In two weeks my stomach stretched. They gave us pajamas to wear, but we had no shoes.

One day I saw the same MP in the Jeep. We said to him, "You gave us freedom, but we have no clothes." He said, "I am 3 kilometers from here; come tomorrow at 7 am." We were there at 6 am.

We saw the soldiers get breakfast. He signaled for us to get breakfast too and he told the Captain about us. The Captain said to bring us in. We were nearly naked in our pajamas and with no shoes. The Captain gave us a paper to go to the PX and we got shoes, pants, shirts and jackets. We were told to come back at lunchtime. We got three meals a day for weeks.

At the Displaced Persons camp in Feldafing a man asked me to bring food to his niece who was in the hospital. I brought her oranges, bread and butter. When she got well, she gave me a pair of white linen pants. "You saved my life," she said.

In Germany Feldafing had a big name as a place where you came to find missing people. They put up lists of names of survivors on the walls. A lot of liberated people came looking for relatives. A friend of mine came with two ladies, one whom I knew from before, and the other, Sofia, was my wife's friend.

Sofia said, "You were in the fur business; my girlfriend's family was in the fur business too. Did you ever hear the name of Bursztyn?" I said, "I used to deal with the Bursztyns." She asked me to come to Turkheim to meet her.

I had nothing to lose. Two brothers from Lodz, tailors, made me a suit with two pairs of pants out of a grey and white blanket. My friend and I put our belongings together in one package and went out on the highway to hitchhike to Turkheim.

I left Feldafing in August of 1945.

The next day my wife, Frieda, came to see Sofia. My wife was shy and wouldn't come downstairs to meet me. So Sofia said to her, "Go to the window and take a look." She looked. Since then I say, "My wife looked through the window and took a fishing rod and she got me."

We got married in November 1946. My wife was from the same town as I was, and I used to deal with her family. With us there was a feeling, like a family.

We were very poor. At that time you had to have a card to buy things. I went to the Burgermeister, who was like the mayor, to get coupons to get a suit.

The problem was that I did not have any money to buy it. My wife and Sofia had a little money that they loaned me to buy a suit, and I loaned this suit to my friend when he got married.

My wife had no dress. We were going to get married on Saturday night. Saturday during the day I knocked on the door of this German woman I knew. I had spoken to her in the street, and we had talked a few times.

She had a daughter who was the same size as Frieda. I got 2 packages of cigarettes, 2 Hershey chocolate bars and a little can of coffee and put them into a paper bag.

When she answered the door, we talked and she said to me, "Oh, I saw at the City Hall that you are going to get married." "Yes," I said, "and I am sorry, but my bride has no dress."

Her daughter said, "Oh, No!" and she jumped to the ceiling. Her mother asked her, "Why do you jump, he never said anything about you?" She said, "He is going to want a dress." I said, "Yes, I want a dress." I told that lady that I did not come to rob her. I came to ask her to help me.

I went over to the cedar robe and opened the door and I saw a sky-blue dress. I took up the dress on the hanger and held it up and saw that it was a beautiful color. The daughter started crying. I took the little bag and turned it over on the table and said, "This is the money. This is all that I have. Later on, if I have some, I am going to pay more."

The mother said, "Take it." I thanked her and walked out. The daughter was crying. Later on when I built myself up I never went back to the house because I did not want the daughter to get angry. I saw the mother on the street and talked to her. I did not say to her "What you people did to us."

We got married on November 11, 1946. All the greeners in our town came to the wedding. My friend left early on Friday and brought home carp fish and ducks and a goose. We had challa and cakes, and there was singing and dancing. There was just one thing missing relatives.

We moved from Turkheim to Landsberg, and after 4 years until we came to the United States. My son was born on May the 13, 1948; the State of Israel was born on May the 14, 1948.

We came to New Orleans in 1949. I could not speak English. I went to a fur shop and they gave me fur and pointed to a sewing machine. I sewed. Then I pointed to a frame for stretching the skins and showed them I could do that. I also picked up a knife and showed them I could cut. They hired me at 50 cents an hour even thought the going rate for beginners was 75 cents an hour.

I bought a sewing machine for $50 and started taking in work. Then I was hired by the Haspel Brothers store where I was a foreman. I built myself up, and we raised and educated our two children. After 28 years Frieda and I went on our first vacation in 1978 to Israel.

There were 375,000 Jews living in Warsaw before the war. I doubt that there are 5,000 living there today. It is very, very important for me to tell this story." [15]

In these three stories you can see the horrors that Invasions bring, not just to countries, but to human lives, just like yours.

Location, Plan and Prepare…..those are the most important words for you to remember right now, and to NEVER forget.

"The quickest way of ending a war is to lose it."
George Orwell

Chapter 9: Escape

The dictionary definition of Escape that applies to the circumstance of finding yourself being occupied by an invading army is to avoid a serious or unwanted outcome.

And that is exactly what you need to do, everything in your power to avoid a serious and unwanted outcome, with the worst outcome being the loss of life of either yourself or your family members.

If you had previously planned and prepared you will find yourself far from the effects of war, but now there is the circumstance of dealing with, and under, an occupying power.

You should not be under any illusions either at to your worth to your new occupiers either. Your wealth, your position in life, your education, your connections nor your skills are any kind of indicators as to what will be your fate under your new masters.

Therefore your first priority is to escape from them. This can also take the form of many shapes, including leaving your country or disappearing within it.

Each family member involved also increases your chances of being caught and killed. Having children, especially young children and babies, decreases your chances of escape enormously.

So, your first decisions are going to be who should escape. If the occupying forces of your country are targeting people because of their race, religion, political positions or for any other reasons, and you find yourself being one of those targeted, then individual and multiple escapes should be planned.

It is better if one of your family members is able to survive than if all were to perish. Someone should always be left behind to tell your story and remember your family.

As small children and babies are the least harmful members of a society to the occupiers, strong consideration should be made to leave them behind.

Religious organizations not being targeted by the occupiers are one such option, complete strangers that are not part of a targeted group would be another.

Whatever your decisions may be it's very important that you know the basics of Escape prior to making a decision of any kind.

Survival, Escape, Resistance, Evasion

"Attitude is everything. What you must realize is that without the proper mental attitude, the other topics will be of use for only a short period of time. Depression, loneliness, feelings of abandonment, despondency, and the feeling that nobody knows where you are or cares will conspire to kill you.

If you have done your homework, practiced the techniques described, there is a very good chance you will survive if you have a positive mental attitude. Tell

154

yourself that you WILL get out of this. You WILL persevere.

I have seen some survival books talk as though collecting water is easy, catching game with snares is simple, and survival is something that can be taught in books. When I was very young, I would leave for the country on Friday afternoons.

I would take water proof matches, a liter of water, my bow and some arrows, ground sheet/blanket, and spend the weekend making snares, fishing with equipment I made, and hunting with my bow.

I used primitive fire making methods and only used matches when I had to. I can tell you that there is nothing easy about any of this. There was much I didn't know at the time, but I had read a lot of books.

I probably knew more at 13 than most people ever do. I was preparing myself for a life in the wilderness as a 'mountain man'. Needless to say, I had not yet discovered girls or beer. Cable TV was unheard of, and computers were magical talking 'entities' as seen on Star Trek and 2001.

For me, society was full of unnecessary trappings that only made men soft and weak.

By Sunday I was ready to return home. My parents would usually drive out to the area I was staying in and give me a ride. It was about a 18 mile trek. Fortunately my mom made sure I took along 'emergency rations', just in case I had trouble finding game.

Emergency rations were about the only things I ate all weekend. I shot a few birds and snakes with my bow. Caught a few fish too. But I learned something that many people do not realize. To survive you must battle three things in this order:

Exposure
Dehydration
Food Gathering

You can die in a few hours if you cannot retain body heat. You can die of exposure in 72 degree weather! You will develop hypothermia when your body loses heat faster than you can produce it. You need calories to generate body heat. People die of hypothermia in warm water.

The water is cooler than they are, subsequently the water absorbs body heat until their body can produce no more. It is a slow death.

When you breath your breath causes water loss.

Perspiration causes water loss. Evaporation from your eyes causes water loss. If you cannot replace these losses you will die. Drink water with little microbes, parasites, etc. and you will develop diarrhea. This will increase your fluid loss and you will die even quicker.

Food is the last thing you will need. In moderate climates, you can survive without food for up to 30 days. You will die without water in one or two in the desert! Finding edible berries and plants are the last things you need to learn. Rescue and conserving fluids and body heat are the primary survival skills.

If you can survive long enough to get real hungry you are doing a good job. In extreme cold food is more important because your body converts food to heat.

Taking Inventory

First examine what you have to work with. Seat cushions from a vehicle are insulation. Shiny glass, mirrors, or polished metal can be used to signal search aircraft. Glass with imperfections, bifocals, binoculars, etc. can be used to focus the suns rays enough to start a fire.

Thread stripped from a from seat cushion and wound together can be used to lash things together, make fishing nets, sutures for stitching wounds, etc. Remember your priorities. Rescue, Shelter, Water, and food. You will have to balance these priorities and make decisions.

Generally, you should stay in the area where you became stranded if there is any chance of a search for you. If you try to walk out, the search party will not find you.

You will burn calories while walking, calories that will be hard to replace. You will also perspire; can you afford the water loss?

If the enemy is searching for you, you will have to move to a safe location.

Exposure and Body Heat – Arctic

Time is running against you here. You must work quickly and conserve energy. After you have taken inventory, build a fire:

Hopefully you will have matches or a lighter. You must conserve these valuable items. Before you build your fire, pick a place for your shelter. (see below). Now gather combustible materials. Cones from pine trees don't burn. Bark doesn't either. DON'T waste matches trying to ignite them. Gather material in this order:

Very small match stick thickness twigs. Have at least a good double handful. They must be dry. To find dry sticks in the rain, look under the overhang of an embankment, under-side of logs, dead dry roots pulled out of an embankment, the center of a stump or dead tree (dug out with a knife).

Small sticks a little bigger than the smallest. You will need more of these, at least a quart - half gallon. Some of these may be a little wet.

Bigger sticks - Twice the thickness of the ones before, even more of these.

Keep moving up in size until you are collecting branches/small logs. If the wood is available you will need as much as you can gather in an hour. Drift wood will work if it's dry.

Now that you have your wood it's time to build your fire. Take your time and do this right. DON'T throw the fire together haphazardly.

This will only waste fuel and increase the risk of the fire not lighting. Every match you have is like gold. Do not waste them. If you do this right you will only need one.

Take a medium size branch and lay it down. Now build a tiny lean-to with the smallest sticks by leaning them up against the branch.

Take more and lay them perpendicular to first layer, and parallel to the big branch. Use lots of very small sticks and leave enough gaps between them for the flames to rise up through and ignite the upper layers. If it's raining or windy cover yourself with something to protect your fire.

Now add the bigger sticks to the top of your neat little lean-to, using a teepee shape, and surrounding the little lean to on all sides. Leave a small gap up close to the big branch to get your match under the pile.

If you have a small slip of paper or lint from pockets, put it under the lean-to and ignite it. As your fire grows, start adding more and more sticks to get the fire very hot.

Now add the larger sticks, the heat will dry them if they are damp. (Not if they are green or soaked through.) Keep building your fire in stages. DON'T wait too long to add the next size larger sticks.

The heat generated from the rapidly burning small ones is needed to dry and ignite the larger ones. As soon as you can, put some bigger stuff on by laying them across the big branch on the ground. Once your fire is going,

DON'T let it go out. If you need more fuel gather more, and start building your shelter.

This is the fastest shelter I know of:

Is there a snow bank nearby? Can you build a small one? You are going to dig a cave in the snow. You want the opening to be away from the wind. The cave has to be very small. For a snow shelter to be effective it must be below freezing.

If not, melting snow will saturate your clothing and you will freeze. Hollow out a place to lie in the snow. If you have something to line the floor with it will be much warmer. If you have nothing but plastic or something, try to find evergreen tree limbs to line it with.

You want as much between you and the cold ground as you can. You will lose more heat by being in contact with the cold ground than you will from the air. The air in your cave will warm and retain heat. If you have a small heat source you can place a vent through the roof to allow gas to escape.

You must ration your heat source. You will need it more at night when the temperature drops. Luxuries to add will be more insulation, seat cushions, etc. and a door.

A Ranger Pile is a shelter used by small parties who lack bulky camping equipment or who for tactical reasons, must not risk fire or shelter construction. First layer of men, four or five lays very close together on two ponchos snapped together. Next layer lies on top of the others, cross ways. Another layer on top of them.

Remaining ponchos are snapped together and pulled over the top and tucked in around the sides.

If a quantity of DRY pine needles, leaves, etc. can be quietly collected, this can be used for insulation stuffing. Just pile it on each layer before the next gets on. This is how small recon teams survive without carrying a lot of bullshit with them. It only gets bad when one of the guys has gas!

A vehicle will block the wind but the compartment is too big to retain body heat. You will freeze if you stay in a car or aircraft. Strip cushions, carpet, floor mats, insulation, etc. from the vehicle to line your shelter with. If you have tools and can remove the hood or trunk lid you can use these for a reflector to direct heat in one direction from a fire.

If you are fortunate enough to have the materials to construct a lean-to, build one similar to the way you built your fire. Keep the openings away from the wind, and towards your fire. Use a reflector to direct the heat into your lean-to.

Clothing, what do you have to work with? Thin material should be put closest to your body, as should wool. If you have extra foam from seat cushions, stuff your shirts and pants with it. It will work as insulation.

Extra clothing can be stripped in to pieces of about 5" x 4' and used as wrapping for extra socks. The Russian army has always used wool strips for field socks. You want to have the material that best holds in heat closest to your skin.

This same concept can be used when you have the luxury of a sleeping bag. Sleeping bags are designed to hold in heat much better than clothes. When you get into a bag, remove all of your clothes and lay on them.

Naked, your body heat will be trapped between your skin and the bag. Otherwise your heat escapes through the thin material of your clothing, and stays between your clothes and the bag, until it dissipates.

If you have no clothes for the environment you find yourself in, you will have to use the shelter for clothing. Keep your shelter VERY small and use insulation. This is your only chance to survive.

If there is plenty of snow/ice you will have a good water supply if you have a fire and a container to melt it in. DO NOT EAT SNOW. It will lower your body temperature and bring on hypothermia. Always melt it and get it warm first.

Do not drink alcohol of any kind. It will thin your blood and increase your urine output. If it's strong enough, you can use it as a disinfectant, or to help start your signal fires if an aircraft approaches.

Now that you have your fire and a shelter it is time to improve the odds of rescue. The international distress signal is three (3) of anything or the letters SOS. Don't build three fires because it wastes fuel.

Scrape out three large circles in the snow by dragging something around. If it snows these will fill in. If you have access to lots of branches or something that provides a good contrast to the white snow, lay them out to form 3 large X's.

162

What looks big to you on the ground looks very small from an aircraft at 10,000 feet. Your X's should be 100 - 150 feet across and 75 feet apart. If you have the wood build three fires in the middle of each but don't light them. Keep your main fire going so that you'll be able to take a torch to the other fires in a hurry.

Smoke will be quite visible from the air also. Large piles of pine needles smoke well, as does rubber, plastic, or oil. Be careful about burning critical supplies however! I would not throw a poncho, sheet of plastic, or rubber boots on the fire in a vain attempt to signal a distant plane. You will have to use common sense.

If the plane cannot land near you, and has to radio for help, you could be there a while longer anyway. With bad weather it might take a rescue party several days to get you. If the pilot is an idiot, or lacks a GPS or LORAN, he might report your location as being 20 miles away from where you actually are.

You may want to find a book named "White Dawn". It chronicles the lives of three men who were lost in their small whaling boat in the arctic back in the 1800's. It is an excellent work of fiction and provides many accurate details of how northern aboriginal peoples survive in their climate.

If you are inland you will not have much opportunity to hunt for seals. In some areas of the north, the only thing you will find are lemmings, lichens, and maybe a fox or two; (if there are enough rats to feed them). Near the sea you will be able to hunt seal.

That far north and you won't find much snow, it is too arid and cold. On the Ice pack you will have to build your shelter with ice, and heat it with animal fat. If you wind up on the ice pack, with no supplies, there is little I can tell you here that will save your life. You will have to stay warm long enough to get rescued, which had better be pretty quick.

Exposure – Desert

Since there is nothing in the desert to hold in the heat, it dissipates quickly after the sun goes down. Deserts can drop to near freezing over night. During the day the temperature will soar and fry your brain, dry you out, and kill you.

For this reason any movement should only be at night. For shelter you must get out of the sun. If you can, dig a hole to get in and cover it. Do not strip off your clothes.

Have you ever wondered why Arabic people wear those long, heavy, hot looking clothing on their heads and bodies? It is because moisture evaporation is your worst enemy in the desert. Clothing helps keep in this moisture and slows evaporation. It must be loose enough to allow heat loss. You will need to stay warm at night, refer to the arctic topic above.

Water is the most important thing to consider in the desert, it must be conserved. Long term drinking of urine can make you sick, but if it's all you have you will have to drink it. Succulent plants like cactus also contain water, as do the bodies of snakes, lizards, and other animals. Suck every drop you can from them, but avoid the poison glands in snakes (they are right behind the head in the neck). The only two parts of animals in North America that cannot be eaten are the livers of the polar bear and bearded seal. They contain toxic amounts of Vitamin A.

If you have plastic or a poncho you can collect water at night in the desert. Dig a hole (or use support sticks) as wide as the plastic. Make a hole in the plastic at the center. Stretch the plastic over the hole and weight down the edges with rocks.

Press down the center of the sheet or tie it to a tock to pull it down. Place a container under the hole. When dew forms on the plastic it will roll down hill through the hole and it into your container. Use your poncho during the day as shade.

Do not drink alcohol, it will increase your urine output and aid in dehydration.

Exposure – Topical

Here, heat and sunlight are your worst enemies. Insects and water contamination are also major problems. The heat and humidity of the jungle makes for rapid bacteria growth. Any untreated wound will fester within a few hours.

In a day or two a cut can become bad enough to cause gangrene. You must protect yourself by turning down sleeves, blousing your pants to keep insects out, and wearing gloves and a hat.

Water must be boiled well to kill parasites. Safe water can be found in water vines. These are very thick vines that hang down from large trees. You know, the ones that Tarzan swings from?

Cut one at a 45 degree angle, move up the vine and cut it off about three feet up or sever it to release the suction. Hold your mouth under the vine and the water will flow out. This water is safe to drink without boiling. Try not to let it run along the exposed outside of the vine though, that area will have tiny creepy crawlies.

Jungle streams are usually as deep as they are wide. Diffenbachia (or 'dumb cane') can be crushed and added to water to stun fish.

Chinese Star Apples, Mangoes, bananas, coconuts, and other fruits are safe to eat if you wash them with sterile water first. The seeds of the Star apple are poisonous.

Any species of tree frogs in the rain forests are highly toxic. They are recognized by there bright vivid colors. If you are very careful not to touch them, you can use their skin secretions for poisonous blow gun darts.

Blow guns are difficult to make, but I'll tell you how for the hell of it. Take a limb and split it length-wise. Scrape the bore of the weapon into both halves. It must be perfect. Allow it to dry and polish the bore halves smooth. The two sides must fit perfectly. (This is harder than it sounds). Bind the two back together with bark or vine strips.

Darts are made from any wood that can be sharpened. To launch the dart a small tuft of fiber (like cotton) from the stem of a (????) tree branch is balled around the basc of the dart.

During the rainy season, grubs can be found in the center of (????) trees. I can't remember their names but I know what they look like.

Build a platform or hammock to get off of the ground when you sleep. Insects will eat you alive if you don't. Mud can be used to keep mosquitoes off.

The jungle is a garden of Eden compared to the desert or the arctic. With a little common sense anyone should be able to survive.

I don't know of any poisonous plants that don't taste extremely bitter and nasty. If the leaf tastes mild it is probably OK to eat. When in doubt, try a little piece first and wait a couple of hours. If nothing bad happens try twice as much and wait again.

Keep doing this until you've tried enough to have made you sick. If you are still OK then it's probably safe to eat. There are exceptions to this rule, most notably among berries. Some berries don't taste too bad but are poisonous.

You should educate yourself before going to a new area. Pictures in books never look like the actual plant. Generally, if it crawls, walks, or slithers on its belly it is safe to eat." [16]

Now as you can see, Escape requires a lot of knowledge about a lot of things. You can't take for granted either that you just have to prepare for once set of circumstances, you have to prepare for them all.

Even though you may live in a temperate zone, you could easily find yourself in a desert, Arctic region or a jungle….and all depending upon where you have made your escape from.

"When men are pure, laws are useless; when men are corrupt, laws are broken."
Benjamin Disraeli

Chapter 10: New Rules, New Laws

Living under the occupation of an invading army, either foreign or domestic, is similar to the life you are living now, with the exception being it is a lot more dangerous and deadly.

Between the time of invasion and when the war ends you can expect virtually no changes in the laws you currently live under. What you can expect though will be a whole lot of new rules you will be expected to abide to should you wish to stay out of trouble.

But whether you are confronted with old laws, new laws, old rules or new rules, you must remember at all times that while you are under the control of occupying forces you are free to do whatever you would like to do.

Your obedience is NOT to laws or rules enforced by those of the occupiers, whether old or new, but rather to the survival of yourself, your family, your society and your country.

Merely by the fact that you are living under occupation has made you a criminal in the minds of your occupiers, you will only be able to remain free till they gather the evidence they need to prove this.

Since you are already considered a criminal you now have to learn how to be one. And your newly acquired skills as a criminal will also be those very skills that will insure yours, and your family's, survival.

In later Chapters I'll cover some these skills you'll have to become acquainted with but for this Chapter I want you to become familiar with the International Laws pertaining to war.

Do not be under any illusions either that the occupying forces around you are going to be abiding by these laws, but in some future time, and when the war is over, and those most responsible for it are being held accountable, you will want to be able to see those responsible for the deaths of your family members prosecuted.

Convention Relative to the Protection of Civilian Persons in Time of War, August 12, 1949

The undersigned Plenipotentiaries of the Governments represented at the Diplomatic Conference held at Geneva from 21 April to 12 August 1949, for the purpose of establishing a Convention for the Protection of Civilians in Time of War, have agreed as follows:

PART I
GENERAL PROVISIONS
Art 1. The High Contracting Parties undertake to respect and to ensure respect for the present Convention in all circumstances.

Art. 2. In addition to the provisions which shall be implemented in peace-time, the present Convention shall apply to all cases of declared war or of any other armed conflict which may arise between two or more of the High Contracting Parties, even if the state of war is not recognized by one of them.

The Convention shall also apply to all cases of partial or total occupation of the territory of a High Contracting Party, even if the said occupation meets with no armed resistance. Although one of the Powers in conflict may not be a party to the present Convention, the Powers who are parties thereto shall remain bound by it in their mutual relations. They shall furthermore be bound by the Convention in relation to the said Power, if the latter accepts and applies the provisions thereof.

Art. 3. In the case of armed conflict not of an international character occurring in the territory of one of the High Contracting Parties, each Party to the conflict shall be bound to apply, as a minimum, the following provisions:

(1) Persons taking no active part in the hostilities, including members of armed forces who have laid down their arms and those placed hors de combat by sickness, wounds, detention, or any other cause, shall in all circumstances be treated humanely, without any adverse distinction founded on race, colour, religion or faith, sex, birth or wealth, or any other similar criteria. To this end the following acts are and shall remain prohibited at any time and in any place whatsoever with respect to the above-mentioned persons: (a) violence to life and person, in particular murder of all kinds, mutilation, cruel treatment and torture; (b) taking of hostages; (c) outrages upon personal dignity, in particular humiliating and degrading treatment; (d) the passing of sentences and the carrying out of executions without previous judgment pronounced by a regularly

constituted court, affording all the judicial guarantees which are recognized as indispensable by civilized peoples. (2) The wounded and sick shall be collected and cared for.

An impartial humanitarian body, such as the International Committee of the Red Cross, may offer its services to the Parties to the conflict.

The Parties to the conflict should further endeavour to bring into force, by means of special agreements, all or part of the other provisions of the present Convention.

The application of the preceding provisions shall not affect the legal status of the Parties to the conflict.

Art. 4. Persons protected by the Convention are those who, at a given moment and in any manner whatsoever, find themselves, in case of a conflict or occupation, in the hands of a Party to the conflict or Occupying Power of which they are not nationals.

Nationals of a State which is not bound by the Convention are not protected by it. Nationals of a neutral State who find themselves in the territory of a belligerent State, and nationals of a co-belligerent State, shall not be regarded as protected persons while the State of which they are nationals has normal diplomatic representation in the State in whose hands they are.

The provisions of Part II are, however, wider in application, as defined in Article 13.

Persons protected by the Geneva Convention for the Amelioration of the Condition of the Wounded and Sick in Armed Forces in the Field of 12 August 1949, or by the Geneva Convention for the Amelioration of the Condition of Wounded, Sick and Shipwrecked Members of Armed Forces at Sea of 12 August 1949, or by the Geneva Convention relative to the Treatment of Prisoners of War of 12 August 1949, shall not be considered as protected persons within the meaning of the present Convention.

Art. 5 Where in the territory of a Party to the conflict, the latter is satisfied that an individual protected person is definitely suspected of or engaged in activities hostile to the security of the State, such individual person shall not be entitled to claim such rights and privileges under the present Convention as would, if exercised in the favour of such individual person, be prejudicial to the security of such State.

Where in occupied territory an individual protected person is detained as a spy or saboteur, or as a person under definite suspicion of activity hostile to the security of the Occupying Power, such person shall, in those cases where absolute military security so requires, be regarded as having forfeited rights of communication under the present Convention.

In each case, such persons shall nevertheless be treated with humanity and, in case of trial, shall not be deprived of the rights of fair and regular trial prescribed by the present Convention. They shall also be granted the full rights and privileges of a protected person under the present Convention at the earliest date consistent with the security of the State or Occupying Power, as the case may be.

Art. 6. The present Convention shall apply from the outset of any conflict or occupation mentioned in Article 2.

In the territory of Parties to the conflict, the application of the present Convention shall cease on the general close of military operations.

In the case of occupied territory, the application of the present Convention shall cease one year after the general close of military operations; however, the Occupying Power shall be bound, for the duration of the occupation, to the extent that such Power exercises the functions of government in such territory, by the provisions of the following Articles of the present Convention: 1 to 12, 27, 29 to 34, 47, 49, 51, 52, 53, 59, 61 to 77, 143.

Protected persons whose release, repatriation or re-establishment may take place after such dates shall meanwhile continue to benefit by the present Convention.

Art. 7. In addition to the agreements expressly provided for in Articles 11, 14, 15, 17, 36, 108, 109, 132, 133 and 149, the High Contracting Parties may conclude other special agreements for all matters concerning which they may deem it suitable to make separate provision. No special agreement shall adversely affect the situation of protected persons, as defined by the present Convention, not restrict the rights which it confers upon them.

Protected persons shall continue to have the benefit of such agreements as long as the Convention is applicable to them, except where express provisions to the contrary are contained in the aforesaid or in subsequent agreements, or where more favourable measures have been taken with regard to them by one or other of the Parties to the conflict.

Art. 8. Protected persons may in no circumstances renounce in part or in entirety the rights secured to them by the present Convention, and by the special agreements referred to in the foregoing Article, if such there be.

Art. 9. The present Convention shall be applied with the cooperation and under the scrutiny of the Protecting Powers whose duty it is to safeguard the interests of the Parties to the conflict. For this purpose, the Protecting Powers may appoint, apart from their diplomatic or consular staff, delegates from amongst their own nationals or the nationals of other neutral Powers. The said delegates shall be subject to the approval of the Power with which they are to carry out their duties.

The Parties to the conflict shall facilitate to the greatest extent possible the task of the representatives or delegates of the Protecting Powers.

The representatives or delegates of the Protecting Powers shall not in any case exceed their mission under the present Convention.

They shall, in particular, take account of the imperative necessities of security of the State wherein they carry out their duties.

Art. 10. The provisions of the present Convention constitute no obstacle to the humanitarian activities which the International Committee of the Red Cross or any other impartial humanitarian organization may, subject to the consent of the Parties to the conflict concerned, undertake for the protection of civilian persons and for their relief.

Art. 11. The High Contracting Parties may at any time agree to entrust to an international organization which offers all guarantees of impartiality and efficacy the duties incumbent on the Protecting Powers by virtue of the present Convention.

When persons protected by the present Convention do not benefit or cease to benefit, no matter for what reason, by the activities of a Protecting Power or of an organization provided for in the first paragraph above, the Detaining Power shall request a neutral State, or such an organization, to undertake the functions performed under the present Convention by a Protecting Power designated by the Parties to a conflict.

If protection cannot be arranged accordingly, the Detaining Power shall request or shall accept, subject to the provisions of this Article, the offer of the services of a humanitarian organization, such as the International Committee of the Red Cross, to assume the humanitarian functions performed by Protecting Powers under the present Convention.

Any neutral Power or any organization invited by the Power concerned or offering itself for these purposes, shall be required to act with a sense of responsibility towards the Party to the conflict on which persons protected by the present Convention depend, and shall be required to furnish sufficient assurances that it is in a position to undertake the appropriate functions and to discharge them impartially.

176

No derogation from the preceding provisions shall be made by special agreements between Powers one of which is restricted, even temporarily, in its freedom to negotiate with the other Power or its allies by reason of military events, more particularly where the whole, or a substantial part, of the territory of the said Power is occupied.

Whenever in the present Convention mention is made of a Protecting Power, such mention applies to substitute organizations in the sense of the present Article.

The provisions of this Article shall extend and be adapted to cases of nationals of a neutral State who are in occupied territory or who find themselves in the territory of a belligerent State in which the State of which they are nationals has not normal diplomatic representation.

Art. 12. In cases where they deem it advisable in the interest of protected persons, particularly in cases of disagreement between the Parties to the conflict as to the application or interpretation of the provisions of the present Convention, the Protecting Powers shall lend their good offices with a view to settling the disagreement.

For this purpose, each of the Protecting Powers may, either at the invitation of one Party or on its own initiative, propose to the Parties to the conflict a meeting of their representatives, and in particular of the authorities responsible for protected persons, possibly on neutral territory suitably chosen. The Parties to the conflict shall be bound to give effect to the proposals made to them for this purpose. The Protecting Powers may, if necessary, propose for approval by the Parties to the conflict a person belonging to a neutral Power, or delegated by the International Committee of the Red Cross, who shall be invited to take part in such a meeting.

PART II
GENERAL PROTECTION OF POPULATIONS AGAINST CERTAIN CONSEQUENCES OF WAR

Art. 13. The provisions of Part II cover the whole of the populations of the countries in conflict, without any adverse distinction based, in particular, on race, nationality, religion or political opinion, and are intended to alleviate the sufferings caused by war.

Art. 14. In time of peace, the High Contracting Parties and, after the outbreak of hostilities, the Parties thereto, may establish in their own territory and, if the need arises, in occupied areas, hospital and safety zones and localities so organized as to protect from the effects of war, wounded, sick and aged persons, children under fifteen, expectant mothers and mothers of children under seven.

Upon the outbreak and during the course of hostilities, the Parties concerned may conclude agreements on mutual recognition of the zones and localities they have created. They may for this purpose implement the provisions of the Draft Agreement annexed to the present Convention, with such amendments as they may consider necessary.

The Protecting Powers and the International Committee of the Red Cross are invited to lend their good offices in order to facilitate the institution and recognition of these hospital and safety zones and localities.

178

Art. 15. Any Party to the conflict may, either direct or through a neutral State or some humanitarian organization, propose to the adverse Party to establish, in the regions where fighting is taking place, neutralized zones intended to shelter from the effects of war the following persons, without distinction: (a) wounded and sick combatants or non-combatants; (b) civilian persons who take no part in hostilities, and who, while they reside in the zones, perform no work of a military character.

When the Parties concerned have agreed upon the geographical position, administration, food supply and supervision of the proposed neutralized zone, a written agreement shall be concluded and signed by the representatives of the Parties to the conflict. The agreement shall fix the beginning and the duration of the neutralization of the zone.

Art. 16. The wounded and sick, as well as the infirm, and expectant mothers, shall be the object of particular protection and respect.

As far as military considerations allow, each Party to the conflict shall facilitate the steps taken to search for the killed and wounded, to assist the shipwrecked and other persons exposed to grave danger, and to protect them against pillage and ill-treatment.

Art. 17. The Parties to the conflict shall endeavour to conclude local agreements for the removal from besieged or encircled areas, of wounded, sick, infirm, and aged persons, children and maternity cases, and for the passage of ministers of all religions, medical personnel and medical equipment on their way to such areas.

Art. 18. Civilian hospitals organized to give care to the wounded and sick, the infirm and maternity cases, may in no circumstances be the object of attack but shall at all times be respected and protected by the Parties to the conflict.

States which are Parties to a conflict shall provide all civilian hospitals with certificates showing that they are civilian hospitals and that the buildings which they occupy are not used for any purpose which would deprive these hospitals of protection in accordance with Article 19.

Civilian hospitals shall be marked by means of the emblem provided for in Article 38 of the Geneva Convention for the Amelioration of the Condition of the Wounded and Sick in Armed Forces in the Field of 12 August 1949, but only if so authorized by the State.

The Parties to the conflict shall, in so far as military considerations permit, take the necessary steps to make the distinctive emblems indicating civilian hospitals clearly visible to the enemy land, air and naval forces in order to obviate the possibility of any hostile action.

In view of the dangers to which hospitals may be exposed by being close to military objectives, it is recommended that such hospitals be situated as far as possible from such objectives.

Art. 19. The protection to which civilian hospitals are entitled shall not cease unless they are used to commit, outside their humanitarian duties, acts harmful to the enemy. Protection may, however, cease only after due warning has been given, naming, in all appropriate cases, a reasonable time limit and after such warning has remained unheeded. The fact that sick or wounded members of the armed forces are nursed in these hospitals, or the presence of small arms and ammunition taken from such combatants which have not yet been handed to the proper service, shall not be considered to be acts harmful to the enemy.

Art. 20. Persons regularly and solely engaged in the operation and administration of civilian hospitals, including the personnel engaged in the search for, removal and transporting of and caring for wounded and sick civilians, the infirm and maternity cases shall be respected and protected.

In occupied territory and in zones of military operations, the above personnel shall be recognizable by means of an identity card certifying their status, bearing the photograph of the holder and embossed with the stamp of the responsible authority, and also by means of a stamped, water-resistant armlet which they shall wear on the left arm while carrying out their duties. This armlet shall be issued by the State and shall bear the emblem provided for in Article 38 of the Geneva Convention for the Amelioration of the Condition of the Wounded and Sick in Armed Forces in the Field of 12 August 1949.

Other personnel who are engaged in the operation and administration of civilian hospitals shall be entitled to respect and protection and to wear the armlet, as provided in and under the conditions prescribed in this Article, while they are employed on such duties. The identity card shall state the duties on which they are employed.

The management of each hospital shall at all times hold at the disposal of the competent national or occupying authorities an up-to-date list of such personnel.

Art. 21. Convoys of vehicles or hospital trains on land or specially provided vessels on sea, conveying wounded and sick civilians, the infirm and maternity cases, shall be respected and protected in the same manner as the hospitals provided for in Article 18, and shall be marked, with the consent of the State, by the display of the distinctive emblem provided for in Article 38 of the Geneva Convention for the Amelioration of the Condition of the Wounded and Sick in Armed Forces in the Field of 12 August 1949.

Art.22. Aircraft exclusively employed for the removal of wounded and sick civilians, the infirm and maternity cases or for the transport of medical personnel and equipment, shall not be attacked, but shall be respected while flying at heights, times and on routes specifically agreed upon between all the Parties to the conflict concerned.

They may be marked with the distinctive emblem provided for in Article 38 of the Geneva Convention for the Amelioration of the Condition of the Wounded and Sick in Armed Forces in the Field of 12 August 1949.

Unless agreed otherwise, flights over enemy or enemy occupied territory are prohibited.

Such aircraft shall obey every summons to land. In the event of a landing thus imposed, the aircraft with its occupants may continue its flight after examination, if any.

Art. 23. Each High Contracting Party shall allow the free passage of all consignments of medical and hospital stores and objects necessary for religious worship intended only for civilians of another High Contracting Party, even if the latter is its adversary. It shall likewise permit the free passage of all consignments of essential foodstuffs, clothing and tonics intended for children under fifteen, expectant mothers and maternity cases.

The obligation of a High Contracting Party to allow the free passage of the consignments indicated in the preceding paragraph is subject to the condition that this Party is satisfied that there are no serious reasons for fearing: (a) that the consignments may be diverted from their destination, (b) that the control may not be effective, or (c) that a definite advantage may accrue to the military efforts or economy of the enemy through the substitution of the above-mentioned consignments for goods which would otherwise be provided or produced by the enemy or through the release of such material, services or facilities as would otherwise be required for the production of such goods.

The Power which allows the passage of the consignments indicated in the first paragraph of this Article may make such permission conditional on the distribution to the persons benefited thereby being made under the local supervision of the Protecting Powers.

Such consignments shall be forwarded as rapidly as possible, and the Power which permits their free passage shall have the right to prescribe the technical arrangements under which such passage is allowed.

Art.24. The Parties to the conflict shall take the necessary measures to ensure that children under fifteen, who are orphaned or are separated from their families as a result of the war, are not left to their own resources, and that their maintenance, the exercise of their religion and their education are facilitated in all circumstances. Their education shall, as far as possible, be entrusted to persons of a similar cultural tradition.

The Parties to the conflict shall facilitate the reception of such children in a neutral country for the duration of the conflict with the consent of the Protecting Power, if any, and under due safeguards for the observance of the principles stated in the first paragraph.

They shall, furthermore, endeavour to arrange for all children under twelve to be identified by the wearing of identity discs, or by some other means.

Art. 25. All persons in the territory of a Party to the conflict, or in a territory occupied by it, shall be enabled to give news of a strictly personal nature to members of their families, wherever they may be, and to receive news from them. This correspondence shall be forwarded speedily and without undue delay.

If, as a result of circumstances, it becomes difficult or impossible to exchange family correspondence by the ordinary post, the Parties to the conflict concerned shall apply to a neutral intermediary, such as the Central Agency provided for in Article 140, and shall decide in consultation with it how to ensure the fulfilment of their obligations under the best possible conditions, in particular with the cooperation of the National Red Cross (Red Crescent, Red Lion and Sun) Societies.

If the Parties to the conflict deem it necessary to restrict family correspondence, such restrictions shall be confined to the compulsory use of standard forms containing twenty-five freely chosen words, and to the limitation of the number of these forms despatched to one each month.

Art. 26. Each Party to the conflict shall facilitate enquiries made by members of families dispersed owing to the war, with the object of renewing contact with one another and of meeting, if possible. It shall encourage, in particular, the work of organizations engaged on this task provided they are acceptable to it and conform to its security regulations.

PART III STATUS AND TREATMENT OF PROTECTED PERSONS
SECTION I
Provisions Common to the Territories of the Parties to the Conflict and to Occupied Territories

Art. 27. Protected persons are entitled, in all circumstances, to respect for their persons, their honour, their family rights, their religious convictions and practices, and their manners and customs. They shall at all times be humanely treated, and shall be protected especially against all acts of violence or threats thereof and against insults and public curiosity.

Women shall be especially protected against any attack on their honour, in particular against rape, enforced prostitution, or any form of indecent assault.

Without prejudice to the provisions relating to their state of health, age and sex, all protected persons shall be treated with the same consideration by the Party to the conflict in whose power they are, without any adverse distinction based, in particular, on race, religion or political opinion.

However, the Parties to the conflict may take such measures of control and security in regard to protected persons as may be necessary as a result of the war.

Art. 28. The presence of a protected person may not be used to render certain points or areas immune from military operations.

Art. 29. The Party to the conflict in whose hands protected persons may be, is responsible for the treatment accorded to them by its agents, irrespective of any individual responsibility which may be incurred.

Art. 30. Protected persons shall have every facility for making application to the Protecting Powers, the International Committee of the Red Cross, the National Red Cross (Red Crescent, Red Lion and Sun) Society of the country where they may be, as well as to any organization that might assist them.

These several organizations shall be granted all facilities for that purpose by the authorities, within the bounds set by military or security considerations.

Apart from the visits of the delegates of the Protecting Powers and of the International Committee of the Red Cross, provided for by Article 143, the Detaining or Occupying Powers shall facilitate, as much as possible, visits to protected persons by the representatives of other organizations whose object is to give spiritual aid or material relief to such persons.

Art. 31. No physical or moral coercion shall be exercised against protected persons, in particular to obtain information from them or from third parties.

Art. 32. The High Contracting Parties specifically agree that each of them is prohibited from taking any measure of such a character as to cause the physical suffering or extermination of protected persons in their hands. This prohibition applies not only to murder, torture, corporal punishments, mutilation and medical or scientific experiments not necessitated by the medical treatment of a protected person, but also to any other measures of brutality whether applied by civilian or military agents.

Art. 33. No protected person may be punished for an offence he or she has not personally committed. Collective penalties and likewise all measures of intimidation or of terrorism are prohibited.

Pillage is prohibited.

Reprisals against protected persons and their property are prohibited.

Art. 34. The taking of hostages is prohibited.

SECTION II
Aliens in the Territory of a Party to the Conflict
Art. 35. All protected persons who may desire to leave the territory at the outset of, or during a conflict, shall be entitled to do so, unless their departure is contrary to the national interests of the State. The applications of such persons to leave shall be decided in accordance with regularly established procedures and the decision shall be taken as rapidly as possible. Those persons permitted to leave may provide themselves with the

necessary funds for their journey and take with them a reasonable amount of their effects and articles of personal use.

If any such person is refused permission to leave the territory, he shall be entitled to have refusal reconsidered, as soon as possible by an appropriate court or administrative board designated by the Detaining Power for that purpose.

Upon request, representatives of the Protecting Power shall, unless reasons of security prevent it, or the persons concerned object, be furnished with the reasons for refusal of any request for permission to leave the territory and be given, as expeditiously as possible, the names of all persons who have been denied permission to leave.

Art. 36. Departures permitted under the foregoing Article shall be carried out in satisfactory conditions as regards safety, hygiene, sanitation and food. All costs in connection therewith, from the point of exit in the territory of the Detaining Power, shall be borne by the country of destination, or, in the case of accommodation in a neutral country, by the Power whose nationals are benefited. The practical details of such movements may, if necessary, be settled by special agreements between the Powers concerned.

The foregoing shall not prejudice such special agreements as may be concluded between Parties to the conflict concerning the exchange and repatriation of their nationals in enemy hands.

Art. 37. Protected persons who are confined pending proceedings or subject to a sentence involving loss of liberty, shall during their confinement be humanely treated.

As soon as they are released, they may ask to leave the territory in conformity with the foregoing Articles.

Art. 38. With the exception of special measures authorized by the present Convention, in particularly by Article 27 and 41 thereof, the situation of protected persons shall continue to be regulated, in principle, by the provisions concerning aliens in time of peace. In any case, the following rights shall be granted to them: (1) they shall be enabled to receive the individual or collective relief that may be sent to them. (2) they shall, if their state of health so requires, receive medical attention and hospital treatment to the same extent as the nationals of the State concerned. (3) they shall be allowed to practise their religion and to receive spiritual assistance from ministers of their faith. (4) if they reside in an area particularly exposed to the dangers of war, they shall be authorized to move from that area to the same extent as the nationals of the State concerned. (5) children under fifteen years, pregnant women and mothers of children under seven years shall benefit by any preferential treatment to the same extent as the nationals of the State concerned.

Art. 39. Protected persons who, as a result of the war, have lost their gainful employment, shall be granted the opportunity to find paid employment. That opportunity shall, subject to security considerations and to the provisions of Article 40, be equal to that enjoyed by the nationals of the Power in whose territory they are.

Where a Party to the conflict applies to a protected person methods of control which result in his being unable to support himself, and especially if such a person is prevented for reasons of security from finding paid employment on reasonable conditions, the said Party shall ensure his support and that of his dependents.

Protected persons may in any case receive allowances from their home country, the Protecting Power, or the relief societies referred to in Article 30.

Art. 40. Protected persons may be compelled to work only to the same extent as nationals of the Party to the conflict in whose territory they are.

If protected persons are of enemy nationality, they may only be compelled to do work which is normally necessary to ensure the feeding, sheltering, clothing, transport and health of human beings and which is not directly related to the conduct of military operations.

In the cases mentioned in the two preceding paragraphs, protected persons compelled to work shall have the benefit of the same working conditions and of the same safeguards as national workers in particular as regards wages, hours of labour, clothing and equipment, previous training and compensation for occupational accidents and diseases.

If the above provisions are infringed, protected persons shall be allowed to exercise their right of complaint in accordance with Article 30.

Art. 41. Should the Power, in whose hands protected persons may be, consider the measures of control mentioned in the present Convention to be inadequate, it may not have recourse to any other measure of control more severe than that of assigned residence or internment, in accordance with the provisions of Articles 42 and 43.

In applying the provisions of Article 39, second paragraph, to the cases of persons required to leave their usual places of residence by virtue of a decision placing them in assigned residence, by virtue of a decision placing them in assigned residence, elsewhere, the Detaining Power shall be guided as closely as possible by the standards of welfare set forth in Part III, Section IV of this Convention.

Art. 42. The internment or placing in assigned residence of protected persons may be ordered only if the security of the Detaining Power makes it absolutely necessary.

If any person, acting through the representatives of the Protecting Power, voluntarily demands internment, and if his situation renders this step necessary, he shall be interned by the Power in whose hands he may be.

Art. 43. Any protected person who has been interned or placed in assigned residence shall be entitled to have such action reconsidered as soon as possible by an appropriate court or administrative board designated by the Detaining Power for that purpose. If the internment or placing in assigned residence is maintained, the court or administrative board shall periodically, and at least twice yearly, give consideration to his or her case, with a view to the favourable amendment of the initial decision, if circumstances permit.

Unless the protected persons concerned object, the Detaining Power shall, as rapidly as possible, give the Protecting Power the names of any protected persons who have been interned or subjected to assigned residence, or who have been released from internment or assigned residence. The decisions of the courts or boards mentioned in the first paragraph of the present Article shall also, subject to the same conditions, be notified as rapidly as possible to the Protecting Power.

Art. 44. In applying the measures of control mentioned in the present Convention, the Detaining Power shall not treat as enemy aliens exclusively on the basis of their nationality de jure of an enemy State, refugees who do not, in fact, enjoy the protection of any government.

Art. 45. Protected persons shall not be transferred to a Power which is not a party to the Convention.

This provision shall in no way constitute an obstacle to the repatriation of protected persons, or to their return to their country of residence after the cessation of hostilities.

Protected persons may be transferred by the Detaining Power only to a Power which is a party to the present Convention and after the Detaining Power has satisfied itself of the willingness and ability of such transferee Power to apply the present Convention. If protected persons are transferred under such circumstances, responsibility for the application of the present Convention rests on the Power accepting them, while they are in its custody. Nevertheless, if that Power fails to carry out the provisions of the present Convention in any important respect, the Power by which the protected persons were transferred shall, upon being so notified by the Protecting Power, take effective measures to correct the situation or shall request the return of the protected persons. Such request must be complied with.

In no circumstances shall a protected person be transferred to a country where he or she may have reason to fear persecution for his or her political opinions or religious beliefs.

The provisions of this Article do not constitute an obstacle to the extradition, in pursuance of extradition treaties concluded before the outbreak of hostilities, of protected persons accused of offences against ordinary criminal law.

Art. 46. In so far as they have not been previously withdrawn, restrictive measures taken regarding protected persons shall be cancelled as soon as possible after the close of hostilities.

Restrictive measures affecting their property shall be cancelled, in accordance with the law of the Detaining Power, as soon as possible after the close of hostilities.

SECTION III
Occupied Territories
Art. 47. Protected persons who are in occupied territory shall not be deprived, in any case or in any manner whatsoever, of the benefits of the present Convention by any change introduced, as the result of the occupation of a territory, into the institutions or government of the said territory, nor by any agreement concluded between the authorities of the occupied territories and the Occupying Power, nor by any annexation by the latter of the whole or part of the occupied territory.

Art. 48. Protected persons who are not nationals of the Power whose territory is occupied, may avail themselves of the right to leave the territory subject to the provisions of Article 35, and decisions thereon shall be taken in accordance with the procedure which the Occupying Power shall establish in accordance with the said Article.

Art. 49. Individual or mass forcible transfers, as well as deportations of protected persons from occupied territory to the territory of the Occupying Power or to that of any other country, occupied or not, are prohibited, regardless of their motive.

Nevertheless, the Occupying Power may undertake total or partial evacuation of a given area if the security of the population or imperative military reasons so demand. Such evacuations may not involve the displacement of protected persons outside the bounds of the occupied territory except when for material reasons it is impossible to avoid such displacement. Persons thus evacuated shall be transferred back to their homes as soon as hostilities in the area in question have ceased.

The Occupying Power undertaking such transfers or evacuations shall ensure, to the greatest practicable extent, that proper accommodation is provided to receive the protected persons, that the removals are effected in satisfactory conditions of hygiene, health, safety and nutrition, and that members of the same family are not separated.

The Protecting Power shall be informed of any transfers and evacuations as soon as they have taken place.

The Occupying Power shall not detain protected persons in an area particularly exposed to the dangers of war unless the security of the population or imperative military reasons so demand.

The Occupying Power shall not deport or transfer parts of its own civilian population into the territory it occupies.

Art. 50. The Occupying Power shall, with the cooperation of the national and local authorities, facilitate the proper working of all institutions devoted to the care and education of children.

The Occupying Power shall take all necessary steps to facilitate the identification of children and the registration of their parentage. It may not, in any case, change their personal status, nor enlist them in formations or organizations subordinate to it.

Should the local institutions be inadequate for the purpose, the Occupying Power shall make arrangements for the maintenance and education, if possible by persons of their own nationality, language and religion, of children who are orphaned or separated from their parents as a result of the war and who cannot be adequately cared for by a near relative or friend.

A special section of the Bureau set up in accordance with Article 136 shall be responsible for taking all necessary steps to identify children whose identity is in doubt. Particulars of their parents or other near relatives should always be recorded if available.

The Occupying Power shall not hinder the application of any preferential measures in regard to food, medical care and protection against the effects of war which may have been adopted prior to the occupation in favour of children under fifteen years, expectant mothers, and mothers of children under seven years.

Art. 51. The Occupying Power may not compel protected persons to serve in its armed or auxiliary forces. No pressure or propaganda which aims at securing voluntary enlistment is permitted.

The Occupying Power may not compel protected persons to work unless they are over eighteen years of age, and then only on work which is necessary either for the needs of the army of occupation, or for the public utility services, or for the feeding, sheltering, clothing, transportation or health of the population of the occupied country. Protected persons may not be compelled to undertake any work which would involve them in the obligation of taking part in military operations. The Occupying Power may not compel protected persons to employ forcible means to ensure the security of the installations where they are performing compulsory labour.

The work shall be carried out only in the occupied territory where the persons whose services have been requisitioned are. Every such person shall, so far as possible, be kept in his usual place of employment. Workers shall be paid a fair wage and the work shall be proportionate to their physical and intellectual capacities. The legislation in force in the occupied country concerning working conditions, and safeguards as regards, in particular, such matters as wages, hours of work, equipment, preliminary training and compensation for occupational accidents and diseases, shall be applicable to the protected persons assigned to the work referred to in this Article.

In no case shall requisition of labour lead to a mobilization of workers in an organization of a military or semi-military character.

Art. 52. No contract, agreement or regulation shall impair the right of any worker, whether voluntary or not and wherever he may be, to apply to the representatives of the Protecting Power in order to request the said Power's intervention.

All measures aiming at creating unemployment or at restricting the opportunities offered to workers in an occupied territory, in order to induce them to work for the Occupying Power, are prohibited.

Art. 53. Any destruction by the Occupying Power of real or personal property belonging individually or collectively to private persons, or to the State, or to other public authorities, or to social or cooperative organizations, is prohibited, except where such destruction is rendered absolutely necessary by military operations.

Art. 54. The Occupying Power may not alter the status of public officials or judges in the occupied territories, or in any way apply sanctions to or take any measures of coercion or discrimination against them, should they abstain from fulfilling their functions for reasons of conscience.

This prohibition does not prejudice the application of the second paragraph of Article 51. It does not affect the right of the Occupying Power to remove public officials from their posts.

Art. 55. To the fullest extent of the means available to it, the Occupying Power has the duty of ensuring the food and medical supplies of the population; it should, in particular, bring in the necessary foodstuffs, medical stores and other articles if the resources of the occupied territory are inadequate.

The Occupying Power may not requisition foodstuffs, articles or medical supplies available in the occupied territory, except for use by the occupation forces and administration personnel, and then only if the requirements of the civilian population have been taken into account. Subject to the provisions of other international Conventions, the Occupying Power shall make arrangements to ensure that fair value is paid for any requisitioned goods.

The Protecting Power shall, at any time, be at liberty to verify the state of the food and medical supplies in occupied territories, except where temporary restrictions are made necessary by imperative military requirements.

Art. 56. To the fullest extent of the means available to it, the public Occupying Power has the duty of ensuring and maintaining, with the cooperation of national and local authorities, the medical and hospital establishments and services, public health and hygiene in the occupied territory, with particular reference to the adoption and application of the prophylactic and preventive measures necessary to combat the spread of contagious diseases and epidemics. Medical personnel of all categories shall be allowed to carry out their duties.

If new hospitals are set up in occupied territory and if the competent organs of the occupied State are not operating there, the occupying authorities shall, if necessary, grant them the recognition provided for in Article 18. In similar circumstances, the occupying authorities shall also grant recognition to hospital personnel and transport vehicles under the provisions of Articles 20 and 21.

In adopting measures of health and hygiene and in their implementation, the Occupying Power shall take into consideration the moral and ethical susceptibilities of the population of the occupied territory.

Art. 57. The Occupying Power may requisition civilian hospitals of hospitals only temporarily and only in cases of urgent necessity for the care of military wounded and sick, and then on condition that suitable arrangements are made in due time for the care and treatment of the patients and for the needs of the civilian population for hospital accommodation.

The material and stores of civilian hospitals cannot be requisitioned so long as they are necessary for the needs of the civilian population.

Art. 58. The Occupying Power shall permit ministers of religion to give spiritual assistance to the members of their religious communities.

The Occupying Power shall also accept consignments of books and articles required for religious needs and shall facilitate their distribution in occupied territory.

Art. 59. If the whole or part of the population of an occupied territory is inadequately supplied, the Occupying Power shall agree to relief schemes on behalf of the said population, and shall facilitate them by all the means at its disposal.

Such schemes, which may be undertaken either by States or by impartial humanitarian organizations such as the International Committee of the Red Cross, shall consist, in particular, of the provision of consignments of foodstuffs, medical supplies and clothing.

All Contracting Parties shall permit the free passage of these consignments and shall guarantee their protection.

A Power granting free passage to consignments on their way to territory occupied by an adverse Party to the conflict shall, however, have the right to search the consignments, to regulate their passage according to prescribed times and routes, and to be reasonably satisfied through the Protecting Power that these consignments are to be used for the relief of the needy population and are not to be used for the benefit of the Occupying Power.

Art. 60. Relief consignments shall in no way relieve the Occupying Power of any of its responsibilities under Articles 55, 56 and 59. The Occupying Power shall in no way whatsoever divert relief consignments from the purpose for which they are intended, except in cases of urgent necessity, in the interests of the population of the occupied territory and with the consent of the Protecting Power.

Art. 61. The distribution of the relief consignments referred to in the foregoing Articles shall be carried out with the cooperation and under the supervision of the Protecting Power. This duty may also be delegated, by agreement between the Occupying Power and the Protecting Power, to a neutral Power, to the International Committee of the Red Cross or to any other impartial humanitarian body.

Such consignments shall be exempt in occupied territory from all charges, taxes or customs duties unless these are necessary in the interests of the economy of the territory. The Occupying Power shall facilitate the rapid distribution of these consignments.

All Contracting Parties shall endeavour to permit the transit and transport, free of charge, of such relief consignments on their way to occupied territories.

Art. 62. Subject to imperative reasons of security, protected persons in occupied territories shall be permitted to receive the individual relief consignments sent to them.

Art. 63. Subject to temporary and exceptional measures imposed for urgent reasons of security by the Occupying Power:

(a) recognized National Red Cross (Red Crescent, Red Lion and Sun) Societies shall be able to pursue their activities in accordance with Red Cross principles, as defined by the International Red Cross Conferences. Other relief societies shall be permitted to continue their humanitarian activities under similar conditions; (b) the Occupying Power may not require any changes in the personnel or structure of these societies, which would prejudice the aforesaid activities.

The same principles shall apply to the activities and personnel of special organizations of a non-military character, which already exist or which may be established, for the purpose of ensuring the living conditions of the civilian population by the maintenance of the essential public utility services, by the distribution of relief and by the organization of rescues.

Art. 64. The penal laws of the occupied territory shall remain in force, with the exception that they may be repealed or suspended by the Occupying Power in cases where they constitute a threat to its security or an obstacle to the application of the present Convention.

Subject to the latter consideration and to the necessity for ensuring the effective administration of justice, the tribunals of the occupied territory shall continue to function in respect of all offences covered by the said laws.

The Occupying Power may, however, subject the population of the occupied territory to provisions which are essential to enable the Occupying Power to fulfil its obligations under the present Convention, to maintain the orderly government of the territory, and to ensure the security of the Occupying Power, of the members and property of the occupying forces or administration, and likewise of the establishments and lines of communication used by them.

Art. 65. The penal provisions enacted by the Occupying Power shall not come into force before they have been published and brought to the knowledge of the inhabitants in their own language. The effect of these penal provisions shall not be retroactive.

Art. 66. In case of a breach of the penal provisions promulgated by it by virtue of the second paragraph of Article 64 the Occupying Power may hand over the accused to its properly constituted, non-political military courts, on condition that the said courts sit in the occupied country. Courts of appeal shall preferably sit in the occupied country.

Art. 67. The courts shall apply only those provisions of law which were applicable prior to the offence, and which are in accordance with general principles of law, in particular the principle that the penalty shall be proportionate to the offence. They shall take into consideration the fact the accused is not a national of the Occupying Power.

Art. 68. Protected persons who commit an offence which is solely intended to harm the Occupying Power, but which does not constitute an attempt on the life or limb of members of the occupying forces or administration, nor a grave collective danger, nor seriously damage the property of the occupying forces or administration or the installations used by them, shall be liable to internment or simple imprisonment, provided the duration of such internment or imprisonment is proportionate to the offence committed. Furthermore, internment or imprisonment shall, for such offences, be the only measure adopted for depriving protected persons of liberty. The courts provided for under Article 66 of the present Convention may at their discretion convert a sentence of imprisonment to one of internment for the same period.

The penal provisions promulgated by the Occupying Power in accordance with Articles 64 and 65 may impose the death penalty on a protected person only in cases where the person is guilty of espionage, of serious acts of sabotage against the military installations of the Occupying Power or of intentional offences which have caused the death of one or more persons, provided that such offences were punishable by death under the law of the occupied territory in force before the occupation began.

The death penalty may not be pronounced on a protected person unless the attention of the court has been particularly called to the fact that since the accused is not a national of the Occupying Power, he is not bound to it by any duty of allegiance.

In any case, the death penalty may not be pronounced on a protected person who was under eighteen years of age at the time of the offence.

Art. 69. In all cases the duration of the period during which a protected person accused of an offence is under arrest awaiting trial or punishment shall be deducted from any period of imprisonment of awarded.

Art. 70. Protected persons shall not be arrested, prosecuted or convicted by the Occupying Power for acts committed or for opinions expressed before the occupation, or during a temporary interruption thereof, with the exception of breaches of the laws and customs of war.

Nationals of the occupying Power who, before the outbreak of hostilities, have sought refuge in the territory of the occupied State, shall not be arrested, prosecuted, convicted or deported from the occupied territory, except for offences committed after the outbreak of hostilities, or for offences under common law committed before the outbreak of hostilities which, according to the law of the occupied State, would have justified extradition in time of peace.

Art. 71. No sentence shall be pronounced by the competent courts of the Occupying Power except after a regular trial.

Accused persons who are prosecuted by the Occupying Power shall be promptly informed, in writing, in a language which they understand, of the particulars of the charges preferred against them, and shall be brought to trial as rapidly as possible. The Protecting Power shall be informed of all proceedings instituted by the Occupying Power against protected persons in respect of charges involving the death penalty or imprisonment for two years or more; it shall be enabled, at any time, to obtain information regarding the state of such proceedings. Furthermore, the Protecting Power shall be entitled, on request, to be furnished with all particulars of these and of any other proceedings instituted by the Occupying Power against protected persons.

The notification to the Protecting Power, as provided for in the second paragraph above, shall be sent immediately, and shall in any case reach the Protecting Power three weeks before the date of the first hearing. Unless, at the opening of the trial, evidence is submitted that the provisions of this Article are fully complied with, the trial shall not proceed. The notification shall include the following particulars: (a) description of the accused; (b) place of residence or detention; (c) specification of the charge or charges (with mention of the penal provisions under which it is brought); (d) designation of the court which will hear the case; (e) place and date of the first hearing.

Art. 72. Accused persons shall have the right to present evidence necessary to their defence and may, in particular, call witnesses. They shall have the right to be assisted by a qualified advocate or counsel of their own choice, who shall be able to visit them freely and shall enjoy the necessary facilities for preparing the defence.

Failing a choice by the accused, the Protecting Power may provide him with an advocate or counsel. When an accused person has to meet a serious charge and the Protecting Power is not functioning, the Occupying Power, subject to the consent of the accused, shall provide an advocate or counsel.

Accused persons shall, unless they freely waive such assistance, be aided by an interpreter, both during preliminary investigation and during the hearing in court. They shall have at any time the right to object to the interpreter and to ask for his replacement.

Art.73. A convicted person shall have the right of appeal provided for by the laws applied by the court. He shall be fully informed of his right to appeal or petition and of the time limit within which he may do so.

The penal procedure provided in the present Section shall apply, as far as it is applicable, to appeals. Where the laws applied by the Court make no provision for appeals, the convicted person shall have the right to petition against the finding and sentence to the competent authority of the Occupying Power.

Art. 74. Representatives of the Protecting Power shall have the right to attend the trial of any protected person, unless the hearing has, as an exceptional measure, to be held in camera in the interests of the security of the Occupying Power, which shall then notify the Protecting Power. A notification in respect of the date and place of trial shall be sent to the Protecting Power.

Any judgement involving a sentence of death, or imprisonment for two years or more, shall be communicated, with the relevant grounds, as rapidly as possible to the Protecting Power. The notification shall contain a reference to the notification made under Article 71 and, in the case of sentences of imprisonment, the name of the place where the sentence is to be served. A record of judgements other than those referred to above shall be kept by the court and shall be open to inspection by representatives of the Protecting Power. Any period allowed for appeal in the case of sentences involving the death penalty, or imprisonment of two years or more, shall not run until notification of judgement has been received by the Protecting Power.

Art. 75. In no case shall persons condemned to death be deprived of the right of petition for pardon or reprieve.

No death sentence shall be carried out before the expiration of a period of a least six months from the date of receipt by the Protecting Power of the notification of the final judgment confirming such death sentence, or of an order denying pardon or reprieve.

The six months period of suspension of the death sentence herein prescribed may be reduced in individual cases in circumstances of grave emergency involving an organized threat to the security of the

Occupying Power or its forces, provided always that the Protecting Power is notified of such reduction and is given reasonable time and opportunity to make representations to the competent occupying authorities in respect of such death sentences.

Art. 76. Protected persons accused of offences shall be detained in the occupied country, and if convicted they shall serve their sentences therein. They shall, if possible, be separated from other detainees and shall enjoy conditions of food and hygiene which will be sufficient to keep them in good health, and which will be at least equal to those obtaining in prisons in the occupied country.

They shall receive the medical attention required by their state of health.

They shall also have the right to receive any spiritual assistance which they may require.

Women shall be confined in separate quarters and shall be under the direct supervision of women.

Proper regard shall be paid to the special treatment due to minors.

Protected persons who are detained shall have the right to be visited by delegates of the Protecting Power and of the International Committee of the Red Cross, in accordance with the provisions of Article 143.

Such persons shall have the right to receive at least one relief parcel monthly.

Art. 77. Protected persons who have been accused of offences or convicted by the courts in occupied territory, shall be handed over at the close of occupation, with the relevant records, to the authorities of the liberated territory.

Art. 78. If the Occupying Power considers it necessary, for imperative reasons of security, to take safety measures concerning protected persons, it may, at the most, subject them to assigned residence or to internment.

Decisions regarding such assigned residence or internment shall be made according to a regular procedure to be prescribed by the Occupying Power in accordance with the provisions of the present Convention. This procedure shall include the right of appeal for the parties concerned. Appeals shall be decided with the least possible delay. In the event of the decision being upheld, it shall be subject to periodical review, if possible every six months, by a competent body set up by the said Power.

Protected persons made subject to assigned residence and thus required to leave their homes shall enjoy the full benefit of Article 39 of the present Convention.

SECTION IV
Regulations for the Treatment of Internees
CHAPTER I
General Provisions
Art. 79. The Parties to the conflict shall not intern protected persons, except in accordance with the provisions of Articles 41, 42, 43, 68 and 78.

Art. 80. Internees shall retain their full civil capacity and shall exercise such attendant rights as may be compatible with their status.

Art. 81. Parties to the conflict who intern protected persons shall be bound to provide free of charge for their maintenance, and to grant them also the medical attention required by their state of health.

No deduction from the allowances, salaries or credits due to the internees shall be made for the repayment of these costs.

The Detaining Power shall provide for the support of those dependent on the internees, if such dependents are without adequate means of support or are unable to earn a living.

Art.82. The Detaining Power shall, as far as possible, accommodate the internees according to their nationality, language and customs. Internees who are nationals of the same country shall not be separated merely because they have different languages.

Throughout the duration of their internment, members of the same family, and in particular parents and children, shall be lodged together in the same place of internment, except when separation of a temporary nature is necessitated for reasons of employment or health or for the purposes of enforcement of the provisions of Chapter IX of the present Section. Internees may request that their children who are left at liberty without parental care shall be interned with them.

Wherever possible, interned members of the same family shall be housed in the same premises and given separate accommodation from other internees, together with facilities for leading a proper family life.

CHAPTER II
Places of Internment
Art. 83. The Detaining Power shall not set up places of internment in areas particularly exposed to the dangers of war.

The Detaining Power shall give the enemy Powers, through the intermediary of the Protecting Powers, all useful information regarding the geographical location of places of internment.

Whenever military considerations permit, internment camps shall be indicated by the letters IC, placed so as to be clearly visible in the daytime from the air. The Powers concerned may, however, agree upon any other system of marking. No place other than an internment camp shall be marked as such.

Art.84. Internees shall be accommodated and administered separately from prisoners of war and from persons deprived of liberty for any other reason.

Art. 85. The Detaining Power is bound to take all necessary and possible measures to ensure that protected persons shall, from the outset of their internment, be accommodated in buildings or quarters which afford every possible safeguard as regards hygiene and health, and provide efficient protection against the rigours of the climate and the effects of the war. In no case shall permanent places of internment be situated in unhealthy areas or in districts, the climate of which is injurious to the internees. In all cases where the district, in which a protected person is temporarily interned, is an unhealthy area or has a climate which is harmful to his health, he shall be removed to a more suitable place of internment as rapidly as circumstances permit.

The premises shall be fully protected from dampness, adequately heated and lighted, in particular between dusk and lights out. The sleeping quarters shall be sufficiently spacious and well ventilated, and the internees shall have suitable bedding and sufficient blankets, account being taken of the climate, and the age, sex, and state of health of the internees.

Internees shall have for their use, day and night, sanitary conveniences which conform to the rules of hygiene, and are constantly maintained in a state of cleanliness. They shall be provided with sufficient water and soap for their daily personal toilet and for washing their personal laundry; installations and facilities necessary for this purpose shall be granted to them. Showers or baths shall also be available. The necessary time shall be set aside for washing and for cleaning.

Whenever it is necessary, as an exceptional and temporary measure, to accommodate women internees who are not members of a family unit in the same place of internment as men, the provision of separate sleeping quarters and sanitary conveniences for the use of such women internees shall be obligatory.

Art. 86. The Detaining Power shall place at the disposal of interned persons, of whatever denomination, premises suitable for the holding of their religious services.

Art. 87. Canteens shall be installed in every place of internment, except where other suitable facilities are available. Their purpose shall be to enable internees to make purchases, at prices not higher than local market prices, of foodstuffs and articles of everyday use, including soap and tobacco, such as would increase their personal well-being and comfort.

Profits made by canteens shall be credited to a welfare fund to be set up for each place of internment, and administered for the benefit of the internees attached to such place of internment. The Internee Committee provided for in Article 102 shall have the right to check the management of the canteen and of the said fund.

When a place of internment is closed down, the balance of the welfare fund shall be transferred to the welfare fund of a place of internment for internees of the same nationality, or, if such a place does not exist, to a central welfare fund which shall be administered for the benefit of all internees remaining in the custody of the Detaining Power. In case of a general release, the said profits shall be kept by the Detaining Power, subject to any agreement to the contrary between the Powers concerned.

Art. 88. In all places of internment exposed to air raids and other hazards of war, shelters adequate in number and structure to ensure the necessary protection shall be installed. In case of alarms, the measures internees shall be free to enter such shelters as quickly as possible, excepting those who remain for the protection of their quarters against the aforesaid hazards. Any protective measures taken in favour of the population shall also apply to them.

All due precautions must be taken in places of internment against the danger of fire.

CHAPTER III
Food and Clothing

Art. 89. Daily food rations for internees shall be sufficient in quantity, quality and variety to keep internees in a good state of health and prevent the development of nutritional deficiencies. Account shall also be taken of the customary diet of the internees.

Internees shall also be given the means by which they can prepare for themselves any additional food in their possession.

Sufficient drinking water shall be supplied to internees. The use of tobacco shall be permitted.

Internees who work shall receive additional rations in proportion to the kind of labour which they perform.

Expectant and nursing mothers and children under fifteen years of age, shall be given additional food, in proportion to their physiological needs.

Art. 90. When taken into custody, internees shall be given all facilities to provide themselves with the necessary clothing, footwear and change of underwear, and later on, to procure further supplies if required. Should any internees not have sufficient clothing, account being taken of the climate, and be unable to procure any, it shall be provided free of charge to them by the Detaining Power.

The clothing supplied by the Detaining Power to internees and the outward markings placed on their own clothes shall not be ignominious nor expose them to ridicule.

Workers shall receive suitable working outfits, including protective clothing, whenever the nature of their work so requires.

CHAPTER IV
Hygiene and Medical Attention
Art. 91. Every place of internment shall have an adequate infirmary, under the direction of a qualified doctor, where internees may have the attention they require, as well as appropriate diet. Isolation wards shall be set aside for cases of contagious or mental diseases.

Maternity cases and internees suffering from serious diseases, or whose condition requires special treatment, a surgical operation or hospital care, must be admitted to any institution where adequate treatment can be given and shall receive care not inferior to that provided for the general population.

Internees shall, for preference, have the attention of medical personnel of their own nationality.

Internees may not be prevented from presenting themselves to the medical authorities for examination. The medical authorities of the Detaining Power shall, upon request, issue to every internee who has undergone treatment an official certificate showing the nature of his illness or injury, and the duration and nature of the treatment given. A duplicate of this certificate shall be forwarded to the Central Agency provided for in Article 140.

Treatment, including the provision of any apparatus necessary for the maintenance of internees in good health, particularly dentures and other artificial appliances and spectacles, shall be free of charge to the internee.

Art. 92. Medical inspections of internees shall be made at least once a month. Their purpose shall be, in particular, to supervise the general state of health, nutrition and cleanliness of internees, and to detect contagious diseases, especially tuberculosis, malaria, and venereal diseases. Such inspections shall include, in particular, the checking of weight of each internee and, at least once a year, radioscopic examination.

CHAPTER V
Religious, Intellectual and Physical Activities
Art. 93. Internees shall enjoy complete latitude in the exercise of their religious duties, including attendance at the services of their faith, on condition that they comply with the disciplinary routine prescribed by the detaining authorities.

Ministers of religion who are interned shall be allowed to minister freely to the members of their community. For this purpose the Detaining Power shall ensure their equitable allocation amongst the various places of internment in which there are internees speaking the same language and belonging to the same religion. Should such ministers be too few in number, the Detaining Power shall provide them with the necessary facilities, including means of transport, for moving from one place to another, and they shall be authorized to visit any internees who are in hospital. Ministers of religion shall be at liberty to correspond on matters concerning their ministry with the religious authorities in the country of detention and, as far as possible, with the international religious organizations of their faith. Such correspondence shall not be considered as forming a part of the quota mentioned in Article 107. It shall, however, be subject to the provisions of Article 112.

When internees do not have at their disposal the assistance of ministers of their faith, or should these latter be too few in number, the local religious authorities of the same faith may appoint, in agreement with the Detaining Power, a minister of the internees' faith or, if such a course is feasible from a denominational point of view, a minister of similar religion or a qualified layman. The latter shall enjoy the facilities granted to the ministry he has assumed. Persons so appointed shall comply with all regulations laid down by the Detaining Power in the interests of discipline and security.

Art. 94. The Detaining Power shall encourage intellectual, educational and recreational pursuits, sports and games amongst internees, whilst leaving them free to take part in them or not. It shall take all practicable measures to ensure the exercice thereof, in particular by providing suitable premises.

All possible facilities shall be granted to internees to continue their studies or to take up new subjects. The education of children and young people shall be ensured; they shall be allowed to attend schools either within the place of internment or outside.

Internees shall be given opportunities for physical exercise, sports and outdoor games. For this purpose, sufficient open spaces shall be set aside in all places of internment. Special playgrounds shall be reserved for children and young people.

Art. 95. The Detaining Power shall not employ internees as workers, unless they so desire. Employment which, if undertaken under compulsion by a protected person not in internment, would involve a breach of Articles 40 or 51 of the present Convention, and employment on work which is of a degrading or humiliating character are in any case prohibited.

After a working period of six weeks, internees shall be free to give up work at any moment, subject to eight days' notice.

These provisions constitute no obstacle to the right of the Detaining Power to employ interned doctors, dentists and other medical personnel in their professional capacity on behalf of their fellow internees, or to employ internees for administrative and maintenance work in places of internment and to detail such persons for work in the kitchens or for other domestic tasks, or to require such persons to undertake duties connected with the protection of internees against aerial bombardment or other war risks. No internee may, however, be required to perform tasks for which he is, in the opinion of a medical officer, physically unsuited.

The Detaining Power shall take entire responsibility for all working conditions, for medical attention, for the payment of wages, and for ensuring that all employed internees receive compensation for occupational accidents and diseases. The standards prescribed for the said working conditions and for compensation shall be in accordance with the national laws and regulations, and with the existing practice; they shall in no case be inferior to those obtaining for work of the same nature in the same district. Wages for work done shall be determined on an equitable basis by special agreements between the internees, the Detaining Power, and, if the case arises, employers other than the Detaining Power to provide for free maintenance of internees and for the medical attention which their state of health may require. Internees permanently detailed for categories of work mentioned in the third paragraph of this Article, shall be paid fair wages by the Detaining Power. The working conditions and the scale of compensation for occupational accidents and diseases to internees, thus detailed, shall not be inferior to those applicable to work of the same nature in the same district.

Art.96. All labour detachments shall remain part of and dependent upon a place of internment. The competent authorities of the Detaining Power and the commandant of a place of internment shall be responsible for the observance in a labour detachment of the provisions of the present Convention. The commandant shall keep an up-to-date list of the labour detachments subordinate to him and shall communicate it to the delegates of the Protecting Power, of the International Committee of the Red Cross and of other humanitarian organizations who may visit the places of internment.

CHAPTER VI
Personal Property and Financial Resources Art. 97. Internees shall be permitted to retain articles of personal use. Monies, cheques, bonds, etc., and valuables in their possession may not be taken from them except in

accordance with established procedure. Detailed receipts shall be given therefor.

The amounts shall be paid into the account of every internee as provided for in Article 98. Such amounts may not be converted into any other currency unless legislation in force in the territory in which the owner is interned so requires or the internee gives his consent.

Articles which have above all a personal or sentimental value may not be taken away.

A woman internee shall not be searched except by a woman.

On release or repatriation, internees shall be given all articles, monies or other valuables taken from them during internment and shall receive in currency the balance of any credit to their accounts kept in accordance with Article 98, with the exception of any articles or amounts withheld by the Detaining Power by virtue of its legislation in force. If the property of an internee is so withheld, the owner shall receive a detailed receipt.

Family or identity documents in the possession of internees may not be taken away without a receipt being given. At no time shall internees be left without identity documents. If they have none, they shall be issued with special documents drawn up by the detaining authorities, which will serve as their identity papers until the end of their internment.

Internees may keep on their persons a certain amount of money, in cash or in the shape of purchase coupons, to enable them to make purchases.

Art. 98. All internees shall receive regular allowances, sufficient to enable them to purchase goods and articles, such as tobacco, toilet requisites, etc. Such allowances may take the form of credits or purchase coupons.

Furthermore, internees may receive allowances from the Power to which they owe allegiance, the Protecting Powers, the organizations which may assist them, or their families, as well as the income on their property in accordance with the law of the Detaining Power. The amount of allowances granted by the Power to which they owe allegiance shall be the same for each category of internees (infirm, sick, pregnant women, etc.) but may not be allocated by that Power or distributed by the Detaining Power on the basis of discriminations between internees which are prohibited by Article 27 of the present Convention.

The Detaining Power shall open a regular account for every internee, to which shall be credited the allowances named in the present Article, the wages earned and the remittances received, together with such sums taken from him as may be available under the legislation in force in the territory in which he is interned. Internees shall be granted all facilities consistent with the legislation in force in such territory to make remittances to their families and to other dependants. They may draw from their accounts the amounts necessary for their personal expenses, within the limits fixed by the Detaining Power. They shall at all times be afforded reasonable facilities for consulting and obtaining copies of their accounts. A statement of accounts shall be furnished to the Protecting Power, on request, and shall accompany the internee in case of transfer.

CHAPTER VII

Administration and Discipline

Art. 99. Every place of internment shall be put under the authority of a responsible officer, chosen from the regular military forces or the regular civil administration of the Detaining Power. The officer in charge of the place of internment must have in his possession a copy of the present Convention in the official language, or one of the official languages, of his country and shall be responsible for its application. The staff in control of internees shall be instructed in the provisions of the present Convention and of the administrative measures adopted to ensure its application.

The text of the present Convention and the texts of special agreements concluded under the said Convention shall be posted inside the place of internment, in a language which the internees understand, or shall be in the possession of the Internee Committee.

Regulations, orders, notices and publications of every kind shall be communicated to the internees and posted inside the places of internment, in a language which they understand.

Every order and command addressed to internees individually must, likewise, be given in a language which they understand.

Art. 100. The disciplinary regime in places of internment shall be consistent with humanitarian principles, and shall in no circumstances include regulations imposing on internees any physical exertion dangerous to their health or involving physical or moral victimization. Identification by tattooing or imprinting signs or markings on the body, is prohibited.

In particular, prolonged standing and roll-calls, punishment drill, military drill and manoeuvres, or the reduction of food rations, are prohibited.

Art. 101. Internees shall have the right to present to the authorities in whose power they are, any petition with regard to the conditions of internment to which they are subjected.

They shall also have the right to apply without restriction through the Internee Committee or, if they consider it necessary, direct to the representatives of the Protecting Power, in order to indicate to them any points on which they may have complaints to make with regard to the conditions of internment.

Such petitions and complaints shall be transmitted forthwith and without alteration, and even if the latter are recognized to be unfounded, they may not occasion any punishment.

Periodic reports on the situation in places of internment and as to the needs of the internees may be sent by the Internee Committees to the representatives of the Protecting Powers.

Art. 102. In every place of internment, the internees shall freely elect by secret ballot every six months, the members of a Committee empowered to represent them before the Detaining and the Protecting Powers, the International Committee of the Red Cross and any other organization which may assist them. The members of the Committee shall be eligible for re-election.

Internees so elected shall enter upon their duties after their election has been approved by the detaining authorities. The reasons for any refusals or dismissals shall be communicated to the Protecting Powers concerned.

Art. 103. The Internee Committees shall further the physical, spiritual and intellectual well-being of the internees.

In case the internees decide, in particular, to organize a system of mutual assistance amongst themselves, this organization would be within the competence of the Committees in addition to the special duties entrusted to them under other provisions of the present Convention.

Art. 104. Members of Internee Committees shall not be required to perform any other work, if the accomplishment of their duties is rendered more difficult thereby.

Members of Internee Committees may appoint from amongst the internees such assistants as they may require. All material facilities shall be granted to them, particularly a certain freedom of movement necessary for the accomplishment of their duties (visits to labour detachments, receipt of supplies, etc.).

All facilities shall likewise be accorded to members of Internee Committees for communication by post and telegraph with the detaining authorities, the Protecting Powers, the International Committee of the Red Cross and their delegates, and with the organizations which give assistance to internees. Committee members in labour detachments shall enjoy similar facilities for communication with their Internee Committee in the principal place of internment. Such communications shall not be limited, nor considered as forming a part of the quota mentioned in Article 107.

Members of Internee Committees who are transferred shall be allowed a reasonable time to acquaint their successors with current affairs.

CHAPTER VIII
Relations with the Exterior
Art. 105. Immediately upon interning protected persons, the Detaining Powers shall inform them, the Power to which they owe allegiance and their Protecting Power of the measures taken for executing the provisions of the present Chapter. The Detaining Powers shall likewise inform the Parties concerned of any subsequent modifications of such measures.

Art. 106. As soon as he is interned, or at the latest not more than one week after his arrival in a place of internment, and likewise in cases of sickness or transfer to another place of internment or to a hospital, every internee shall be enabled to send direct to his family, on the one hand, and to the Central Agency provided for by Article 140, on the other, an internment card similar, if possible, to the model annexed to the present Convention, informing his relatives of his detention, address and state of health. The said cards shall be forwarded as rapidly as possible and may not be delayed in any way.

Art. 107. Internees shall be allowed to send and receive letters and cards. If the Detaining Power deems it necessary to limit the number of letters and cards sent by each internee, the said number shall not be less than two letters and four cards monthly; these shall be drawn up so as to conform as closely as possible to the models annexed to the present Convention. If limitations must be placed on the correspondence addressed to internees, they may be ordered only by the Power to which such internees owe allegiance, possibly at the request of the Detaining Power. Such letters and cards must be conveyed with reasonable despatch; they may not be delayed or retained for disciplinary reasons.

Internees who have been a long time without news, or who find it impossible to receive news from their relatives, or to give them news by the ordinary postal route, as well as those who are at a considerable distance from their homes, shall be allowed to send telegrams, the charges being paid by them in the currency at their disposal. They shall likewise benefit by this provision in cases which are recognized to be urgent.

As a rule, internees' mail shall be written in their own language. The Parties to the conflict may authorize correspondence in other languages.

Art. 108. Internees shall be allowed to receive, by post or by any other means, individual parcels or collective shipments containing in particular foodstuffs, clothing, medical supplies, as well as books and objects of a devotional, educational or recreational character which may meet their needs. Such shipments shall in no way free the Detaining Power from the obligations imposed upon it by virtue of the present Convention.

Should military necessity require the quantity of such shipments to be limited, due notice thereof shall be given to the Protecting Power and to the International Committee of the Red Cross, or to any other organization giving assistance to the internees and responsible for the forwarding of such shipments.

The conditions for the sending of individual parcels and collective shipments shall, if necessary, be the subject of special agreements between the Powers concerned, which may in no case delay the receipt by the internees of relief supplies. Parcels of clothing and foodstuffs may not include books. Medical relief supplies shall, as a rule, be sent in collective parcels.

Art. 109. In the absence of special agreements between Parties to the conflict regarding the conditions for the receipt and distribution of collective relief shipments, the regulations concerning collective relief which are annexed to the present Convention shall be applied.

The special agreements provided for above shall in no case restrict the right of Internee Committees to take possession of collective relief shipments intended for internees, to undertake their distribution and to dispose of them in the interests of the recipients. Nor shall such agreements restrict the right of representatives of the Protecting Powers, the International Committee of the Red Cross, or any other organization giving assistance to internees and responsible for the forwarding of collective shipments, to supervise their distribution to the recipients.

Art. 110. An relief shipments for internees shall be exempt from import, customs and other dues.

All matter sent by mail, including relief parcels sent by parcel post and remittances of money, addressed from other countries to internees or despatched by them through the post office, either direct or through the

Information Bureaux provided for in Article 136 and the Central Information Agency provided for in Article 140, shall be exempt from all postal dues both in the countries of origin and destination and in intermediate countries. To this effect, in particular, the exemption provided by the Universal Postal Convention of 1947 and by the agreements of the Universal Postal Union in favour of civilians of enemy nationality detained in camps or civilian prisons, shall be extended to the other interned persons protected by the present Convention. The countries not signatory to the above-mentioned agreements shall be bound to grant freedom from charges in the same circumstances.

The cost of transporting relief shipments which are intended for internees and which, by reason of their weight or any other cause, cannot be sent through the post office, shall be borne by the Detaining Power in all the territories under its control. Other Powers which are Parties to the present Convention shall bear the cost of transport in their respective territories.

Costs connected with the transport of such shipments, which are not covered by the above paragraphs, shall be charged to the senders.

The High Contracting Parties shall endeavour to reduce, so far as possible, the charges for telegrams sent by internees, or addressed to them.

Art. 111. Should military operations prevent the Powers concerned from fulfilling their obligation to ensure the conveyance of the mail and relief shipments provided for in Articles 106, 107, 108 and 113, the Protecting Powers concerned, the International Committee of the Red Cross or any other organization duly approved by the Parties to the conflict may undertake to ensure the conveyance of such shipments by suitable means (rail, motor vehicles, vessels or aircraft, etc.). For this purpose, the High Contracting Parties shall endeavour to supply them with such transport, and to allow its circulation, especially by granting the necessary safe-conducts.

Such transport may also be used to convey: (a) correspondence, lists and reports exchanged between the Central Information Agency referred to in Article 140 and the National Bureaux referred to in Article 136; (b) correspondence and reports relating to internees which the Protecting Powers, the International Committee of the Red Cross or any other organization assisting the internees exchange either with their own delegates or with the Parties to the conflict.

These provisions in no way detract from the right of any Party to the conflict to arrange other means of transport if it should so prefer, nor preclude the granting of safe-conducts, under mutually agreed conditions, to such means of transport.

The costs occasioned by the use of such means of transport shall be borne, in proportion to the importance of the shipments, by the Parties to the conflict whose nationals are benefited thereby.

Art. 112. The censoring of correspondence addressed to internees or despatched by them shall be done as quickly as possible.

The examination of consignments intended for internees shall not be carried out under conditions that will expose the goods contained in them to deterioration. It shall be done in the presence of the addressee, or of a fellow-internee duly delegated by him. The delivery to internees of individual or collective consignments shall not be delayed under the pretext of difficulties of censorship.

Any prohibition of correspondence ordered by the Parties to the conflict either for military or political reasons, shall be only temporary and its duration shall be as short as possible.

Art. 113. The Detaining Powers shall provide all reasonable execution facilities for the transmission, through the Protecting Power or the Central Agency provided for in Article 140, or as otherwise required, of wills, powers of attorney, letters of authority, or any other documents intended for internees or despatched by them.

In all cases the Detaining Powers shall facilitate the execution and authentication in due legal form of such documents on behalf of internees, in particular by allowing them to consult a lawyer.

Art. 114. The Detaining Power shall afford internees all facilities to enable them to manage their property, provided this is not incompatible with the conditions of internment and the law which is applicable. For this purpose, the said Power may give them permission to leave the place of internment in urgent cases and if circumstances allow.

Art. 115. In all cases where an internee is a party to proceedings in any court, the Detaining Power shall, if he so requests, cause the court to be informed of his detention and shall, within legal limits, ensure that all necessary steps are taken to prevent him from being in any way prejudiced, by reason of his internment, as regards the preparation and conduct of his case or as regards the execution of any judgment of the court.

Art.116. Every internee shall be allowed to receive visitors, especially near relatives, at regular intervals and as frequently as possible.

As far as is possible, internees shall be permitted to visit their homes in urgent cases, particularly in cases of death or serious illness of relatives.

CHAPTER IX
Penal and Disciplinary Sanctions
Art. 117. Subject to the provisions of the present Chapter, the laws in force in the territory in which they are detained will continue to apply to internees who commit offences during internment.

If general laws, regulations or orders declare acts committed by internees to be punishable, whereas the same acts are not punishable when committed by persons who are not internees, such acts shall entail disciplinary punishments only.

No internee may be punished more than once for the same act, or on the same count.

Art. 118. The courts or authorities shall in passing sentence take as far as possible into account the fact that the defendant is not a national of the Detaining Power. They shall be free to reduce the penalty prescribed for the offence with which the internee is charged and shall not be obliged, to this end, to apply the minimum sentence prescribed.

Imprisonment in premises without daylight, and, in general, all forms of cruelty without exception are forbidden.

Internees who have served disciplinary or judicial sentences shall not be treated differently from other internees.

The duration of preventive detention undergone by an internee shall be deducted from any disciplinary or judicial penalty involving confinement to which he may be sentenced.

Internee Committees shall be informed of all judicial proceedings instituted against internees whom they represent, and of their result.

Art. 119. The disciplinary punishments applicable to internees shall be the following: (1) a fine which shall not exceed 50 per cent of the wages which the internee would otherwise receive under the provisions of Article 95 during a period of not more than thirty days. (2) discontinuance of privileges granted over and above the treatment provided for by the present Convention (3) fatigue duties, not exceeding two hours daily, in connection with the maintenance of the place of internment. (4) confinement.

In no case shall disciplinary penalties be inhuman, brutal or dangerous for the health of internees. Account shall be taken of the internee's age, sex and state of health.

The duration of any single punishment shall in no case exceed a maximum of thirty consecutive days, even if the internee is answerable for several breaches of discipline when his case is dealt with, whether such breaches are connected or not.

Art. 120. Internees who are recaptured after having escaped or when attempting to escape, shall be liable only to disciplinary punishment in respect of this act, even if it is a repeated offence.

Article 118, paragraph 3, notwithstanding, internees punished as a result of escape or attempt to escape, may be subjected to special surveillance, on condition that such surveillance does not affect the state of their health, that it is exercised in a place of internment and that it does not entail the abolition of any of the safeguards granted by the present Convention.

Internees who aid and abet an escape or attempt to escape, shall be liable on this count to disciplinary punishment only.

Art. 121. Escape, or attempt to escape, even if it is a repeated offence, shall not be deemed an aggravating circumstance in cases where an internee is prosecuted for offences committed during his escape.

The Parties to the conflict shall ensure that the competent authorities exercise leniency in deciding whether punishment inflicted for an offence shall be of a disciplinary or judicial nature, especially in respect of acts committed in connection with an escape, whether successful or not.

Art. 122. Acts which constitute offences against discipline shall be investigated immediately. This rule shall be applied, in particular, in cases of escape or attempt to escape. Recaptured internees shall be handed over to the competent authorities as soon as possible.

In cases of offences against discipline, confinement awaiting trial shall be reduced to an absolute minimum for all internees, and shall not exceed fourteen days. Its duration shall in any case be deducted from any sentence of confinement.

The provisions of Articles 124 and 125 shall apply to internees who are in confinement awaiting trial for offences against discipline.

Art. 123. Without prejudice to the competence of courts and higher authorities, disciplinary punishment may be ordered only by the commandant of the place of internment, or by a responsible officer or official who replaces him, or to whom he has delegated his disciplinary powers.

Before any disciplinary punishment is awarded, the accused internee shall be given precise information regarding the offences of which he is accused, and given an opportunity of explaining his conduct and of defending himself. He shall be permitted, in particular, to call witnesses and to have recourse, if necessary, to the services of a qualified interpreter. The decision shall be announced in the presence of the accused and of a member of the Internee Committee.

The period elapsing between the time of award of a disciplinary punishment and its execution shall not exceed one month.

When an internee is awarded a further disciplinary punishment, a period of at least three days shall elapse between the execution of any two of the punishments, if the duration of one of these is ten days or more.

A record of disciplinary punishments shall be maintained by the commandant of the place of internment and shall be open to inspection by representatives of the Protecting Power.

Art. 124. Internees shall not in any case be transferred to penitentiary establishments (prisons, penitentiaries, convict prisons, etc.) to undergo disciplinary punishment therein.

The premises in which disciplinary punishments are undergone shall conform to sanitary requirements: they shall in particular be provided with adequate bedding. Internees undergoing punishment shall be enabled to keep themselves in a state of cleanliness.

Women internees undergoing disciplinary punishment shall be confined in separate quarters from male internees and shall be under the immediate supervision of women.

Art. 125. Internees awarded disciplinary punishment shall be allowed to exercise and to stay in the open air at least two hours daily.

They shall be allowed, if they so request, to be present at the daily medical inspections. They shall receive the attention which their state of health requires and, if necessary, shall be removed to the infirmary of the place of internment or to a hospital.

They shall have permission to read and write, likewise to send and receive letters. Parcels and remittances of money, however, may be withheld from them until the completion of their punishment; such consignments shall meanwhile be entrusted to the Internee Committee, who will hand over to the infirmary the perishable goods contained in the parcels.

No internee given a disciplinary punishment may be deprived of the benefit of the provisions of Articles 107 and 143 of the present Convention.

Art. 126. The provisions of Articles 71 to 76 inclusive shall apply, by analogy, to proceedings against internees who are in the national territory of the Detaining Power.

CHAPTER X
Transfers of Internees
Art. 127. The transfer of internees shall always be effected humanely. As a general rule, it shall be carried out by rail or other means of transport, and under conditions at least equal to those obtaining for the forces of the Detaining Power in their changes of station. If, as an exceptional measure, such removals have to be effected on foot, they may not take place unless the internees are in a fit state of health, and may not in any case expose them to excessive fatigue.

The Detaining Power shall supply internees during transfer with drinking water and food sufficient in quantity, quality and variety to maintain them in good health, and also with the necessary clothing, adequate shelter and the necessary medical attention. The Detaining Power shall take all suitable precautions to ensure their safety during transfer, and shall establish before their departure a complete list of all internees transferred.

Sick, wounded or infirm internees and maternity cases shall not be transferred if the journey would be seriously detrimental to them, unless their safety imperatively so demands.

If the combat zone draws close to a place of internment, the internees in the said place shall not be transferred unless their removal can be carried out in adequate conditions of safety, or unless they are exposed to greater risks by remaining on the spot than by being transferred.

When making decisions regarding the transfer of internees, the Detaining Power shall take their interests into account and, in particular, shall not do anything to increase the difficulties of repatriating them or returning them to their own homes.

Art. 128. In the event of transfer, internees shall be officially advised of their departure and of their new postal address. Such notification shall be given in time for them to pack their luggage and inform their next of kin.

They shall be allowed to take with them their personal effects, and the correspondence and parcels which have arrived for them. The weight of such baggage may be limited if the conditions of transfer so require, but in no case to less than twenty-five kilograms per internee.

Mail and parcels addressed to their former place of internment shall be forwarded to them without delay.

The commandant of the place of internment shall take, in agreement with the Internee Committee, any measures needed to ensure the transport of the internees' community property and of the luggage the internees are unable to take with them in consequence of restrictions imposed by virtue of the second paragraph.

CHAPTER XI
Deaths

Art. 129. The wills of internees shall be received for safe-keeping by the responsible authorities; and if the event of the death of an internee his will shall be transmitted without delay to a person whom he has previously designated.

Deaths of internees shall be certified in every case by a doctor, and a death certificate shall be made out, showing the causes of death and the conditions under which it occurred.

An official record of the death, duly registered, shall be drawn up in accordance with the procedure relating thereto in force in the territory where the place of internment is situated, and a duly certified copy of such record shall be transmitted without delay to the Protecting Power as well as to the Central Agency referred to in Article 140.

Art. 130. The detaining authorities shall ensure that internees who die while interned are honourably buried, if possible according to the rites of the religion to which they belonged and that their graves are respected, properly maintained, and marked in such a way that they can always be recognized.

Deceased internees shall be buried in individual graves unless unavoidable circumstances require the use of collective graves. Bodies may be cremated only for imperative reasons of hygiene, on account of the religion of the deceased or in accordance with his expressed wish to this effect. In case of cremation, the fact shall be stated and the reasons given in the death certificate of the deceased. The ashes shall be retained for safe-keeping by the detaining authorities and shall be transferred as soon as possible to the next of kin on their request.

As soon as circumstances permit, and not later than the close of hostilities, the Detaining Power shall forward lists of graves of deceased internees to the Powers on whom deceased internees depended, through the Information Bureaux provided for in Article 136. Such lists shall include all particulars necessary for the identification of the deceased internees, as well as the exact location of their graves.

Art. 131. Every death or serious injury of an internee, caused or suspected to have been caused by a sentry, another internee or any other person, as well as any death the cause of which is unknown, shall be immediately followed by an official enquiry by the Detaining Power.

A communication on this subject shall be sent immediately to the Protecting Power. The evidence of any witnesses shall be taken, and a report including such evidence shall be prepared and forwarded to the said Protecting Power.

If the enquiry indicates the guilt of one or more persons, the Detaining Power shall take all necessary steps to ensure the prosecution of the person or persons responsible.

CHAPTER XII
Release, Repatriation and Accommodation in Neutral Countries
Art. 132. Each interned person shall be released by the Detaining Power as soon as the reasons which necessitated his internment no longer exist.

The Parties to the conflict shall, moreover, endeavour during the course of hostilities, to conclude agreements for the release, the repatriation, the return to places of residence or the accommodation in a neutral country of certain classes of internees, in particular children, pregnant women and mothers with infants and young children, wounded and sick, and internees who have been detained for a long time.

Art. 133. Internment shall cease as soon as possible after the close of hostilities.

Internees in the territory of a Party to the conflict against whom penal proceedings are pending for offences not exclusively subject to disciplinary penalties, may be detained until the close of such proceedings and, if circumstances require, until the completion of the penalty. The same shall apply to internees who have been previously sentenced to a punishment depriving them of liberty.

By agreement between the Detaining Power and the Powers concerned, committees may be set up after the close of hostilities, or of the occupation of territories, to search for dispersed internees.

Art. 134. The High Contracting Parties shall endeavour, upon the Repatriation close of hostilities or occupation, to ensure the return of all internees to their last place of residence, or to facilitate their residence repatriation.

Art. 135. The Detaining Power shall bear the expense of returning released internees to the places where they were residing when interned, or, if it took them into custody while they were in transit or on the high seas, the cost of completing their journey or of their return to their point of departure.

Where a Detaining Power refuses permission to reside in its territory to a released internee who previously had his permanent domicile therein, such Detaining Power shall pay the cost of the said internee's repatriation. If, however, the internee elects to return to his country on his own responsibility or in obedience to the Government of the Power to which he owes allegiance, the Detaining Power need not pay the expenses of his journey beyond the point of his departure from its territory. The Detaining Power need not pay the cost of repatriation of an internee who was interned at his own request.

If internees are transferred in accordance with Article 45, the transferring and receiving Powers shall agree on the portion of the above costs to be borne by each.

The foregoing shall not prejudice such special agreements as may be concluded between Parties to the conflict concerning the exchange and repatriation of their nationals in enemy hands.

SECTION V
Information Bureaux and Central Agency
Art. 136. Upon the outbreak of a conflict and in all cases of occupation, each of the Parties to the conflict

shall establish an official Information Bureau responsible for receiving and transmitting information in respect of the protected persons who are in its power.

Each of the Parties to the conflict shall, within the shortest possible period, give its Bureau information of any measure taken by it concerning any protected persons who are kept in custody for more than two weeks, who are subjected to assigned residence or who are interned. It shall, furthermore, require its various departments concerned with such matters to provide the aforesaid Bureau promptly with information concerning all changes pertaining to these protected persons, as, for example, transfers, releases, repatriations, escapes, admittances to hospitals, births and deaths.

Art. 137. Each national Bureau shall immediately forward information concerning protected persons by the most rapid means to the Powers in whose territory they resided, through the intermediary of the Protecting Powers and likewise through the Central Agency provided for in Article 140. The Bureaux shall also reply to all enquiries which may be received regarding protected persons.

Information Bureaux shall transmit information concerning a protected person unless its transmission might be detrimental to the person concerned or to his or her relatives. Even in such a case, the information may not be withheld from the Central Agency which, upon being notified of the circumstances, will take the necessary precautions indicated in Article 140.

All communications in writing made by any Bureau shall be authenticated by a signature or a seal.

Art. 138. The information received by the national Bureau and transmitted by it shall be of such a character as to make it possible to identify the protected person exactly and to advise his next of kin quickly. The information in respect of each person shall include at least his surname, first names, place and date of birth, nationality last residence and distinguishing characteristics, the first name of the father and the maiden name of the mother, the date, place and nature of the action taken with regard to the individual, the address at which correspondence may be sent to him and the name and address of the person to be informed.

Likewise, information regarding the state of health of internees who are seriously ill or seriously wounded shall be supplied regularly and if possible every week.

Art. 139. Each national Information Bureau shall, furthermore, be responsible for collecting all personal valuables left by protected persons mentioned in Article 136, in particular those who have been repatriated or released, or who have escaped or died; it shall forward the said valuables to those concerned, either direct, or, if necessary, through the Central Agency. Such articles shall be sent by the Bureau in sealed packets which shall be accompanied by statements giving clear and full identity particulars of the person to whom the articles belonged, and by a complete list of the contents of the parcel. Detailed records shall be maintained of the receipt and despatch of all such valuables.

Art. 140. A Central Information Agency for protected persons, in particular for internees, shall be created in a neutral country. The International Committee of the Red Cross shall, if it deems necessary, propose to the Powers concerned the organization of such an Agency, which may be the same as that provided for in Article 123 of the Geneva Convention relative to the Treatment of Prisoners of War of 12 August 1949.

The function of the Agency shall be to collect all information of the type set forth in Article 136 which it may obtain through official or private channels and to transmit it as rapidly as possible to the countries of origin or of residence of the persons concerned, except in cases where such transmissions might be detrimental to the persons whom the said information concerns, or to their relatives. It shall receive from the Parties to the conflict all reasonable facilities for effecting such transmissions.

The High Contracting Parties, and in particular those whose nationals benefit by the services of the Central Agency, are requested to give the said Agency the financial aid it may require.

The foregoing provisions shall in no way be interpreted as restricting the humanitarian activities of the International Committee of the Red Cross and of the relief Societies described in Article 142.

Art. 141. The national Information Bureaux and the Central Information Agency shall enjoy free postage for all mail, likewise the exemptions provided for in Article 110, and further, so far as possible, exemption from telegraphic charges or, at least, greatly reduced rates.

PART IV
EXECUTION OF THE CONVENTION
SECTION I
General Provisions

Art. 142. Subject to the measures which the Detaining Powers may consider essential to ensure their security or to meet any other reasonable need, the representatives of religious organizations, relief societies, or any other organizations assisting the protected persons, shall receive from these Powers, for themselves or their duly accredited agents, all facilities for visiting the protected persons, for distributing relief supplies and material from any source, intended for educational, recreational or religious purposes, or for assisting them in organizing their leisure time within the places of internment. Such societies or organizations may be constituted in the territory of the Detaining Power, or in any other country, or they may have an international character.

The Detaining Power may limit the number of societies and organizations whose delegates are allowed to carry out their activities in its territory and under its supervision, on condition, however, that such limitation shall not hinder the supply of effective and adequate relief to all protected persons.

The special position of the International Committee of the Red Cross in this field shall be recognized and respected at all times.

Art. 143. Representatives or delegates of the Protecting Powers shall have permission to go to all places where protected persons are, particularly to places of internment, detention and work.

They shall have access to all premises occupied by protected persons and shall be able to interview the latter without witnesses, personally or through an interpreter.

Such visits may not be prohibited except for reasons of imperative military necessity, and then only as an exceptional and temporary measure. Their duration and frequency shall not be restricted.

Such representatives and delegates shall have full liberty to select the places they wish to visit. The Detaining or Occupying Power, the Protecting Power and when occasion arises the Power of origin of the persons to be visited, may agree that compatriots of the internees shall be permitted to participate in the visits.

The delegates of the International Committee of the Red Cross shall also enjoy the above prerogatives. The appointment of such delegates shall be submitted to the approval of the Power governing the territories where they will carry out their duties.

Art. 144. The High Contracting Parties undertake, in time of peace as in time of war, to disseminate the text of the present Convention as widely as possible in their respective countries, and, in particular, to include the study thereof in their programmes of military and, if possible, civil instruction, so that the principles thereof may become known to the entire population.

Any civilian, military, police or other authorities, who in time of war assume responsibilities in respect of protected persons, must possess the text of the Convention and be specially instructed as to its provisions.

Art. 145. The High Contracting Parties shall communicate to one another through the Swiss Federal Council and, during hostilities, through the Protecting Powers, the official translations of the present

Convention, as well as the laws and regulations which they may adopt to ensure the application thereof.

Art. 146. The High Contracting Parties undertake to enact any legislation necessary to provide effective penal sanctions for persons committing, or ordering to be committed, any of the grave breaches of the present Convention defined in the following Article.

Each High Contracting Party shall be under the obligation to search for persons alleged to have committed, or to have ordered to be committed, such grave breaches, and shall bring such persons, regardless of their nationality, before its own courts. It may also, if it prefers, and in accordance with the provisions of its own legislation, hand such persons over for trial to another High Contracting Party concerned, provided such High Contracting Party has made out a prima facie case.

Each High Contracting Party shall take measures necessary for the suppression of all acts contrary to the provisions of the present Convention other than the grave breaches defined in the following Article.

In all circumstances, the accused persons shall benefit by safeguards of proper trial and defence, which shall not be less favourable than those provided by Article 105 and those following of the Geneva Convention relative to the Treatment of Prisoners of War of 12 August 1949. Art. 147. Grave breaches to which the preceding Article relates shall be those involving any of the following acts, if committed against persons or property protected by the present Convention: wilful killing, torture or inhuman treatment, including biological experiments, wilfully causing great suffering or serious injury to body or health, unlawful deportation or transfer or unlawful confinement of a protected person, compelling a protected person to serve in the forces of a hostile Power, or wilfully depriving a protected person of the rights of fair and regular trial prescribed in the present Convention, taking of hostages and extensive destruction and appropriation of property, not justified by military necessity and carried out unlawfully and wantonly.

Art. 148. No High Contracting Party shall be allowed to absolve itself or any other High Contracting Party of any liability incurred by itself or by another High Contracting Party in respect of breaches referred to in the preceding Article.

Art. 149. At the request of a Party to the conflict, an enquiry shall be instituted, in a manner to be decided between the interested Parties, concerning any alleged violation of the Convention.

If agreement has not been reached concerning the procedure for the enquiry, the Parties should agree on the choice of an umpire who will decide upon the procedure to be followed.

Once the violation has been established, the Parties to the conflict shall put an end to it and shall repress it with the least possible delay.

SECTION II
Final Provisions
Art. 150. The present Convention is established in English and in French. Both texts are equally authentic.

The Swiss Federal Council shall arrange for official translations of the Convention to be made in the Russian and Spanish languages.

Art. 151. The present Convention, which bears the date of this day, is open to signature until 12 February 1950, in the name of the Powers represented at the Conference which opened at Geneva on 21 April 1949.

Art. 152. The present Convention shall be ratified as soon as possible and the ratifications shall be deposited at Berne.

A record shall be drawn up of the deposit of each instrument of ratification and certified copies of this record shall be transmitted by the Swiss Federal Council to all the Powers in whose name the Convention has been signed, or whose accession has been notified.

Art. 153. The present Convention shall come into force six months after not less than two instruments of ratification have been deposited.

Thereafter, it shall come into force for each High Contracting Party six months after the deposit of the instrument of ratification.

Art. 154. In the relations between the Powers who are bound by the Hague Conventions respecting the Laws and Customs of War on Land, whether that of 29 July 1899, or that of 18 October 1907, and who are parties to the present Convention, this last Convention shall be supplementary to Sections II and III of the Regulations annexed to the above-mentioned Conventions of The Hague.

Art. 155. From the date of its coming into force, it shall be open to any Power in whose name the present Convention has not been signed, to accede to this Convention.

Art. 156. Accessions shall be notified in writing to the Swiss Federal Council, and shall take effect six months after the date on which they are received.

The Swiss Federal Council shall communicate the accessions to all the Powers in whose name the Convention has been signed, or whose accession has been notified.

Art. 157. The situations provided for in Articles 2 and 3 shall effective immediate effect to ratifications deposited and accessions notified by the Parties to the conflict before or after the beginning of hostilities or occupation. The Swiss Federal Council shall communicate by the quickest method any ratifications or accessions received from Parties to the conflict.

Art. 158. Each of the High Contracting Parties shall be at liberty to denounce the present Convention.

The denunciation shall be notified in writing to the Swiss Federal Council, which shall transmit it to the Governments of all the High Contracting Parties.

The denunciation shall take effect one year after the notification thereof has been made to the Swiss Federal Council. However, a denunciation of which notification has been made at a time when the denouncing Power is involved in a conflict shall not take effect until peace has been concluded, and until after operations connected with release, repatriation and re-establishment of the persons protected by the present Convention have been terminated.

The denunciation shall have effect only in respect of the denouncing Power. It shall in no way impair the obligations which the Parties to the conflict shall remain bound to fulfil by virtue of the principles of the law of nations, as they result from the usages established among civilized peoples, from the laws of humanity and the dictates of the public conscience.

Art. 159. The Swiss Federal Council shall register the present Convention with the Secretariat of the United Nations. The Swiss Federal Council shall also inform the Secretariat of the United Nations of all ratifications, accessions and denunciations received by it with respect to the present Convention.

In witness whereof the undersigned, having deposited their respective full powers, have signed the present Convention.

Done at Geneva this twelfth day of August 1949, in the English and French languages. The original shall be deposited in the Archives of the Swiss Confederation. The Swiss Federal Council shall transmit certified copies thereof to each of the signatory and acceding States.

ANNEX I
Draft Agreement Relating to Hospital and Safety Zones and Localities

Art. 1. Hospital and safety zones shall be strictly reserved for the persons mentioned in Article 23 of the Geneva Convention for the Amelioration of the

Condition of the Wounded and Sick in Armed Forces in the Field of 12 August 1949, and in Article 14 of the Geneva Convention relative to the Protection of Civilian Persons in Time of War of 12 August 1949, and for the personnel entrusted with the organization and administration of these zones and localities, and with the care of the persons therein assembled.

Nevertheless, persons whose permanent residence is within such zones shall have the right to stay there.

Art. 2. No persons residing, in whatever capacity, in a hospital and safety zone shall perform any work, either within or without the zone, directly connected with military operations or the production of war material.

Art. 3. The Power establishing a hospital and safety zone shall take all necessary measures to prohibit access to all persons who have no right of residence or entry therein.

Art. 4. Hospital and safety zones shall fulfil the following conditions: (a) they shall comprise only a small part of the territory governed by the Power which has established them (b) they shall be thinly populated in relation to the possibilities of accommodation (c) they shall be far removed and free from all military objectives, or large industrial or administrative establishments (d) they shall not be situated in areas which, according to every probability, may become important for the conduct of the war.

Art. 5. Hospital and safety zones shall be subject to the following obligations: (a) the lines of communication and means of transport which they possess shall not be used for the transport of military personnel or material, even in transit (b) they shall in no case be defended by military means.

Art. 6. Hospital and safety zones shall be marked by means of oblique red bands on a white ground, placed on the buildings and outer precincts.

Zones reserved exclusively for the wounded and sick may be marked by means of the Red Cross (Red Crescent, Red Lion and Sun) emblem on a white ground.

They may be similarly marked at night by means of appropriate illumination.

Art. 7. The Powers shall communicate to all the High Contracting Parties in peacetime or on the outbreak of hostilities, a list of the hospital and safety zones in the territories governed by them. They shall also give notice of any new zones set up during hostilities.

As soon as the adverse party has received the above-mentioned notification, the zone shall be regularly established.

If, however, the adverse party considers that the conditions of the present agreement have not been fulfilled, it may refuse to recognize the zone by giving immediate notice thereof to the Party responsible for the said zone, or may make its recognition of such zone dependent upon the institution of the control provided for in Article 8.

Art. 8. Any Power having recognized one or several hospital and safety zones instituted by the adverse Party shall be entitled to demand control by one or more

Special Commissions, for the purpose of ascertaining if the zones fulfil the conditions and obligations stipulated in the present agreement.

For this purpose, members of the Special Commissions shall at all times have free access to the various zones and may even reside there permanently. They shall be given all facilities for their duties of inspection.

Art. 9. Should the Special Commissions note any facts which they consider contrary to the stipulations of the present agreement, they shall at once draw the attention of the Power governing the said zone to these facts, and shall fix a time limit of five days within which the matter should be rectified. They shall duly notify the Power which has recognized the zone.

If, when the time limit has expired, the Power governing the zone has not complied with the warning, the adverse Party may declare that it is no longer bound by the present agreement in respect of the said zone.

Art. 10. Any Power setting up one or more hospital and safety zones, and the adverse Parties to whom their existence has been notified, shall nominate or have nominated by the Protecting Powers or by other neutral Powers, persons eligible to be members of the Special Commissions mentioned in Articles 8 and 9.

Art. 11. In no circumstances may hospital and safety zones be the object of attack. They shall be protected and respected at all times by the Parties to the conflict.

Art. 12. In the case of occupation of a territory, the hospital and safety zones therein shall continue to be respected and utilized as such.

Their purpose may, however, be modified by the Occupying Power, on condition that all measures are taken to ensure the safety of the persons accommodated.

Art. 13. The present agreement shall also apply to localities which the Powers may utilize for the same purposes as hospital and safety zones.

ANNEX II
Draft Regulations concerning Collective Relief

Art. 1. The Internee Committees shall be allowed to distribute collective relief shipments for which they are responsible to all internees who are dependent for administration on the said Committee's place of internment, including those internees who are in hospitals, or in prison or other penitentiary establishments.

Art. 2. The distribution of collective relief shipments shall be effected in accordance with the instructions of the donors and with a plan drawn up by the Internee Committees. The issue of medical stores shall, however, be made for preference in agreement with the senior medical officers, and the latter may, in hospitals and infirmaries, waive the said instructions, if the needs of their patients so demand. Within the limits thus defined, the distribution shall always be carried out equitably.

Art. 3. Members of Internee Committees shall be allowed to go to the railway stations or other points of arrival of relief supplies near their places of internment so as to enable them to verify the quantity as well as the quality of the goods received and to make out detailed reports thereon for the donors.

Art. 4. Internee Committees shall be given the facilities necessary for verifying whether the distribution of collective relief in all subdivisions and annexes of their places of internment has been carried out in accordance with their instructions.

Art. 5. Internee Committees shall be allowed to complete, and to cause to be completed by members of the Internee Committees in labour detachments or by the senior medical officers of infirmaries and hospitals, forms or questionnaires intended for the donors, relating to collective relief supplies (distribution, requirements, quantities, etc.). Such forms and questionnaires, duly completed, shall be forwarded to the donors without delay.

Art. 6. In order to secure the regular distribution of collective relief supplies to the internees in their place of internment, and to meet any needs that may arise through the arrival of fresh parties of internees, the Internee Committees shall be allowed to create and maintain sufficient reserve stocks of collective relief. For this purpose, they shall have suitable warehouses at their disposal; each warehouse shall be provided with two locks, the Internee Committee holding the keys of one lock, and the commandant of the place of internment the keys of the other.

Art. 7. The High Contracting Parties, and the Detaining Powers in particular, shall, so far as is in any way possible and subject to the regulations governing the food supply of the population, authorize purchases of goods to be made in their territories for the distribution of collective relief to the internees. They shall likewise facilitate the transfer of funds and other financial measures of a technical or administrative nature taken for the purpose of making such purchases.

Art. 8. The foregoing provisions shall not constitute an obstacle to the right of internees to receive collective relief before their arrival in a place of internment or in the course of their transfer, nor to the possibility of representatives of the Protecting Power, or of the International Committee of the Red Cross or any other humanitarian organization giving assistance to internees and responsible for forwarding such supplies, ensuring the distribution thereof to the recipients by any other means they may deem suitable. [17]

With your understanding of all of your rights as a civilian living under the occupation of a foreign military power there is always the possibility that your KNOWLEDGE of these laws could prevent harm coming to either yourself or your family.

You must KNOW more about these things than your occupiers do. Many a life has been saved by a lower ranking soldier refusing to break these laws, even if contrary to his own orders.

DO NOT assume that all of the occupying soldiers are monsters, they aren't.

Know all of these Laws; they may save your life one day.

"Truly, to tell lies is not honorable;
but when the truth entails tremendous ruin,
To speak dishonorably is pardonable."
Sophocles

Chapter 11: Bribery

To Bribe is to give someone something, such as money or a favor, in a position of trust, to influence that person's views or conduct. During times of war, especially living under occupation, knowing how to bribe, who to bribe and when to bribe will frequently mean the difference between you living and dying.

The first thing you have to determine is what do you have to bribe someone with? It has to be something that not only has value but is also able to benefit the person who you are bribing.

It must also be something that is universally transferable and portable enough to be quickly concealed upon a person's body.

No matter how much your grand piano is worth, your televisions, your vehicles, or other such large items, they are not going to be your first choice as an exchange item for bribing someone, and shouldn't even be your last choice.

A bribe you may offer to a low ranking solider doing guard duty will also be different from that being offered to the higher ranking officer who is in control of a checkpoint.

A bribe also has to match the favor being asked for to keep from arousing suspicion or fear of punishment. A lower ranking solider will most likely let you pass his guard station for a carton of cigarettes, but will hold you under arrest if you offer him $1,000 in gold.

You should also understand that the soldiers of many armies, and maybe the one that is occupying your country, are masters in the arts of extortion and bribery, and as this report from the Human Rights Organization shows:

"Russian soldiers along the newly-opened escape route out of Grozny are forcing displaced persons from Chechnya to pay bribes in order to cross checkpoints, Human Rights Watch said today.

Chechen displaced persons, as well as returnees seeking to go back to their homes, have been subjected to extortion, beatings, and insults along the two main exit routes from Chechnya--the northern route toward Russia, opened by Russian forces on December 11, as well as the western route toward Ingushetia.

Russian forces opened the northern corridor with much fanfare as a protective measure for the civilian population. But the beatings, extortion, and threats are a serious obstacle to their safe exit from the war zone."

"Russian forces opened the northern corridor with much fanfare as a protective measure for the civilian population," said Holly Cartner, executive director of Human Rights Watch's Europe and Central Asia division. "But the beatings, extortion, and threats are a serious obstacle to their safe exit from the war zone."

"Malik" (not the man's true name), a twenty-four-year-old man who left Grozny on December 13, told Human Rights Watch researchers that he decided to use the northern route--which passes through Pervomayskaya--because he had heard it was a safe route, but was forced to pay border soldiers 1,000 rubles [approximately U.S.$40] in order to cross:

"My neighbor told us that [Minister of Emergency Situations Sergei] Shoigu was promising safe passage, but when we came to the checkpoint there was no Shoigu, so I had to pay a bribe."

According to Malik, about fifty people were waiting at the checkpoint when he arrived, and were prevented from crossing because they could not pay the required bribe.

Malik said that border soldiers brought him to the passport verification booth, and told him: "See all those people who can't get through the checkpoint? If you want to go, you have to pay."

Malik also told Human Rights Watch that the soldiers insulted and threatened him and his wife: "They wanted to take away my wife, and put a gun to my head and said that if I moved they would shoot me.

They insulted me and my wife, because my wife was never touched by anyone else. They were hinting very strongly at what they wanted to do, but I am too ashamed to repeat what they said."

Malik had sought shelter in a cellar in Grozny's Kalinin district for the past two weeks to escape bombing and shelling. He estimated that about thirty people were staying in the shelter on the eve of his departure, mostly the elderly, who were running out of food.

In another border incident, on December 9 Russian soldiers at the Kavkaz-1 checkpoint (about 30 miles west of Grozny near the Ingush border) detained and beat several Chechen men to coerce bribes.

The men were driving trucks transporting displaced persons and their belongings from displaced persons camps in Ingushetia to their homes in Sernovodsk, a Chechen town close to the border with Ingushetia.

The column of about fifteen trucks and numerous passenger cars filled with Sernovodsk residents arrived at the checkpoint around 2:00 p.m. Human Rights Watch separately interviewed three women from Sernovodsk who gave consistent accounts that checkpoint soldiers waved through passenger cars, but ordered trucks to pull over.

Seeing that the trucks had been stopped, those riding in passenger cars pulled over and got out. The soldiers then fired at the ground to chase the passengers back, but later relented and allowed the passengers to approach.

All three women said that the checkpoint soldiers took truck drivers aside to the command post to coerce bribes. Fifty-year-old "Tamara" (not her real name) told Human Rights Watch that soldiers beat her husband when he said he had no money: "They took my husband over inside their tent and said, 'It's impossible that you don't have any money. Go find some wherever you [can].' He was in there for about forty minutes. [When he came out] his eye was [all beaten], a black eye. His nose was bleeding.

He looked out [from the tent] and shouted to me, 'Ask someone for 410 rubles.' He only had 90." After Tamara gathered the money, her husband was released.

The soldiers also detained the son of fifty-year-old "Leyla" (not real name) and at first demanded that he pay a bribe of U.S. $500; Leyla related to Human Rights Watch what her son had told her: "They went up to my son and said 'Come on, give us $500 bucks.' That's exactly what they said, 'bucks' [or]. . . you'll end up waiting here until morning.

If you want to pay, pay; if not we'll find some reason to detain you." The soldiers later settled on as much money as the women gathered around could collect, about 500 to 600 rubles.

A third witness, sixty-year-old "Pata" (not her real name), said that her son Ruslan Arsuyev was detained for two hours until he agreed to pay a bribe. He reportedly told her that other men in the tent had been beaten, although he was not.

All three women told Human Rights Watch that checkpoint soldiers unloaded the trucks containing household articles until the people agreed to pay a bribe. Tamara told Human Rights Watch that the soldiers said, "If you don't want us to toss your things out give us money."

Leyla confirmed this: "All of our things were thrown on the ground. They were stamping on them . . ., undoing [all the bundles]. They had to look over everything. If you tried to say anything it was, 'Get out of here or we'll shoot.' And then they start cursing. We paid them and they stopped." According to Pata, after one truck driver, Khajiyev, agreed to pay they were allowed to reload the trucks." [18]

It is also interesting to know the history of bribery, and here is very short one:

"The word bribery itself starts in medieval French, where bribe meant "a piece of bread". A linguistic game of consequences led the sense from this to "a piece of bread given to a beggar", then more generally to "alms" and "living upon alms", to "begging" and so to associations with mendicancy and vagabondage. By a further very short step the meaning arrived at "theft; stealing".

It was with the last of these senses that the word first appeared in English in the fourteenth century, in the works of Chaucer and his contemporaries. It soon evolved further to take in the idea of extortion, or demanding money with menaces.

Only in this usage did bribe finally come to mean a sum of money, though at this time briber meant the person doing the menacing and so getting the money. The worst offenders were often judges and public officials, who extorted money from claimants in order to pass down a favorable outcome.

It was in the sixteenth century that the meaning flipped completely over so that briber meant instead the person handing over the money. Nobody seems to know quite how this happened.

In the process bribe changed to mean a supposedly voluntary inducement instead of something extracted by force, so arriving at the sense which it has retained ever since." [19]

However you look upon bribery, or what you may feel about it, you must be prepared to be able to do it.

Some of the simple rules are:

Bribe only with something of value to the person you are bribing. If you don't know what that may be, ask them.

Know the ranking and position of anyone you are attempting to bribe, there are those military forces and others (like intelligence officers) who are never able to be bribed.

As distasteful as this may be to you, you should be prepared to offer sexual favors as a bribe, even if it may be your husband, wife, mother, son or daughter. This can sometimes mean the difference between life and death. You must remember that some soldiers are going to rape anyway, so you might as well extract favors from them beforehand.

You're exact and specific instructions on who to bribe, how to bribe and when to bribe are going to depend on your own individual circumstances too. Therefore you will have to acquire a great deal of knowledge into the nature of your occupying forces before attempting to bribe them.

The further you are away from cities and urban areas also increase your chances of successfully bribing guards and soldiers manning checkpoints and roadblocks.

Never attempt to bribe a group, only individuals. An exception to this could be a checkpoint manned by a few lower ranking soldiers.

Let the person you are bribing suggest the amount of money or whatever you are bribing with, the value he puts on this transaction is better than you putting your own value on it. If you make the first offer and he believes it is too high for what he is able to do for you, this will make him suspicious and will lead to your arrest and detention.

"Trust thyself only, and another shall not betray thee."
Thomas Fuller

Chapter 12: Who to Trust

The first general rule about trusting anyone during wartime is simple, trust no one.

To those you give your trust to you also give your life, and those of your family. If there is a possibility of you being betrayed, you will be betrayed.

No matter what position you find yourself in during wartime occupation, you must never forget that in the eyes of your occupiers you are a criminal. You may have value to them, but you will never cease being a criminal in their eyes.

You must not only learn how to lie but you must also become a master at doing so, able to convince your own wife, husband, mother or father of any lie you tell them. Yours and their lives will depend on this.

If you are planning an escape this becomes even more critical because when they start looking for you who do you think they are going to visit first?

Another way to look at this issue is, it's not to whom you give your trust, but rather how that trust is given.

One Escapees Story

"Cyril Rofé seldom feels strange in strange countries. Born in Cairo on April 11, 1916, he was educated at

266

Clifton and Chillon College, trained for the hotel business at the Swiss Hotel School in Lausanne and, after a period at the May Fair Hotel in London, went to the Bristol, in Vienna, where he acquired a love of opera and skiing.

He got out ten days after Hitler marched into Austria, and on the outbreak of war volunteered for aircrew. While waiting for training he joined the Scots Guards special ski battalion, which was intended for Norway, and when this was disbanded went into the Air Force and trained as an observer (navigator and bomb aimer).

Short, wiry and always determined, he was in the crew of a Wellington bomber of No.40 Squadron which was shot down into the Maas Estuary on, June 11, 1941.

The first time he escaped Cyril Rofé tried walking to Switzerland, where his mother was living, but after ten days' tramping through woods and hills towards Czechoslovakia some week end blackberry pickers pointed him out to a forester armed with a shotgun.

Back in the cells at Lamsdorf, the Germans regarded him with the customary distaste shown to Palestinian soldiers in the British Army, unaware that the Jewish private whose name he had assumed was fraudulently bearing Rofé's name, rank and status as a flight sergeant navigator in the well guarded R.A.F. compound. Rofé of course, like James Dowd, welcomed the soldier's obligation of going out on the lightly guarded working parties.

His friends considered that, if he was so keen to escape by walking through Germany, it was asking for trouble to go as a Jewish soldier, but Rofé's attitude was a kind of stubborn loyalty to his race. He himself was an English Jew, though his small, wiry frame and broken nose looked untypical.

After the cells he went out with another working party to a Polish coal mine, where, as a most reluctant miner, he took to absenteeism and headed on foot for Danzig to stow away on a boat for Sweden. Half way to Danzig a Polish collaborator gave him away and, back in the Lamsdorf cells, the Germans said that if he made any more trouble he was liable to find himself next time in one of the special camps for Jews.

Enough rumors had come out of Auschwitz to make their meaning clear. A couple of guards hinted with satisfaction that all Jewish prisoners would finish up in the special camps anyway.

The winter stopped escape activities for a while, and in the spring of 1944 the arm that was badly broken when he was shot down gave him more trouble, so that it was summer before he went out on another working party, this time to help build wooden barracks near Schomberg and Kattowitz, in the far east of Germany, the so called "Little Ruhr" where the borders of Poland and Czechoslovakia ran down towards the Tatra Mountains.

It was a long way from either Switzerland or Sweden, and he was wryly pondering that point when it occurred to him that only two hundred miles to the east was the advancing Russian Army, and that this distance was liable to be less before long.

He had been caught twice trying to escape in the obvious direction; why not, he thought, go the unexpected way? The longest way round might be the quickest way home. He asked Karl Hillebrand, a thin, studious looking Palestinian corporal on the working party, if he would like to try it with him. "Might be Auschwitz if we're caught," Hillebrand said. "It might be Auschwitz anyway," Rofé answered. "The only way we can make sure of never seeing Auschwitz is to get away from the Huns."

"What about getting through the German lines?" "Well, the whole area's chaotic. Even if we can't get through we can hide up somewhere and wait till the Russians bust through." "O.K.," Hillebrand said, "I'm game."

By August 20, through exercising P.O.W. talents for bribery, ingenuity and theft, they each had forged papers showing them to be Belgian electrical workers with permits to travel to Saybusch, a hundred marks and a store of chocolate, biscuits and cigarettes. Rofé had an old grey suit, grey trilby and a brief case, and Hillebrand had a black jacket, grey trousers and also a trilby.

At 5.30 a.m. on that day the German guard clumped through the barracks yelling, "Raus! Raus!" and as soon as he had gone they pulled their civilian clothes from under the wood-wool palliasses, put them on, pulled borrowed overalls over them and straggled out with the other hundred or so prisoners to the untidy patch where they had been (not very efficiently) putting up the prefabricated huts.

The others, well briefed, started milling around in confusion and Rofé and Hillebrand slipped into one of the finished huts, where they tore off the overalls, put on their hats and walked out of the hut like honest Germans.

A couple of the prisoners winked, though most of them were clustering round the guards asking silly questions and diverting their attention. Rofé passed, poker faced, within five yards of one of the guards, forcing himself to walk naturally, but the guard did not even look at him, and then he and Hillebrand had turned the corner of the last but and were away.

They waited in the silent streets of Schomberg for the cross country tram to Beuthen, and as a man walked down the street towards them Hillebrand quietly swore, grabbed Rofé's arm and swung him so that they both faced away. "He was working on the wiring at the huts the other day," Hillebrand hissed. "He would remember me."

The man stopped just behind them, and they stayed looking nervously and self consciously the other way till the tram arrived and the man climbed into the front compartment. They got into the rear, and the man never glanced round all the way to Beuthen.

In Beuthen they were waiting for another tram to Kattowitz, and a policeman stopped and eyed them speculatively. Rofé turned half away and out of the corner of his eye saw the policeman walking towards him. Sometimes dread is paralyzing and nauseous.

The policeman was standing by his elbow and said something in German, evidently a question. Rofé's German was not very good and he did not understand it. He looked dumbly.

The German spoke again, more slowly.

Ah, the time Rofé looked at his watch and said, with an attempt at a smile, "Sechs Uhr and Halb."

The policeman smiled; he spoke slowly again and Rofé incredulous, understood that he was apologising for not speaking German properly. He was Ukrainian; the policeman was saying, not German. It seemed to give him an inferiority complex. Hillebrand, who's German was faultless, had moved to the rescue and was telling the policeman kindly that everyone could not be German.

They chatted amiably until the tram arrived and the policeman got in with them and talked all the way to Kattowitz, which was reassuring when two more police got in at a little village and looked arrogantly round the tram.

At Kattowitz they boarded a train for Saybusch, and a woman in the opposite seat insisted on telling them about the time she was bombed out of Berlin and what she would do to any R.A.F. airman she got her hands on. Rofé left most of the talking to Hillebrand, bracing himself to agree with the woman now and then.

He thought they were getting away with it nicely, but that made the shock all the worse when a railway policeman swung through the far door and moved from person to person, examining travel permits. There was no escape and their papers were not expert; when the man stood by the seat Rofé handed over the two permits, not bringing himself to look directly at him.

The man looked and said something, and as Rofé lifted his eyes fearfully he vanished behind the seat with the papers.

They heard him in amazement talking to the people behind, explaining that these were the sort of papers they must have to travel, and they had better have them next time.

And then the policeman was back, handing them their passes with a polite smile, and moving on. At Saybusch they walked briskly east out of the town and not till they were out of sight of the houses did Rofé feel confidence seeping back into him.

At dusk they slept in a small wood and at dawn walked again, cutting across fields towards the peak of Rabingora that rose out of the flat, Silesian plain miles ahead. Somewhere near Rabingora Germany ended, though their home made map did not indicate exactly where. Skirting fields where peasants worked, they came at night to the foot of the mountain and rested.

At midnight Rofé woke Hillebrand; a hush lay over the country and a thin slice of moon shed just enough light to outline the black tree trunks. Hillebrand pulled on his boots and they walked up the mountain.

At first light they climbed over a saddleback and came to a swathe about five yards wide cut through the forest; a few yards along it lay a white stone shaped like a tiny pyramid. They could see the letter "D" on the side facing them.

"This is it," Rofé said excitedly. He ran up to the stone and saw on another side the letter "S," felt a momentary dismay, and on the last side was "P." "Polska," he said, as though he had found a gold mine. The "S," he guessed, was for Slowakei (Slovakia).

They must be a little south of course at the point where Germany, Slovakia and Poland met. He kicked some dirt over the letter "D," said "Good bye, Deutschland" with great feeling and they walked east through the trees into Poland. Poland was thickly occupied by Germans and the "Quisling" Polish police, but that could not damp the joy of being out of Germany.

The next eight days were remarkable not for narrow escapes, but for swift progress and lack of drama. They walked by day along dusty roads, across fields, through woods and sometimes, boldly, through primitive little villages, and nothing went wrong.

They tramped steadily south east through the foothills of the Tatra Range, avoiding the main roads to the north on the plain where the Germans were, and in the quiet valleys behind the first ridges made good time along the rough cart tracks, averaging nearly fifteen miles a day.

At night they slept, sometimes in woods and sometimes in peasant barns and hayricks. Every day they walked boldly up to lonely farmhouses and asked for food, finding the peasants simple and friendly.

After a day or two Rofé felt it was safe enough to tell them that he was R.A.F. and the effect was invariably gratifying. The peasants almost worshipped him. They gave him and Hillebrand what food they could, but that was not much; they had so little themselves. Usually it was a few potatoes and some milk; sometimes a little bread. Rofé had never seen such poor people.

273

Their houses were of baked mud, brick and thatch, usually divided into two rooms with hard earth floors, and the women went barefoot, dressed in shawls and simple homespun dresses that hung on them like sugar bags.

The market town of Markowa straddled a valley road they were following and rather than climb out of the deep valley to go round it, Rofé suggested they walk straight through. It was the last time they made that mistake.

Coming up to the town they saw an S.S. officer standing by the roadside. It was too late to turn back without looking guilty; they walked on, passing within two yards of him and felt his eyes following them. For a terrifying moment he looked as though he were going to challenge them, and then he seemed to relax and they walked thankfully on through the town.

On the other side they were dismayed to see a line of German soldiers supervising gangs of Poles digging trenches obviously a new defence line. Veering away from the road they found more Germans and Poles stretched across the valley and had to climb for two hours over the hills to the side before they struck a clear path through.

Some of the peasants spoke a little German and Rofé and Hillebrand had learned a few pat Polish phrases for asking food and shelter. Isolated in the valleys the farms were self contained little units of life and in the first farm they tried after Markowa the peasant wife was sitting at a spinning wheel producing thread from flax grown by her husband; she also weaved the thread herself and dyed it with home made dyes.

The husband grew his own tobacco and wore home made slippers. Rofé and Hillebrand dined with this family, sitting round a big bowl of mashed potato. Each had a spoon and cup of milk, and dinner consisted of dipping the spoon in the communal bowl of potato and then dipping it again in one's own milk.

On the eighth morning, ambling casually through a wood, they heard voices through the trees over to the left and stopped abruptly, hunting for cover, but saw only the thin trunks of the pines where a cat could hardly have hidden. Through the trees three men in dark clothes filed into sight; two of them carried rifles.

"Polish police," Rofé whispered in alarm. He grabbed Hillebrand and as they turned to run one of the men shouted. Two rifles were pointing at them and the third man with a revolver in his hand was running to cut them off.

"Take it easy. Don't run," Hillebrand said. Rofé hesitated a moment and then it was too late.

The one with the revolver, a tall man in his middle thirties, said something sharply in Polish. Rofé and Hillebrand shook their heads. Hillebrand said something in German and the man demanded (also in German), "Who are you?" Hillebrand said frankly, "Escaping British prisoners" and Rofé wanted to strangle him.

He had braced himself to bluff it out and now, he thought bitterly, it was all over in a moment without even a show of fight. Hillebrand and the Pole were talking in German but it was too fast for Rofé to follow.

Hillebrand handed over his P.O.W. identity disc; the Pole looked at it and spoke again, and this time Rofé understood "We will help you all we can," the Pole said, and Rofé gaped at him and turned to Hillebrand: "They're going to help us?" "Of course," Hillebrand said, puzzled. "We always thought the partisans would."

"They're partisans?"

"Police have uniforms," Hillebrand said patiently. "These chaps don't. It's the first thing I noticed." He told the Pole with the revolver that Rofé had thought they were pro German police and the Pole nearly wept with laughter, then shook his big fist at Rofé and said slowly in German that he was mortally offended. He introduced himself as Tadek and said he would lead them to a partisan hide out.

As they wound through the trees Tadek said they were lucky he had found them; a mile further on lay the wide Poprad River, swarming with Germans building a new defence line.

The hide out was a small clearing where the partisans had built a wooden hut. Sentries were posted around in the woods and about six more men and a girl were in the hut. Rofé as a member of the famous R.A.F. was given a hero's welcome; Tadek brought out a bottle of brandy and they all drank individual toasts to the R.A.F. and themselves till the bottle was empty. The front line, according to Tadek, was about sixty kilometres away.

"We will try and get you across the Poprad," he said, "but it will be dangerous to try and get through the front. Why do you not stay with us till the battle goes past? "

Neither Rofé nor Hillebrand would think about it. Having come more than a hundred miles in eight days they were too full of confidence, so Tadek shrugged and started telling them about a man called Kmicic who had a partisan band on a mountain called Jaworze, miles across the river.

At midnight, two nights later, he gave them a letter to Kmicic and led them through the woods to the river. The moon was like a cheddar cheese behind a veil of wispy cloud and they lay in the trees and watched a German patrol march along the river bank.

"Now," whispered Tadek, and they ran crouching through undergrowth, across newly dug trenches, down to the water and into a punt. Tadek poled them across while others of his band watched over the gunwales with rifles at the ready. On the far bank Tadek briefly wished them luck and poled the punt back.

The first day was easy walking and that night the wind came from the east and they heard the rumble of guns. In the morning on a dust laden road just below the foothills something stirred in the long grass beside the road and two German policemen rose up out of it, blinking sleep from their eyes.

One of them called sharply and Rofé and Hillebrand stopped. There was no option. The police, suspicious from the start, demanded to know who they were, where they had come from, where going, what for, where they had slept the previous night and so on.

They snapped the questions one after the other and Hillebrand, impassive but pale, was struggling to answer them. After seeing their papers the police wanted to know what two Belgians were doing so close to the East Front.

By some miracle Hillebrand knew the name of the next village and said they were detailed for work in Binczarowa. At that moment three Poles came along the road; the police stopped them and asked if there was any work for electricians in Binczarowa and the Poles, after hesitating, said "Yes." God, the relief as the police sourly waved them all on.

For days the two of them tramped around Jaworze mountain, and one night, at a friendly farm, they came face to face with Kmicic, an elusive, blue eyed, dynamic young man who was the hero of the district.

Hearing that they wanted to get through to the Russians, he frowned and said they should wait till the Russian lines over ran them. Only when both Rofé and Hillebrand insisted they were going through did he admit that there was, perhaps, one way.

Both armies, he said, were massing for a battle round Tarnów, to the north, and due east of Jaworze was a hilly, wooded area where the front seemed to be fluid. One of his band, a Russian soldier called Achmetow who had escaped from the Germans, might be able to lead them through.

In another hut in the woods he introduced them to Achmetow, a cherubic little man in remnants of tattered Russian uniform. Achmetow spoke a little German and

278

his round apple of a face grinned obligingly at the risky prospect of rejoining his own troops.

Kmicic drew them a map and on the morning of September 17 Rofé Hillebrand and Achmetow, keyed up, started east. The guns were thumping louder at night now but still sounded far away.

All the first day they kept asking peasants where the line was, but the peasants shook their heads vaguely until a farmer who had lived years in America and spoke fluent English with an American accent, said, shrugging and throwing his hands out expressively, that there was no line. Some Russians had broken through not far away and scattered patrols of both sides were ranging over the country.

Two days ago some Russians had been reported only three kilometers away. Rofé said, when they had left the farmer, "I don't like this. There must be a line somewhere."

"It can't be very near or we'd be seeing Germans," Hillebrand answered. "The guns must have been a good ten miles away last night."

A small river meandered across their path the Visloka, according to the map and they were walking along the winding bank when, a hundred yards ahead, three men stepped out of the shade of some trees and stared at them.

Rofe had stopped dead. "What sort of uniform is that?" he asked. It was just too far to pick out the details.

"I don't know," Hillebrand said uncertainly.

Achmetow, very excited, swung round to them and said, "Russki! Russki!"

"They can't be," Rofe said, but Achmetow was running madly ahead. They watched him talking excitedly to the three men and then he turned and beckoned wildly. As he went cautiously forward Rofe could see that the three men had medals on both sides of their chests, black fur caps and dark uniforms with rather full cut trousers tucked into riding boots.

"My God, they are Russians," he yelled, and broke into a run. He could make out the officer's tabs on their shoulders and as he came up to them one of them, a middle aged man, said in German: "You are British?"

"Royal Air Force," Rofe announced.

"We are the Red Army," declared the officer and Rofe said breathlessly, "Deutschland kaput! Deutschland kaput!" It was all he could think of to say.

He was grinning and shaking hands and he and Hillebrand were both talking at once while the Russians regarded them tolerantly.

"I can't understand it," Rofe marvelled when things were a little quieter. "We've come right through the German lines and not seen a German. I thought it was terrible fighting on this front."

"This is not the front," said the middle aged officer, shaking his head. "There are plenty of Germans back there." He turned and pointed behind, east, and added soberly, "We have been cut off for three weeks.

The Germans are behind us trying to …..." He pulled a finger across his throat, and Rofe felt as though he had been hit in the stomach. The Russian sensed the shock he had delivered and said cheerfully, "It is not the first time we have been cut off. The Cossacks are used to it."

"You are Cossacks?" Hillebrand asked, and the Russian nodded and took off his black fur cap, showing the red top and the crossed gold braid over it.

Waving his hand behind, he said that the rest of the Cossacks were camped in the fields and suggested they go back with Achmetow to join them. Rofé and Hillebrand said a wry farewell and walked off with Achmetow.

"No peace in this bloody war," Hillebrand said disconsolately and Rofé had to laugh at the unconscious humour. Half a mile on they came to the first Cossack units, scores of men in dark, coarse uniforms, lounging on the ground, nearly all with tommy guns beside them; nearby were horse lines and narrow farm type waggons with sloping sides. Achmetow spoke to some of the men and they pointed down a cart track that cut between the fields.

For two hours they followed the track, staggered at the thousands of Russians camped in the fields. They looked so peaceful, as though no war existed and no enemy encircled them. Achmetow said they were a division of the Fourth Cossack Corps and he was trying to find division headquarters.

At a field kitchen a grinning Russian soldier with a three days' beard stubble gave them hunks of bread and a plate of meat, and it occurred to Rofé that he, himself, must look even worse. He suggested to Hillebrand that they freshen up to meet the general and a little later, when they came to a stream, he made Achmetow wait while they stripped and swam and shaved.

In the shelter of a fringe of wood they came to a low, white farmhouse; Achmetow vanished inside and a minute later Rofé was startled to see a girl coming out. She was about twenty three, rather heavily built and dressed in the olive green officer's uniform, including riding boots, though instead of trousers she wore a neat pleated skirt. Walking straight up to them she introduced herself briskly in English as a headquarters' interpreter and asked, politely, if they would wait till the colonel was ready to see them.

Rofé mumbled facetiously about having nowhere else to go, but she did not seem to think that was particularly amusing. Rofé trying hard, said he was surprised to see such a pretty girl in such a dangerous position in the front line of a war, but she took that solemnly, too, saying disconcertingly, "I am not pretty and I do not think it unusual that a Russian girl should be in the front line.

There are many of us here. It is our duty." She wanted to know if they were "workers" and when Rofé virtuously said they were she smiled for the first time.

They waited a long time for the colonel. Dusk settled over the fields and they were still waiting when they heard the drone of aircraft, growing louder.

The dark shape of what looked like a Dakota slid over the trees towards them and over the field a cloud of parachutes broke from the plane and floated down.

A dozen more planes came over and dropped more supplies and then several antiquated single engined biplanes puttered over the field. Someone flashed a torch at them and one by one they switched on landing lights, side slipped steeply and made miraculous uphill dusk landings in the field. Under the wings on each side were little nacelles like overload tanks and Cossacks went up with stretchers of wounded men and loaded them into the nacelles like mummies. One by one the planes turned, roared over the field and lifted into the darkness. It was unbelievably quick and efficient.

The girl came out and led them into the house, and, in a low ceilinged room, a dark, heavily built colonel greeted them with grave friendliness. The girl interpreted while they told him of their trip, and in particular of the work of the partisans and the lack of Germans they had encountered.

They talked for an hour before the colonel said, "Now you must eat." He called a soldier and they followed the soldier into the woods, coming after a while to another farmhouse. In a warm living room a dozen Russian officers crowded round them with dazzling smiles of welcome. Most were be-medaled and looking very spruce.

One produced a bottle of schnapps and while they were drinking another officer brought in two plates of fresh meat and eggs, and bread and butter, and made Rofé and Hillebrand sit at the table and start eating.

Rofé thought it was the best food he had eaten since he was shot down but one of the officers, a major called Fyodor, who spoke some German, apologized that it was the best they could do.

They talked for a couple of hours about their adventures and afterwards the major said, "Well, you are all right now. Enjoy yourselves."

"But we are cut off," Rofé said. "We can't very well relax yet, can we?"

"Nichevo," said Major Fyodor explosively, rolling his eyes to the ceiling. He translated Rofé's words to the others and they laughed gaily. "We have been surrounded before," Fyodor said. "We will fight our way back."

"When?" Rofé wanted to know and the major shrugged and said, "Soon. Very soon."

There were two small double beds in the house and around midnight Fyodor bowed Rofé and Hillebrand towards one of them. They both protested strongly, having seen two Russian officers lying on the bed before and guessing that the two usually slept there, but Fyodor insisted. He kept saying,

"You are our guests. We will look after you."

Rofé and Hillebrand got on to the bed, almost purring with the luxury of it and thinking that the Russians would find a bed elsewhere. Again they were shaken to see the two displaced officers take off their boots, stretch out on the hard floor and pull blankets over themselves.

Hillebrand, the humble corporal, whispered to Rofé: "I was just trying to imagine a couple of Russian soldiers as grubby as us going up to a British officers' mess and getting this sort of thing."

284

In the morning an orderly brought them eggs and meat soup for breakfast. Another orderly came in with letters from home and newspapers for the Russians, dropped by the planes the previous night; Rofé was most intrigued when the Russians, instead of reading the papers, tore them into strips, brought out tobacco pouches and began rolling cigarettes in the newsprint. One of them explained that they had already heard all the news on the radio.

Rofé and Hillebrand had many surprises in the next few days. After breakfast they went for a walk among the troops in the fields with a German speaking Russian and gazed fascinated at the number of girl soldiers who had been lying down on their groundsheets to sleep among the other soldiers in the night.

They watched curiously, but apparently nothing questionable went on. Nothing came off either. The Russians explained that no one ever took their clothes off in the battle line. When they fought their way back, he said, they would all hand their clothes in to a depot, have a bath and be given new uniforms.

"The girls they fight too?" Rofé asked.

The Russian laughed and shook his head, explaining that they were headquarters' secretaries, nurses, interpreters and traffic controllers.

"No trouble among the men?" Rofé persisted, and the Russian said solemnly: "There is no sex in battle. Russian girls in battle are comrades."

He added, a little sadly, that things had not always been quite the same since the advance because the Russian girls had seen Polish girls with waved hair and cosmetics. "It has disturbed them a little," he lamented, and added gravely, "Some of them have been buying dresses."

Relations between the soldiers and the girls seemed completely impersonal. The girls never tried to be coquettish and the soldiers virtually ignored them.

When Nature called, the girls went behind a hedge like the soldiers (though not the same hedge). Apart from the skirts they acted and looked just like the men; like the men, too, some of them had lice, though there was nothing remarkable in that. They had not been able to take their clothes off for three weeks. Rofé had lice himself; it was part of the life.

The whole scene seemed so strange and peaceful he could hardly believe they were surrounded by enemies until, on the way back to the farmhouse, heavy guns opened up somewhere across the woods and shells screamed overhead. The Russians paid no attention whatsoever.

More meat for lunch, more meat for supper and they were just finishing when a tall Cossack officer wearing a beautifully cut astrakhan fur coat, sword and spurs clumped into the house and said that everyone must prepare to move.

They slept that night in their boots and at 5 a.m. Fyodor, unshaven and brisk, woke them and said, "We are going to break through."

Outside the door a convoy of wagons was assembling and Rofé and Hillebrand, tense and tingling, climbed into one of them. There was a lot of shouting and bustle and they were jolting over the fields on to a dirt road. Once they stopped and a patrol ran past carrying long, anti tank rifles. Later, explosions and machine gun fire sounded about a mile ahead and after a while the wagons moved on again.

In the afternoon they sheltered in a wood and at darkness moved out along a road down into a valley. The moon was thin but bright and a mile or two away in front and on each side flares were bursting in the sky and distant thumps and the rattle of machine guns reached them.

A quarter of a mile ahead a brilliant flash lit the darkness; there was a heavy explosion and then more flashes and explosions. The drivers yelled and whipped at the horses and in a few seconds they were galloping; Rofé crouched against the side of the wagon, clinging grimly as the wagon bucked on the rutted surface.

He had a terrifying impression of flashes .and explosions, shouts and hoof beats and the clattering of wheels and then the convoy was slowing up; the wagon stopped and the driver screamed at them to jump off. They did not know what he meant till they saw officers jumping off the other wagons and running up the hill towards the woods.

They jumped off and ran after them, and in the cover of the trees found Fyodor, some of the other headquarters' men and several girl officers. In a long line they filed among the trunks up the steep side of the valley until the crashes of the shells sounded fainter and well below. Rofé was breathless and quiet but all the Russians, girls included seemed to be in wonderful spirits, laughing and joking, straggling along as if they were on a midnight picnic.

Without warning, flashes winked a hundred yards ahead and a machine gun rattled terrifyingly. Red streaks of tracer darted at them, the air was full of angry "zips" and Rofé instinctively dived to the side and went rolling down an embankment with the Russians. They lay in a huddle at the bottom.

Fyodor was shouting and some Russians ran off into the trees.

A little later they heard a quick burst from the machine gun and then cracks of rifle fire and some sharp explosions. Someone shouted from above and they were climbing back up the embankment. All the Russians were laughing cheerfully again (including the girl officers) and Rofé gathered that an isolated German machine gun post ahead had been wiped out. A little later more machine gun fire rattled well ahead and Fyodor said they would lie down in the woods where they were and sleep.

Dawn broke grey and wet and they climbed to the heights over the valley and walked east for several miles till they reached a clear saddleback where a road ran just below.

Almost immediately machine gun bullets came at them from across the far heights and they scuttled over the saddleback and went on walking east. Rofé could not get over the attitude of the girls they seemed as cheerful as ever and utterly oblivious of their danger. Tired and edgy, he found himself wishing he had their outlook.

288

At dusk they came down from the ridge to a farmhouse in the valley and there, unbelievably, were the wagons they had left the previous day. A field kitchen served meat stew; they slept again in the woods and stayed there all the next day. Confused as to what was happening, Rofé could not shake off the fear that the purposeful Germans were closing in all round them.

They were. The attack came an hour after darkness. First there were some dull thumps a few hundred yards away. In a few seconds mortar bombs were bursting among the trees; then the machine guns started. Rofé heard shouting and the skin on the back of his neck crawled as he recognized German words.

All round in the darkness the Cossacks were screeching. A bullet smacked into a tree trunk two yards from his head. It seemed to go on unnervingly for a long time, and then gradually the firing and the shouting died away. He lay down to sleep but at midnight a Russian roused him and he and Hillebrand followed the others into the wagons which jolted off into the darkness.

At dawn they were sheltering on the edge of a birch wood when the Germans attacked again. First they were shelled, then mortared and then the machine guns and shouting again. The shouts died away and some scattered German JU88's screamed over and the bombs fell. Most were wide but one exploded deafeningly fifty yards away and the blast knocked Rofé off his feet.

With a stub of pencil he noted on a scrappy diary he had started a few days before: "It is terrible being so helpless. I'm unarmed and don't understand a word that's being said so I don't know where we are or where we're going or whether we'll ever get there. I do know that we're nearly out of ammunition."

He and Hillebrand spent another miserable wet and wakeful night among the birch trees and in the morning he could have wept with joy when a bloodstained and bandaged Achmetow walked up to them.

They had not seen him for days and he said, not grinning quite so much now and so tired he could hardly stand, that he had been helping to man machine guns. There were so many wounded now, he said, that the wounded had to fight too.

Rofé could have guessed that; he had watched the wounded being brought in and loaded into the wagons till the wagons were full. Achmetow said that the doctors had run out of medical supplies.

They moved off at noon, cramming into the wagons among the wounded and breaking out of the wood at a crazy gallop along a valley road. Machine guns spat at them from the heights but the range was too far to be effective and the sweating horses dragged most of the wagons to a pine wooded ridge where they huddled again during the night.

It rained all night and Rofé lay awake the whole time, a groundsheet wrapped tightly round him like a shroud, but the rain soaked through so that he was lying in a puddle, shivering with cold.

In the dawn he was stiff and muzzy with tiredness. A Russian gave him a piece of bread it was the first food he had had for twenty four hours. Chewing at the bread he walked briskly around with Achmetow to get warm;

Hilllebrand brand said he was too exhausted to walk so they left him propped against a tree trunk.

The earth in the woods was churned into mud by the rain, the wagons and the horses, and they slogged around the confused scene till they came to the fringe of the trees where the hillside sloped gently away to a broad meadowland, grey under mist. Achmetow pointed to a vague line of trees far across the fields and said, "Red Army … there." About a mile on each side the woods straggled down into broken ground, framing the meadows in a wide, shallow saucer.

Achmetow waved vaguely from side to side, shrugged and said, "Germans" It looked deserted and peaceful. "We will know very soon," he added. "Perhaps by noon" He spoke stolidly but Rofé became conscious that the hollow feeling in his stomach was not only hunger. They turned back into the woods

Shouts and the jingle of harness sounded through the trees; they started running and saw officers cantering about yelling at the soldiers scattered thickly for hundreds of yards through the woods.

Some of the wagons were already lurching through the mud, straggling into line and moving parallel to the edge of the woods. Rofé could not find the tree where he had left Hillebrand and ran anxiously through the mud looking for him, but Hillebrand had vanished.

He met Fyodor who pointed ahead at the wagons and said he had seen Hillebrand moving up. Rofé ran along looking in the wagons and suddenly there was a tremendous explosion off to the right followed by the tearing sound of falling trees.

More shells came crashing into the woods and some of the horses were plunging about whinnying with fear. A wagon turned over, spilling the wounded into the mud; the next two wagons picked them up.

Rofé ran past two horses lying dead with their bellies ripped open, and then the pines opened into a small gully where a troop of about a hundred Cossacks sat quietly on their horses under the wet trees.

On one of the horses Rofé recognized the tall officer in the astrakhan coat who had come into the divisional mess days ago. He ran across and asked if he had seen Hillebrand. The officer, who could apparently just understand the German, shook his head and as Rofé turned to follow the wagons the officer reached out of the saddle and grabbed his shoulder.

He shouted something in Russian and one of the Cossacks walked his horse towards them, leading a brown mare with an empty saddle. The officer grinned gaily at Rofé and jerked his thumb towards the mare. He said in rough German, "Sic kommen mit uns."

Rofé tried to get his foot into the stirrup and a burly Cossack leaned over, grabbed his belt and hoisted him into the saddle. He grinned back at the Cossacks around him, trying to remember how long it was since he had last sat on a horse.

They waited while the wagons went crashing past the gully and it must have been half an hour after the last one had gone that the officer stood up in his stirrups, raised his fist and waved it forward, and the troop moved off in single file through the trees.

They were heading a different way from the wagons and Rofé realized with a flutter round his heart that they were moving towards the fringe of the forest. The wet trees pressed all round and no one spoke. The mare seemed to sense the tension; she was whinnying a little, pricking her ears and then laying them back.

They were moving downhill, the horses slithering on the slimy earth. Shots sounded in the distance. Some bodies of men and dead horses lay scattered among the trees and the, mare shied nervously. The trees were thinning and the Cossacks started to fan out on each side.

Rofé saw the officer ahead with his fist raised, motionless; he veered to one side reined in alongside the others and saw drat they were lining up on the edge of the trees. Now the mist was gone and two miles across the sunlit meadows he saw clearly the trees where the Red Army was and liberty. Over the flat fields there was no shred of cover.

The horses were flank to flank, bobbing their heads nervously so that the harness jingled, and he had the weird feeling that he was in a Hollywood film that had suddenly become real.

Over to the left the tall officer had drawn his saber; he was waving it round his head so that the blade glinted in the sun and then with a wild yell he slashed it forward and spurred his horse. Wild shouts broke from the line and the horses surged forward, plunged out of the trees in a ragged line and galloped down the slope.

They rode like demons, yelling, spreading out in a long line. Rofé sensed the brutal strength of the mare's shoulders flexing under him, felt gladly that he was firm in the saddle and became conscious of his own yells in the wild chorus that mingled with the drumming of the hooves. Exhilaration swept him.

A horse went down a few yards to one side and he saw fleetingly the rider rolling over and over.

Somewhere, heavy explosions were thumping and he bent lower in the saddle. Puffs of dirt spurted out of the ground and once he heard a "zip" past his ear.

The Cossacks were waving their arms and the officer, drawn a little ahead on a beautiful black horse, slashed his sword in a circle over his head. They were pounding over the flat meadows full of fierce joy. The head of a Cossack in front seemed to split and his hat spun crazily back. A fleeting glimpse...

Bullet or shell. He rolled sideways off the horse and the horse was galloping rider less with them. Two more horses went down and Rofé crazily thought he was part of a film again; they were Red Indians, the Light Brigade, the gallant Six Hundred charging into the cannons and the cameras.

And yet the taste of reality like iron on the tongue: an R.A.F. Sergeant in a Cossack cavalry charge. Confusion, but madly, madly exciting. Something buzzed sharply by his ear; another horse and rider were down. The mare was blowing hard but still stretched out in the mad gallop.

Now only a spasmodic cry sounded and the rest was the thunder of hooves. He heard more bangs and was shocked to see a tank crawling over the grass ahead.

Beyond it more tanks were crawling and beside him a Cossack was screaming: "Nasha! Nasha!" The shouting spread along the line and Rofé saw the big red stars on the side of the tanks. They raced straight for them and then they were past the first tank, weaving past the others and dunning up to the trees.

He was reining back and the half crazed mare was breaking the gallop reluctantly, pulling iron mouthed and slowly dropping to a canter while he dragged savagely on the reins.

She broke down to a trot as she took him into the trees and he pulled her up and found he was perspiring and shaking. The Cossacks were milling around, laughing and shouting at Russian soldiers spread out in the woods. Rofé saw the slit trenches, a big mortar half hidden by branches, knew he was free, and felt warm joy soaking quietly through him.

An hour later he was drinking vodka with the riotously happy Cossacks in a large tent near a headquarters outside a village, and there, a couple of days later, he met Hillebrand, who had come through on the wagons.

Ten weeks later he was still waiting at another village a few miles back feeling he would go mad soon if something did not happen. The Russians kept saying, "Nichevo," claiming they must wait for orders from Moscow, and one day in December the orders came.

A Russian Dakota flew them to Moscow; they went on by train to Murmansk and sailed aboard an aircraft carrier in a convoy. That was almost the worst part; aircraft bombed them and then they ran into a U boat pack and lost several ships.

On Christmas Eve Rofé reached London and an intelligence officer, welcoming him with admirable detachment and no interest whatsoever, asked, "Have you come from the other side?"

It sounded for a moment like "The Other Side," and Rofé said dryly, "Yes, I feel in a way I have." [20]

Whatever situation you find yourself in remember, your trust is both a life saving and a life ending thing, give it wisely.

"The chief value of money lies in the fact that one lives in a world in which it is overestimated."
H. L. Mencken

Chapter 13: Underground Economy

In all of my life's experiences I have failed to find one home in a war torn land where the inhabitants are sitting around their table eating money.

Though they may have a lot of money it remains nothing but pieces of metal and paper who's only value lies in what others are willing to trade for it, and during wars and occupations most are willing to trade nothing.

Prior to war even actually reaching your homeland you will begin to see the effects of this being so as one by one national currencies begin to be devalued and the prices of everything keep going up.

Once war does reach homeland your national currency will be worth exactly what it is in your hand, worthless, and that is why you need to educate yourself with a lot of new words and concepts, such as; Underground Economy, Black-marketing and Bartering.

During the chaos of war and occupation these are going to be those things which keep you and your family clothed, fed and sheltered.

You should also plan for this coming Underground Economy beforehand by accumulating those things which others are going to need on a daily or weekly basis, regardless of the fact they won't have the money to buy them.

Alcohol of any kind, tobacco products of all kinds, toilet paper, disposable diapers, heath products (such as medicines, medical supplies and tampons) and all such other types of commodities should be gathered in as great as quantities as possible and stored away for future use.

And not just for your own personal use, for in times of war and occupation these things will be worth more than money itself.

The accumulation of food should be only for the use of you and your family, but items such as salt, sugar, coffee, tea, etc. should also be put into your storage for items of future barter.

If you are able to raise crops and/or animals of any kind you should start this as soon as possible. During occupations farmers of all kinds are rarely bothered as they provide food to both the citizens living under occupation and the soldiers who are guarding them.

I'll remind you again that simply by the fact that you're living under occupation makes you a criminal in the eyes of your occupiers, so do not be concerned about the laws and rules that you are being told to abide by.

The storage of these items should also never be near you, especially in your home or on your property. These are the first places that will be searched, and even if buried they will be found. Don't forget that no matter how much you believe you are a good hider of things, those soldiers searching for what you have hidden have hidden away are that much better, and have much more experience than you do.

Never underestimate your enemy, and remember your own countrymen can be some of your worst ones in an Underground Economy. That is because they have been at it much longer than you have, have been criminals much longer than you have and the only difference an occupation means to them is different types of police and soldiers they have to look out for.

And these present criminals, as you will find out under occupation life, will become some of your greatest allies. Where before an occupation they were drug dealers, illegal aliens, thieves, prostitutes and criminals, under an occupation they frequently become freedom fighters, and you will need them so now is the time to know them.

How do underground economies get started in the first place?

Overview of United States Underground Economy

"There is a bustling and shadowy world where jobs, services, and business transactions are conducted by word of mouth and paid for in cash to avoid scrutiny by government officials. It is called the "underground economy," which is as old as government itself. It springs from human nature that makes man choose between given alternatives.

Facing the agents of government and their exactions, man will weigh the alternatives and may choose to go "underground." In the ancient world, most rulers were tyrants who commanded the laws and lorded over their subjects. They set just and "fair" prices for labor and commodities, and enforced them with arbitrary power and terror.

The people either suffered degrading submission or sought escape in countless ways and directions. Many went "underground" or moved elsewhere in search of better conditions. They reacted to edicts of the Egyptian dynasties and the Roman emperors, as they did later to the mandates of their Medieval feudal lords. Immutable in his nature, man is forever acting on and reacting to the world around him. In our era, man has again become a subject under the watchful eye of government.

Guided by ancient notions and prejudices he depends on his rulers for mandates and directives. When government intervention fails to satisfy him, or even works evil, he is slow to relinquish his notions and prejudices. He may cling to them with tenacity and perseverance, but may seek to avoid the ill effects through circumvention, evasion, and escape.

He may find his way to the "black market," where economic transactions take place in violation of price control and ration laws. Or he may descend to the "underground" where political edicts are ignored and exactions avoided through word-of-mouth dealings and cash transactions. The underground economy must be distinguished clearly and unmistakably from the criminal activities of the underworld.

Government officials and agents are ever eager to lump both together, the criminals and their organization with the producers in the underground. Both groups are knowingly violating laws and regulations and defying political authority. But they differ radically in the role they play in society. The underworld comprises criminals who are committing acts of bribery, fraud, and racketeering, and willfully inflicting wrongs on society.

The underground economy involves otherwise law-abiding citizens who are seeking refuge from the wrongs inflicted on them by government. They are employers and employees who are rendering valuable services without a license or inspection sticker, or failing to report their productive activities to the political authorities. Underground activities can be grouped into four main categories:

1. Economic activity yielding income that is not reported to the tax authorities.

2. Economic production that violates one or several other mandates, such as compulsory government licensing and rate making, inspection and label laws, labor laws, government regulations of agriculture, export and import controls, government control over money and banking, governmental control of energy production and distribution, and countless others. Violators may or may not evade taxes, but they all work illegally, hiding from swarms of government inspectors.

3. Productive activity by transfer beneficiaries who draw Social Security benefits or receive public assistance. Their freedom to work is severely restricted.

4. Productive activity by illegal aliens without residence status. They may pay income taxes and other taxes, but must remain underground for fear of deportation.

A tax is a compulsory payment of income or wealth to the government to defray the expenses incurred in performing services and to finance income and wealth transfer to tax consumers. It impairs the economic conditions of producers and thereby reduces their ability to consume and invest.

By reducing the returns from productive effort it lowers the marginal utility of such effort, and raises that of leisure. It makes many taxpayers prefer leisure to work. It is difficult to estimate the magnitude of this shift to leisure in recent years of rising taxation. Many millions of elderly people have gone "into retirement' consuming their savings and idling their days away searching for fun and play. They have flocked to resort and retirement centers, especially in Florida, Arizona, California, and Hawaii, where they support thriving entertainment and amusement industries and kindle unbridled real estate booms.

In reaction to ever-rising levels of taxation, younger workers may choose to work fewer hours and take longer vacations. Many may seek to reduce the number of weekly hours from forty to thirty-five, or even to thirty. Others may seek benefits that are tax-exempt, such as expense accounts, stock purchase options, club memberships, health care and insurance benefits, and countless other gratuities. They all are seeking escape and shelter from the tax collector.

In recent years millions of law-abiding American workers escaped by illegal methods; they joined the underground economy. High tax rates, soaring inflation, and a growing distrust of government led them to take this desperate step. No one can know with certainty just how many Americans actually participate in the underground. Yet it is common knowledge that vast amounts of goods and services are produced without being reported to government authorities, that the unemployment rate is a lot lower than the official rates of the Labor Department, and that the actual savings rate is much higher that commonly thought.

Taxation lowers the marginal utility of productive labor and reduces economic output; the underground economy raises the marginal utility of labor and increases economic output. But it does so at the risk of discovery by government officials and agents and potential retribution by the courts and penal institutions.

The risk is directly proportional to the productivity of the underground worker. It is minimal for a common laborer who is earning a few dollars working "off the books" over weekends. His income-tax return may not even warrant an audit by IRS agents. But the weekend entrepreneur who may earn thousands of dollars of profits is a moving target for auditors and, when found to labor in the underground economy, a ready-made object of fines and imprisonment.

It is easy to foresee the wrath of a federal judge and the cruel punishment he is likely to mete out to a businessman who evaded a million dollars in taxes. The different degrees of risk of discovery and government retribution may explain the different intensities of underground activity. Millions upon millions of factory workers, painters, electricians, plumbers, cab drivers, farmers, and others, whose risk exposure is minimal, are engaged in legal activities but fail to report part or all of their income to avoid paying taxes.

Thousands of doctors, lawyers, accountants, contractors, restaurateurs, and small manufacturers are working "off the books," trying to conceal income and evade tax exactions. But it is unlikely that many large entrepreneurs or their corporations are engaged in work on the side. They are rather visible not only to the IRS and its army of auditors and investigators, but also to many envious and resentful employees who eagerly report all irregularities to the authorities.

It is difficult to imagine, therefore, General Motors or U.S. Steel engaging in subterranean activity. There is little room for income tax evasion and underground activity where employers are forced to withhold taxes from wage and salary payments. Approximately two-thirds of federal individual income tax revenue is withheld by employers and transmitted directly to the U.S. Treasury.

The employees never take possession of this part of income, which thus is kept out of reach for tax evasion. And employers are rarely tempted to hold on to the withholdings because they are not employer property. Yet the withholding of taxes is enlisting ever more workers in the underground. While it may reduce their tax consciousness, it creates a visible difference between the after-tax income and untaxed underground income.

With rising tax withholdings this difference tends to grow, which may tempt more and more workers to forego taxable employment and descend to the underground. A master electrician who may suffer the withholding of 30 to 40 percent of his earned income may substantially raise his net income and improve his level of living by working independently and "off the books."

The underground economy is thriving wherever, in the judgment of taxpayers, the government exactions are exorbitant and unjust. It shuns written receipts, bank accounts, and other kinds of evidence that might reveal the activity. It makes a mockery of the popular forecast that the U.S. is headed toward a cashless society fueled by credit cards and electronic bank transfers. On the contrary, the underground, which is thriving on cash, is pointing towards a "cash only" economy where individuals shun all bank deposits.

After all, the IRS, which has ready access to all bank records, usually begins its audits with bank deposit tests, and proceeds on the assumption that bank deposits are taxable income. It is quick to levy income taxes on all individual deposits, to impose fines and charge interest — unless the taxpayer can prove convincingly that his deposits were loans, transfers, or other "legitimate" receipts. In the early years of federal income taxation when the rates were relatively low, it worked rather well for the U.S. Treasury.

A high degree of taxpayer compliance characterized the American system. But rising tax exactions, together with soaring rates of inflation, caused public attitude toward tax evasion to change notably. The interaction between inflation and the progressive federal income tax system gradually weakened taxpayer compliance and encouraged underground activity.

Inflation raises incomes and thereby pushes taxpayers into higher marginal tax brackets. Since 1965 the marginal tax rate for a family of four earning the median income has risen from 17 to 24 percent in 1980.1By now it is probably approaching 30 percent although real income is declining steadily. For double-median incomes it rose from 26 percent to 43 percent and now probably stands at 50 percent despite the 1981 tax rate reduction.

To avoid or limit the decline in levels of living many taxpayers partly or completely descended to the underground where the effective tax rate is zero. In the coming years of raging inflation that is bound to follow the colossal budget deficits, the interaction between inflation and taxation may doom the regulated and taxed economy, but undoubtedly will fortify the underground economy.

Circumventing Regulations and Licensing Requirements Progressive federal and state taxation, in conjunction with soaring rates of inflation, provide an important motive power for underground economic activity. But the mainspring of the underground is yet more substantial and reputable than tax evasion. It is the inalienable right to life and property, which comprises the right to sustain both life and property through honest work. It is a basic right that precedes and supersedes all rules and regulations that would deny it.

It takes precedence over minimum wage laws, license restrictions, union rules, and many other mandates that are denying the right to work. There is no doubt that the underground economy is essentially an employment phenomenon. Where government causes disemployment the underground offers ample opportunities for employment. It offers jobs to the officially unemployable. It does so although it is besieged and harassed by government officials and their spokesmen in the media.

It functions admirably although it is handicapped by a legal system that not only denies protection to its contract parties, but also threatens to fine and imprison them. Minimum wage laws are nothing more than government orders to workers that they must not work for less than the stated minimum, and to employers that they must pay the minimum, or not employ at all.

But such mandates may deny millions of workers the right to work, which is synonymous with the basic right to sustain their lives through their own efforts. What is a worker to do who lacks the training and experience to earn the mandated minimum? If he is young and healthy he may join the armed forces.

If he is intelligent and industrious he may seek the training that may permit him to earn the minimum. But if he is short any one of these attributes the minimum mandates condemn him to an empty life on charity and public assistance. The underground economy offers to suspend his life sentence and promises new hope and opportunity.

Many Americans enter the labor market via the underground. As young children they may earn their pocket money through odd chores that make them think, and teach them to be attentive, industrious, and confident. Many parents are convinced that children should labor to be healthy and happy. But if they should work they probably violate some child-labor law. And if they should neglect to file an income tax return and fail to pay the levies, the children are actually working in the underground.

Surely, there is a minimum amount that is exempt from income taxation. But the self-employment tax, which provides funds for Social Security and Medicare benefits, is levied on annual incomes of $400 or more, or just $1.13 per day. Many high school and college students are earning more than this. In a climate of economic stagnation and decline the underground economy serves a useful economic and social function.

It provides jobs to millions of willing workers, affords opportunities for learning and training, and teaches the importance of individual initiative. It constitutes an important safety valve that relieves discontent and tension in a world wracked by political disruptions. During the 1960s and 1970s, the U.S. Government, in cooperation with the state governments, destroyed millions of jobs.

It forcibly raised the cost of labor through sizeable boosts in Social Security levies, unemployment taxes, Workman's Compensation expenses, Occupational Safety and Health Act expenses, and many other production costs. The mandated raises inevitably reduced the demand for labor and added millions of workers to the unemployment rolls. The boosts also reduced the take-home pay of the remaining workers as market adjustments shifted the new costs to the workers themselves. Both effects, the rising unemployment and falling net wages, provided powerful stimuli to off-the-books employment.

The underground economy offers a new way of life that is very attractive to many young people. As the primary victims of stagnation and unemployment they react against frustration and boredom by seeking off-the-books jobs, which may be irregular but profitable. After a while they learn to like their new freedom and lifestyle.

They are turning a necessity into a new way of life that offers great opportunities to improve their skills, learn several trades and, at last, find self-fulfillment. Many of these young people on the edge of the regulated society are budding entrepreneurs who are earning not only labor income that is undiminished by tax withholdings and mandated costs, but also entrepreneurial profits.

They are everywhere, in towns and in the country, and are numbering hundreds of thousands. Underground producers revive economic life where government is disrupting and thwarting it. In many occupations state and local governments require licenses or other types of permits.

These requirements are designed to favor some producers at the expense of others, and although they are imposed under the pretense of consumer protection, actually limit the freedom of choice and impair economic wellbeing. Permits and licenses reduce the supply of goods and services and raise prices. Unlicensed individuals observing the high prices may be tempted to fill the gaps through underground activity.

In many cities, a shortage of medallion taxis produces large fleets of so-called gypsy cabs to provide car service to the community. The gypsy operators must hide not only from the local police, but also from the tax collectors. In most communities strict building codes and permit requirements make housing construction and renovation extraordinarily expensive.

They are designed to favor "licensed" craftsmen, especially members of labor unions, at the expense of outsiders and the public. To avoid exorbitant charges and safeguard their economic conditions, many builders learn to do it themselves. Physicians and dentists, attorneys, accountants, professors and business executives may become carpenters, electricians, or painters in their own homes, often in violation of license and permit requirements.

Or they may engage unlicensed craftsmen who make the desired improvements without a government permit. Although no one can know the magnitude of this underground activity, it probably comprises more than one-half of all renovating and remodeling of owner-occupied homes. In larger, more visible projects its share is probably smaller.

But there cannot be any doubt that underground construction constitutes a significant energizing part of the American construction industry. Illegal self-employment is on the rise throughout the United States. For many people it is their sole occupation—for officially unemployed and retired workers, students, and housewives; for many it is a part-time occupation that provides supplemental income. Countless Americans are forced to join the underground economy by the Fair Labor Standards Act, which limits the hours of regular work to 40 hours a week.

Work in excess of these hours must be paid for at not less than 1 ½ times the regular wage rate. This mandate obviously reduces the demand for labor beyond 40 hours a week and severely limits overtime production. But there are millions of industrious Americans who are not content with working just forty hours per week. They prefer income over leisure time, more convenience and amenities for their families rather than idleness.

310

Seeking fulfillment and happiness from work they may find work in the underground economy. It is estimated that one-fourth of the American working population is engaged in double-jobbing.2While some declare their extra earnings and pay additional federal, state, and local income taxes and Social Security charges, many choose to overlook the extra take.

They are laboring in the underground. Certain occupations and professions have a long tradition of "moonlighting." Many teachers, policemen, firemen, and watchmen whose jobs make few demands on their physical strength hold supplementary jobs. After regular hours they are tutors, salesmen, construction workers, chauffeurs, truck drivers, and wear many other hats.

It is ironic that, in their classes, many teachers propagate the wisdom and virtue of government regulations, but in their private lives, they readily ignore the regulations and diligently moonlight off-the-books. Many policemen who on duty must arrest and prosecute violators of economic regulations, join the underground as soon as they sign off.

It is difficult to estimate the number of hours per week moonlighters spend on their second job. They probably work from a few hours on regular work days to ten or more hours on weekends, and forty hours during vacations. A National Education Association survey in 1981 found that 11 percent of teachers were moonlighting, up from 6 percent in 1971.

A Texas NEA poll showed nearly 30 percent of teachers were working after class an average of 12 hours weekly. Some people are avoiding cash payment in any form. They are bartering one service or product for another. But barter usually violates license and permit requirements and invites tax evasion. A car dealer trades a jalopy for a plumbing or electrical job at his home.

A dentist trades his services for a construction job at his home or an overhaul of his antique car. Organized barter groups and barter exchanges, which offer their customers a large variety of goods and services, advise their members that licenses and permits may need to be obtained and income taxes be paid on the value received in the exchange.

But many who barter routinely ignore this advice. Flea markets which are shops or fairs selling antiques, new and used household goods, clothing, curios, and the like, are thriving on the fringes of the regulated economy. They are growing in "backward" communities that choose not to impose government ordinances restricting merchandising, jobbing, vending, and peddling. They are prospering on the outskirts of "progressive" metropolitan areas that suffer from such restrictions.

State governments like to raid the flea markets, exact sales taxes, and impose heavy penalties on vendors who violate regulations or fail to collect sales taxes. Countless homemakers operate profitable businesses out of their homes. They turn "garage" or "yard" sales into paying ventures by buying items at other sales and reselling them.

On a nice day, from March to November, there may be more yard sales in progress than there are licensed business establishments in a rural community. Most sales openly violate zoning ordinances, license and permit regulations, reporting requirements, and, last but not least, fail to charge sales taxes and pay income taxes to the federal, state, or local governments. Few homemakers, if any, report their income from garage sales. Most are probably unaware that they are participating in the underground economy.

Reaping Transfer Benefits While Working in the Underground

The transfer society is a conflict society in which the political beneficiaries are ever eager for more benefits and entitlements, while the victims bitterly oppose every new exaction. The transfer battle is fought in all media of communication and education and on the floors of the legislature, where, in a democratic manner, the majority of representatives decide the issue.

Whatever we may say about the consequences of the transfer battle, there cannot be any doubt that the victims react by seeking to escape. They become refugees in their own country, dismayed and frightened, always on the run from agents of the transfer system. They seek to realize income that is tax exempt, qualify for deductions and tax credits, shift incomes to various types taxed at lower rates, try to get even by joining the lines of beneficiaries, or simply evade the burdens by going underground.

The beneficiaries and their spokesmen eagerly engage in the transfer battle. They applaud and elect the politicians who legislate the distribution by political force. But all their victories are just temporary as the political battle continues. In every session of the legislature, whether it is federal, state, or local, the

313

transfer process needs to be fed by new appropriations and allocations, and new victims need to be found in order to bestow new benefits.

Countless regulations need to be formulated and enforced in order to organize the distribution process. Most government income security programs are based on a "means" test that determines eligibility and benefit levels. If earned incomes exceed a specific level the beneficiaries may no longer qualify for all or part of their benefits, which creates a powerful incentive for understating their incomes and working "off the books." The underground economy thus reunites both victims and beneficiaries in a common effort to improve their economic conditions.

During the last two decades the Social Security System has expanded to a vast distribution system upon which 54 million Americans depend for basic retirement and disability income and health care services. It now provides average federal benefits of $10,000 per couple per year and finances average annual health care expenditures ranging between $1,700 and $2,200 per beneficiary under Medicaid and Medicare, respectively. But the beneficiaries lose 50 cents in benefits for every one dollar they earn through labor over a certain amount unless they are 70 years of age or older.

To the beneficiaries this reduction may amount to an extremely harsh tax or penalty. It may discourage some people from seeking productive employment, preferring the pleasures of leisure over potential labor income. Other highly productive individuals, such as physicians, dentists, attorneys, and business executives, may simply ignore the entire system and continue labor as long as they are physically fit.

Others yet may ignore the reporting requirements and conceal their labor incomes in order to collect their undiminished benefits. They are laboring in the underground. A few beneficiaries actually report their earnings and suffer the reductions. In 1977, the Social Security Administration withheld benefits from 1.2 million recipients, or 12 percent of those subject to the earnings test, because of reported incomes. If twelve percent of recipients report some income and suffer painful benefit reductions, how many are understating their incomes or hiding them altogether?

Transfer payments by way of pensions, unemployment compensation, aid to families with dependent children, medical care, food stamps, and so on, provide powerful stimuli to off-the-books activity. Surely, they also may buy more leisure and act as a disincentive to work on the part of recipients capable of working. But they do not bar the beneficiaries from working as such, they merely discourage them from taking on-the-books jobs. Unemployed workers draw compensation that amounts to about one-half their previous wage or salary.

While they are receiving compensation they may legally earn up to 40 percent of their weekly benefit rates through full-time or part-time employment. Any amount earned over 40 percent of benefits is deducted from their benefit checks. To remain eligible for benefits, unemployed workers must report all wages earned during the week for which benefits are claimed.

Wages include cash, allowances for meals, lodging, tips, credit on purchases, and any other kind of payment received in exchange for work or services rendered. In the fanciful world of government statistics, the millions of unemployed workers receiving compensation never

315

do a day's work. They are officially out of work, waiting to be called back to work, or searching for other employment. In the world of reality, many actually do work, but fail to report their income to the authorities.

They work off the books, so as not to jeopardize their government checks. There is a ready underground market for services by people drawing unemployment compensation. They are offering "home-related" services including lawn care, painting, carpentry, plumbing, electrical work, cleaning, washing, cooking, and babysitting. Surely some service workers dutifully report their earnings to the Office of Employment Security and consequently suffer benefit reductions. But many fail to report their wages to their claims interviewers and neglect to inform the IRS.

They prefer to labor in the underground economy. Urban slums are centers of transfer and strongholds of the underground economy. They are the homes of immigrant workers from foreign countries or from rural parts of the United States, of blacks from the rural South, or other minority groups, such as Mexicans, Puerto Ricans, and Orientals.

Labor legislation and economic regulation render them useless and unemployable; the underground economy welcomes them with many jobs and entrepreneurial opportunities. Urban slums are areas in which economic legislation, regulation, and taxation have made economic production legally impossible.

The minimum wage law prohibits the employment of most slum inhabitants. Labor legislation that bestows legal immunities and privileges on labor unions denies employment even to skilled minority workers. License and permit laws deny them the right to carry on any business. Zoning ordinances bar the construction of productive facilities.

Rent controls and housing ordinances prevent the construction of new housing and the maintenance of old housing. Confiscatory taxation compounds the destruction by turning assets into liabilities and forcing many owners to abandon their property. The slum situation is further aggravated by the inability of political authority to distinguish between budding underground activity that tends to spring forth throughout the slums, and juvenile delinquency and crime which are clearly associated with slum environment. Municipal costs for policing are significantly higher in slum areas than in other neighborhoods.

But it is difficult to determine whether the policing effort is aimed primarily at the suppression of underground economic activity or the prevention of crime against persons and property. Since government fails to draw this important distinction it cannot be surprising that many juvenile delinquents are unable to make the distinction and, therefore, may move freely from one activity to another. If it were not for underground production there would be little or no productive activity in urban slums.

The underground springs forth from human nature despite all the obstacles which political authority may erect. It may even give rise to organized business activity in the form of partnerships and cooperatives that operate under laws of their own. Successful entrepreneurs may become slum employers who give jobs to the unemployable and pay wages and salaries.

For employers the risk of detection and the severity of potential penalty are likely to be significantly greater than for underground workers. Employers must weigh the inherent risk against the pecuniary advantages which, in their judgment, compensate them for the risk involved, and the satisfaction they may derive from offering income and opportunity to otherwise "unemployable" individuals.

While millions of able workers are officially unemployed, there are countless opportunities for capable entrepreneurs willing to ignore the rules and regulations that are causing the unemployment. In fact, there is no greater need than entrepreneurial activity that puts the idle labor to productive use rendering valuable service and earning labor income.

While they may ignore the minimum wage mandate, underground employers do pay the market wage that reflects a worker's contribution to production. They pay wages undiminished by payroll taxes, such as employer contributions to Social Security, federal and state unemployment taxes, and workman's compensation premiums, and unshorn by income tax withholdings. Underground take-home pay, therefore, is often higher than that paid in the regulated labor market.

Few Americans fully appreciate the valuable contributions to their economic wellbeing that are made by illegal aliens. Millions of them are laboring in the citrus groves in Florida, California, Arizona, and Texas, in the fruit orchards in Oregon and Washington, the vineyards of California and the southeastern states, on the farms and ranches in Colorado, Wyoming, and Idaho, in restaurants, motels and hotels in New York,

Chicago, and Houston, and in countless other endeavors from coast to coast.

No one can possibly know their numbers, whether five, ten, or twenty million. But we do know that they all chose to enter the United States in violation of U.S. laws, and that, despite all laws and regulations, they are making a living by adding their productive efforts to our economic lives. Many are laboring in the underground economy.

Never in history did so many aliens enter the United States illegally as in recent years. It took the combined efforts of two powerful governments to create the mass migration: the Mexican government that ravished and impoverished its people and drove millions across the border, and the U.S. government that sought to stem the tide by making it illegal.

The Mexican government under Lopez Portillo wrecked willful economic destruction. It ruined the peso, confiscated the banks and the people's savings, wasted billions of dollars on nationalized industries, and created mass unemployment. Wrecking Mexican economic life, it set into motion a mass exodus of its poor and downtrodden people.

The underground economy probably represents the most serious challenge and danger to all government planners and regulators. It defies their authority and control, escapes their tax exactions, misleads them in fiscal and monetary policy deliberations, and misguides them in other areas such as manpower, housing, welfare, and industrial policies.

They would crush it with every means at their disposal. In totalitarian societies, underground workers when apprehended may be flogged, hanged, decapitated, gassed, or shot. In the United States, they may be fined and imprisoned. Numerous bills have been introduced to suppress underground activity by punishing employers for hiring illegal aliens, by removing the Social Security earnings test, and by withdrawing $100 bills from circulation. In a free society without economic planners and regulators, there would be no regulated economy and no underground.

All productive activity would be free. Most analyses of the underground economy deal with the lost revenue that is slipping by federal and state tax agents. The Internal Revenue Service estimates that it is losing some 100 billion dollars a year. In desperation it is seeking ever more powers to search for income, prosecute tax evaders, and impose stiff fines and penalties.

But despite all its efforts at intimidation and coercion the underground economy continues to grow and prosper as if it were driven by the very forces that seek to suppress it. Sober reflection on underground economic activity casts serious doubt not only on official statistics and pronouncements, but on government actions and policies as well.

The unemployment rate is probably the most politically sensitive economic indicator that stirs public opinion and affects public policy. But it is a spurious conclusion based on unrealistic assumptions and beliefs. The Bureau of the Census conducts a monthly interview survey of 56,000 households to determine the unemployment rate. If an individual admits to being engaged in work as an employee or in his own business, he is considered employed.

If he contends he is actively seeking paid employment, he is considered unemployed. In the May 1983, interview, 5,656 individuals, or 10.1 percent of the sample, claimed to be unemployed, which, according to the Bureau of the Census, makes for 11.2 million jobless workers in a labor force of 110.8 million, or 10.1 percent. Do underground workers admit their work activity to the census interviewer? If they do not, the census data, especially the unemployment rate, is seriously flawed.

An untruthful answer by just one percent of the 56,000 people interviewed would inflate the national rate by one percent, or 1.1 million. A deceptive answer by 10.1 percent would cast doubt on any and all unemployment. As no one can possibly determine the deception rate, no one can possibly know the true unemployment rate.

The U.S. Government, which until 1965 had sanctioned the employment of some 4.8 million Mexican farm workers under the Bracero Program, closed its borders at the moment of greatest Mexican need. The Immigration and Nationality Act of 1965 established bureaucratic controls for the protection of American workers from foreign competition.

It gave all powers to the Secretary of Labor by authorizing him to certify, before any quota immigration visa can be issued, that there is a shortage of native labor and that the employment of an alien will not adversely affect the wages and employment conditions of American workers. Obviously, the

Secretary of Labor has never issued such a certification for factory workers and agricultural laborers.

However, he has welcomed thousands of professional people, artists and scientists who are filling the national quotas. Many illegal immigrants find the underground economy most congenial. To minimize the danger of detection and deportation they hide from all government authorities. The underground offers the best shield of anonymity. But many are forced by American employers who are fearful of becoming accomplices to illegal employment and tax evasion, to pay.

They are forced to emerge from the underground economy, but must continue to hide from the immigration authorities. The apprehension rate of illegal aliens who surface from the underground is significantly higher than that of aliens who remain consistently off the books.

The rate probably rises in direct proportion to alien surfacing and claiming the transfer entitlements of legal residents. The illegal alien who dares to claim unemployment compensation or public assistance, or sends his foreign-born children to public school, is jeopardizing his anonymity and inviting his apprehension.

Most illegal aliens, therefore, find underground work congenial. But if employers force them to surface through withholdings of Social Security and income taxes, they tend to shy away from entitlement agencies, which after all are government authorities. Millions of illegal aliens have expanded the overall dimensions of the underground economy.

Even if only one-half or one-quarter are working off-the-books, the number is significant. It incites American labor leaders and their spokesmen in the U.S. Congress who are ever eager to find culprits for the unemployment they themselves create. They would impose heavy penalties on employers who hire illegal aliens, introduce national ID cards, issue government work permits, and deport as many illegal aliens as they could catch.

Other politicians who loathe the underground economy because it escapes their dominion are inclined to offer U.S. citizenship to illegal aliens. But they blithely overlook the pernicious effects of U.S. labor legislation. To offer citizenship is to subject the aliens to minimum wage legislation and labor market regulation that are causing mass unemployment, and to authorize them to partake of the transfer entitlements that are paralyzing the regulated economy.

In short order, it would add five to ten million workers to the unemployment and welfare rolls, invite millions of dependents to join their parents in the U.S., and trigger a tidal wave of new illegal aliens.

And to the dismay of these champions of economic regulation, the underground economy would soon receive reinforcement not only from new citizens now drawing unemployment compensation and public assistance, but also from millions of illegal newcomers. In most months less than half of the officially jobless collect unemployment compensation.

Why don't they claim their benefits? Have they run out of their legal entitlement which, at the present, amounts to 55 weeks of full benefits? They may have fallen on public assistance or private charity. Or, they may be working off the books, but when the Census interviewer calls, are searching for employment.

If countless individuals who are drawing unemployment compensation are also laboring in the underground economy, is it unreasonable to assume that many of the five to six million jobless workers without compensation are laboring side by side with the compensated workers? Their need for gainful employment and labor income may be as pressing as that of those with benefits. And there are countless opportunities in a labor market that is free from government regulations and controls.

Many individuals who indicate to their Census interviewer that they are self-employed may actually be laboring in the underground economy. At least, this was the finding of a special IRS study. It found that 47 percent of the workers who were classified as independent contractors did not report any taxable income. And 22 percent of independent contractors who were professionals failed to report any of their earnings. If so many failed to report any income at all, how many others neglected to report most or part of their incomes?

There cannot be any doubt that the underground economy offers permanent employment to millions of individuals. They live by the motto, which is also a fundamental principle of market economics, that anyone willing to work can find a job.

Millions of illegal aliens live by that principle and prosper in their own way, which makes many more aliens want to follow in their footsteps. In the underground economy the alien workers cooperate with millions of American workers who permanently or irregularly, full-time or part-time, render useful services and earn underground incomes." [21]

"I'd rather get my brains blown out in the wild than wait in terror at the slaughterhouse."
Craig Volk

Chapter 14: To Kill or Not to Kill

I deliberately chose the quote that begins this chapter for the purpose of you fully coming to realize and understand that in living under occupation you are no different than sheep and cattle to those soldiers guarding you.

They will kill you, your family, your friends, and your church, anyone they perceive as being a threat, and feel absolutely no remorse about it afterwards.

There may still exist in the world today those police officials who's duties are to protect and serve, but do not ever ascribe these attributes of humanity to soldiers fighting in war.

Their sole purpose for being is to kill human beings and destroy property. Their missions do not take into account bystanders or non-combatants.

If you find yourself, or your family, between them and whatever objective they may have, you can rest assured they will kill you as surely as you are reading these words on this page.

Police are trained to hesitate, to make absolutely sure they are right and justified before taking a human life. Soldiers are trained to kill and destroy on sight, never, ever forget this.

With this all being understood you now have to make those decisions necessary to ascertaining whether or not you are able to be the same.

There is no harder human action that can be contemplated than the taking of the life of another human being, but in a war that is exactly what you have to be prepared to do, and without hesitation.

Matching yourself, and whatever marksmanship skills you may have, against a modern combat soldier on an equal basis is beyond foolish, it's downright insanity.

However, there are countless examples throughout both ancient and modern history where civilian freedom fighters can actually have the advantage over well trained soldiers on the battlefield.

To the occupying forces you will be labeled a terrorist, but there are differences and distinctions between terrorism and insurgency.

Differences between Terrorism and Insurgency

"If no single definition of terrorism produces a precise, unambiguous description, we can approach the question by eliminating similar activities that are not terrorism, but that appear to overlap.

For the U.S. military, two such related concepts probably lead to more confusion than others. Guerilla warfare and insurgencies are often assumed to be synonymous with terrorism. One reason for this is that insurgencies and terrorism often have similar goals. However, if we examine insurgency and guerilla warfare, specific differences emerge.

A key difference is that an insurgency is a movement - a political effort with a specific aim. This sets it apart from both guerilla warfare and terrorism, as they are both methods available to pursue the goals of the political movement.

Another difference is the intent of the component activities and operations of insurgencies versus terrorism. There is nothing inherent in either insurgency or guerilla warfare that requires the use of terror.

While some of the more successful insurgencies and guerilla campaigns employed terrorism and terror tactics, and some developed into conflicts where terror tactics and terrorism became predominant; there have been others that effectively renounced the use of terrorism.

The deliberate choice to use terrorism considers its effectiveness in inspiring further resistance, destroying government efficiency, and mobilizing support.

Although there are places where terrorism, guerilla warfare, and criminal behavior all overlap, groups that are exclusively terrorist, or subordinate "wings" of insurgencies formed to specifically employ terror tactics, demonstrate clear differences in their objectives and operations.

Disagreement on the costs of using terror tactics, or whether terror operations are to be given primacy within the insurgency campaign, have frequently led to the "urban guerilla" or terrorist wings of an insurgency splintering off to pursue the revolutionary goal by their own methods.

The ultimate goal of an insurgency is to challenge the existing government for control of all or a portion of its territory, or force political concessions in sharing political power. Insurgencies require the active or tacit support of some portion of the population involved.

External support, recognition or approval from other countries or political entities can be useful to insurgents, but is not required. A terror group does not require and rarely has the active support or even the sympathy of a large fraction of the population.

While insurgents will frequently describe themselves as "insurgents" or "guerillas", terrorists will not refer to themselves as "terrorists" but describe themselves using military or political terminology ("freedom fighters", "soldiers", "activists").

Terrorism relies on public impact, and is therefore conscious of the advantage of avoiding the negative connotations of the term "terrorists" in identifying themselves.

Terrorism does not attempt to challenge government forces directly, but acts to change perceptions as to the effectiveness or legitimacy of the government itself.

This is done by ensuring the widest possible knowledge of the acts of terrorist violence among the target audience. Rarely will terrorists attempt to "control" terrain, as it ties them to identifiable locations and reduces their mobility and security.

Terrorists as a rule avoid direct confrontations with government forces. A guerilla force may have something to gain from a clash with a government combat force, such as proving that they can effectively challenge the military effectiveness of the government.

A terrorist group has nothing to gain from such a clash. This is not to say that they do not target military or security forces, but that they will not engage in anything resembling a "fair fight", or even a "fight" at all.

Terrorists use methods that neutralize the strengths of conventional forces.

Bombings and mortar attacks on civilian targets where military or security personnel spend off-duty time, ambushes of undefended convoys, and assassinations of poorly protected individuals are common tactics.

Insurgency need not require the targeting of non-combatants, although many insurgencies expand the accepted legal definition of combatants to include police and security personnel in addition to the military.

Terrorists do not discriminate between combatants and non-combatants, or if they do, they broaden the category of "combatants" so much as to render it meaningless. Defining all members of a nation or ethnic group, plus any citizen of any nation that supports that nation as "combatants" is simply a justification for frightfulness.

Deliberate de-humanization and criminalization of the enemy in the terrorists' mind justifies extreme measures against anyone identified as hostile. Terrorists often expand their groups of acceptable targets, and conduct operations against new targets without any warning or notice of hostilities.

330

Ultimately, the difference between insurgency and terrorism comes down to the intent of the actor. Insurgency movements and guerilla forces can adhere to international norms regarding the law of war in achieving their goals, but terrorists are by definition conducting crimes under both civil and military legal codes.

Terrorists routinely claim that were they to adhere to any "law of war" or accept any constraints on the scope of their violence, it would place them at a disadvantage vis-à-vis the establishment. Since the nature of the terrorist mindset is absolutist, their goals are of paramount importance, and any limitations on a terrorist's means to prosecute the struggle are unacceptable." [22]

Now the differences between being an insurgent and a terrorist are significant and need to be understood by you, and the consequences associated with these differences.

Whether acting alone for the protection of your own life, or those your family, or by participation in a larger group of likeminded citizens, the occupying authorities are not going to care. They are going to ruthlessly hunt you down and try to kill you before you can kill them.

Once you take that first human life an enemy solider, or anyone cooperating with the occupation, a clock starts clicking on your life and from that moment on you are in a fight for survival.

So, before you being that fight you must be absolutely certain that not only can you take one human life, you must be prepared to continue taking human lives until the war ends or you escape.

These not only applies to yourself but to each and every member of your family that is able to shoot, stab, throw a bomb or in any other like fashion is prepared to defend their families lives against their enemies.

You and your family should also be prepared to act as your own killing operation.

There may be a checkpoint manned by two soldiers that you have to go through. There is yourself, your spouse and your two children. The children should be trained to approach the soldiers at a designated time and after which the two parents have concealed themselves.

As the children approach the checkpoint and distract the guards the parents would then make their attack, either by sniper fire or close combat with pistols or knives.

The choices of attack would depend upon many factors including terrain, adjacent soldiers, weather, etc.

Now, just by this short example you can see that it is not just the contemplation of killing that has to be considered but also many other factors.

And if there is a main point that I can stress to you it is this, killing takes preparation and training. If you are able to kill another human being to defend yourself, and your family, then train and prepare yourself, and your family to be able to do so effectively.

You should never put the mind set of either yourself or your family members as one being of self defense, which is dangerous and foolhardy.

Physiology/Psychology of a Gun Fight

In a self defense situation, your normal goal is not to maim or kill your assailant. It is rather to stay alive, and survive a desperate confrontation. If flight is possible you would normally escape by any means.

If you are trapped, be prepared to fight. Proper application of deadly force, through use of a firearm, may represent the only viable means by which the intended victim can expect to have a chance of living through an assault by an aggressively determined, physically powerful, possibly armed attacker.

The mere presence of a gun in the hands of an occupied citizen will not prevent the occurrence of bloodshed on either side.

If you are ever required to fire a gun to save innocent lives, including your own, keep shooting the assailant in the chest and head until the conflict is over and the criminal no longer represents a threat.

Do not issue any warnings. You should not be firing unless the situation has degenerated to a matter of life or death.

Before bringing a firearm to bear for personal protection, quickly determine if the following three conditions exist:

By means of their language, actions, behavior, or demeanor, another person has demonstrated their intent to kill or severely injure you;

This person has the means at hand to carry out their intent, because they are armed with a knife, gun, club, or other lethal weapon, or, if unarmed, they are physically capable of overpowering you;

The physical conditions of the encounter are such that the other person has the opportunity to carry out the attack.

These conditions warrant the use of deadly force on your part. Keep in mind that all three criteria should exist in most normal circumstances.

In self defense, preparedness and practice are paramount. Become familiar with your firearms operation.

In a like manner, it is just as important to understand and anticipate the instinctual alarm reactions your mind and body will likely assume in the event you are about to experience a violent attack.

In a life threatening situation, the intended victim's "fight or flight" reflex manifests itself. This reflex, honed by millenniums of adaptive human survival behavior, results in increased heart rate and cardiac output, higher blood pressure, accelerated respiration, greater carbohydrate metabolism, and virtually instantaneous supercharging of the body.

This stimulation is attributable to the adrenal glands above the kidneys which produce steroidal hormones, and the hormones and neurotransmitters epinephrine (adrenaline) and norepinephrine, responsible for constricting blood vessels and dilating bronchi in the lungs.

The stress, rage, and fear which overwhelm the intended victim thus create a bodily alarm reaction which expresses itself as a period of greater strength and faster speed, accompanied by near impervious reaction to pain.

At the same time, fine motor skills grossly deteriorate, dexterity noticeably decreases, and the hands, arms and legs may tremble. The intended victim will also likely experience an altered state of perception as well. One, indeed, is not calm, cool and collected.

The perception of time may become distorted. With the body alarm reaction, the mind processes stimuli at a fantastically accelerated rate when compared to normal. The result may be the perception that activities are occurring in slow motion, even though movements of the event may actually be extremely fast. The reverse may also occur: the event may seem to transpire faster than one would expect.

In its in incredibly heightened state of awareness, the mind of the intended victim tends to focus with tunnel vision on the identified threat. This results in the exclusion of normal peripheral vision. Knowledge of this potential visual reaction to an attack is valuable in the event one is ever faced with multiple assailants.

The perception of hearing, like vision, may also be drastically affected during a life threatening encounter. The mind screens out everything that is extraneous to immediate survival, resulting in auditory exclusion. The distorted perception of hearing may mute shouts, sirens and screams. You may not even hear your own gun fire.

(This sensory response was employed with considerable dramatic effect by Steven Spielberg in his motion picture "Saving Private Ryan".)

The "fight or flight" reflex allows the mind to draw upon memory resources that are not normally used. The intended victim may experience a sense of precognition, an anticipation response to a subconsciously perceived sequence of circumstances. You "see it coming", even though to the casual observer no violent threat as yet exists.

Be prepared to experience a denial response to a life or death situation. One tends to seek mental and emotional shelter in normalcy. When this state of mind is horrifically shattered, the intended victim's reaction may be "this can't be happening".

One may experience "hysterical blindness" during or after an attack. Essentially, the mind refuses to visualize any longer a terrifying event perceived by the eyes. This may translate into fleeing the scene of an attack, even if one successfully, and legally, used lethal force to survive the incident. Needless to say, law enforcement officials will take a dim view of this evasion.

In a highly trained person who has practiced to a degree that the body's reaction to a stimulus is automatic, the "fight or flight" reflex may create the illusion of "watching one's self". The body movement is so fast, without the guidance of deliberate thought, which one's conscious mind can't keep up.

The highest manifestation of the phenomenon of observing oneself occurs as an "out of body" experience. Due to trauma, the mind's survival instinct drives all senses into a state of profound and unparalleled perception. From sounds and recalled sights, the mind is able to generate three dimensional images.

The out of body experience is often combined with a "celestial death". During this state, one sees a brilliant, bright tunnel or vortex of intense white light. One may also spiritually encounter loved ones who have passed on.

The celestial death may be experienced by those who are clinically dead, who miraculously recover, as well as by those victims of an attack who believe themselves to be mortally wounded, near imminent death.

After a life threatening encounter, the intended victim may occasionally revert to a state similar to that of sleep walking, seeming to be in a zombie-like trance.

Confusion is a state of mind commonly experienced by an intended victim who has survived a life or death encounter. Manifestations include remembering events out of sequence, exaggerating the importance of trivial incidents, and forgetting important events due to short term memory loss.

The ramifications of the foregoing physical-psychological aspects of encountering, enduring, and evading a life threatening violent attack are obvious:

recognize in yourself how your body and mind may react, and prepare yourself accordingly to the extent possible. Mental preparedness is one aspect of self defense.

Physically, the adrenalin rush which supercharged the body has given way to a precipitous decline in energy, and the intended victim is likely exhausted and confused.

HOW A BULLET DETERS AN ASSAILANT

A bullet may be effective in incapacitating an aggressor by any of five mechanisms:

Disrupting or impairing the supply of blood carrying oxygen to the brain;

Disrupting the central nervous system;

Breaking bones and the skeletal support structure;

Psychological reasons;

Neural shock.

The respiratory system consists of the nose, mouth, upper throat, larynx, trachea, bronchi, lungs, diaphragm, and the muscles of the chest. Oxygen passes through the lungs into the blood, and carbon dioxide is given off.

The body requires a constant supply of oxygen. Certain cells, such as those in the brain and nervous system, can be injured or die after four to six minutes without oxygen. Such damage is irreparable, because these

338

cells are not regenerated or replaced. The cardiovascular system distributes oxygen throughout the body.

Damage to the vascular system is the most likely occurrence to result from a shooting. Blood vessels will be either severed or torn.

Usually blood loss, hence unconsciousness, is a very gradual process. An assailant must lose at least twenty percent (one quart) of the body's total blood supply in order to be incapacitated. A blood loss of 50 percent usually results in death. However, even with the heart totally destroyed, an assailant can remain functional for full and complete voluntary action for 10-15 seconds, due to the presence of oxygen already in the brain.

The fact that the brain can survive for a very brief period of time after the body is technically dead has been known for centuries. During the French Revolution, the mob found great delight in the grisly sport of finding a head freshly severed by the guillotine that blinked or grimaced.

Consider that a man with a 44-inch chest will measure approximately 13- to 14-inches in diameter through the torso.

It is generally regarded that penetration of ten to twelve inches of soft tissue by a bullet is the acceptable minimum performance standard for a self defense cartridge. Penetration in excess of eighteen inches is excessive, and represents a waste of wounding potential, particularly if the bullet exits the attacker's body.

The foregoing criteria are not hard and fast, and common sense should prevail. For example, penetration of 8 inches is usually adequate to inflict effective wound trauma capable of terminating criminal hostilities when conditions are favorable, such as a shot placed front to back through the sternum.

In most defense situations, shots to an assailant will likely be frontal or quartering frontal. Major blood vessels and vital organs will be encountered at bullet penetration from six to eight inches.

The ten- to twelve-inch minimum criteria provide a degree of insurance in the unfavorable event that a bullet requires abnormally deep penetration to reach vital areas.

This can, and does, happen quite often in real life homicidal encounters.

Examples include the presence of non critical tissue, such as a shielding or obstructing arm which must be traversed by the bullet, an unusual angle of the bullet path through the criminal's torso which increases distance to be traveled to vital areas, or the fact that one's attacker is exceptionally chunky or huge.

Disruption of the central nervous system is produced by a shot to the brain or cervical spinal cord. Instantaneous collapse will result.

The most effective shot placement is to the cranial vault of the head or to the brain stem. The problem with a skull shot is that the head of an assailant is a relatively small and rapidly moving target. Also, the bones of the skull are extremely tough.

There are numerous incidences where a head shot has resulted only in a superficial glancing blow when the bullet ricochet off. Should the bullet actually enter the brain, crushing and hydrostatic shock will induce immediate incapacitation. The cervical spinal cord is only about the thickness of one's little finger, offering a very elusive target indeed.

While most bullets of reasonably sized caliber are capable of breaking bones, this occurrence alone is not likely to bring about a termination of hostility by incapacitating the aggressor. A shot to the pelvis will tend to cripple, but not kill.

Psychological predisposition may cause some people to collapse or capitulate when shot. This "Oh my God, I've been shot" reaction may greatly outweigh the effects of any actual physical trauma. The psychological response to being shot is extremely variable.

Emotional fainting may occur. This type of neurogenic shock is a physiological mechanism attributable to a psychological cause. The walls of the blood vessels possess muscle fibers which allow the vessels to constrict or dilate. This enables the body to adjust blood flow in response to external conditions such as heat and cold. Intense emotions such as fear can also cause widespread dilation of bodily blood vessels.

The vascular capacity may increase greatly, beyond the capability of the blood supply to fill it. The force exerted by gravity may draw blood into the legs and lower torso to the extent that the brain is deprived of oxygen, resulting in unconsciousness.

341

In addition to emotional fainting, psychological incapacitation can result in a situation whereby the attacker may voluntarily decide to cease aggression and surrender.

The psychological reaction is very erratic, unpredictable, and unreliable. It may not occur in everyone, especially in a highly motivated criminal bent on death and destruction (yours).

Consciousness can be lost due to neural shock. An area at the lower part of the brain-stem largely controls human consciousness.

This area, called the reticular activating system, can be disrupted by physical damage, by pressure from the cranial vault, by intense emotion, or by physical pain.

It is speculated that various organs of the body can send pain impulses to the brain stem indicating a severe or overwhelming bodily injury. The reticular activating system responds by producing a functional "shut down", which results in loss of consciousness within a second or two. PCP, heroin, and to a lesser extent alcohol and adrenalin, are known to impair this function.

This sometimes results in cases where a high or intoxicated aggressor seems immune to gunshots and will not stop hostilities even though wounded by multiple handgun, rifle, or even shotgun rounds.

To reiterate and emphasize:

The ability to produce instant incapacitation is not possible with any handgun round, unless the central

342

nervous system is hit. This involves penetrating the brain or hitting the cervical spine.

Blood loss resulting from a shooting is the primary cause of incapacitation. The greater the tissue damage and disruption, the greater the bleeding.

The process can be slow. Bodily blood loss on the order of twenty percent is required to produce unconsciousness. One's assailant may be fully functional during the time preceding unconsciousness.

Incapacitation depends on the physical, emotional, and psychological state of the assailant.

The onset of incapacitation can be delayed by the presence of narcotics, alcohol or adrenalin in the assailant's blood.

Cardiovascular organs and vessels will only be destroyed if they are directly hit by the bullet. Hence, the ability of a bullet to penetrate is extremely important. Minimum penetration is regarded to be 10-12 inches of soft tissue.

The intended victim should keep shooting as long as the assailant poses a threat.

The shooting skill acquired with practice promotes the confidence and resolution which allows one to prevail in an armed encounter with a criminal aggressor. Hence, familiarity with one's firearm of choice is essential." [23]

Normal human beings are not born with an instinct to kill other human beings, this is an acquired skill. So, if you are planning on killing your enemies in order to protect the life of yourself and your family, you must start preparing now.

Your preparations are simple too, practice, practice and then practice some more.

"You can take from every experience what it has to offer you. And you cannot be defeated if you just keep taking one breath followed by another. "
Oprah Winfrey

Chapter 15: Forced Labor

Without having made plans for escape and not being able to bring yourself to kill in the defense of your family or your occupied country, you then join the largest group of humanity during times of war, the victims.

The quote I've begun this chapter with are from the words of an American Media Icon who by her past history has gone through great trials and tribulations but, and in her words kept taking 'one breath followed by another'.

But in the circumstances you will find yourself in as you are being marched towards the labor camps of your enemies even these breaths will not belong to you, but to your enemies and for their purposes will they be owned too.

In the best of circumstances your enemies will feed, clothe and house you so as to keep you alive and in good health. In the worst of circumstances they will not have any caring for your life as you are not only replaceable, but your death and burial in some nameless pit are actually a part of their overall plan for you and your fellow countrymen.

In either case you are reduced to nothing more than expedient and cheap sources of human labor to further their war and occupation goals.

You could find yourself doing hard manual labor as readily as you would find yourself behind a desk doing mundane paperwork, the difference between the two being how well your Labor Camp is being run and what their primary objectives are.

If you have a skill that you know that your Labor Camp leaders are short of you should by all means make this known to them. Never assume that they have read all of the files on all of their inmates, they haven't and most likely they won't.

While imprisoned you will also have to adapt to this life, and though it will be a strange new life to you it is not the same for those hundreds of millions who were once standing in the very shoes you will be standing in yourself.

The Labor Camp Memories of Janina Sulkowska-Gladun

"In the Soviet Union there are only three categories of people: those who were in prison, those who are in prison, and those who will be in prison." Soviet maxim brought to Poland.

It was late evening as I was bundled into the car between guards and driven to our former police building which was now NKVD headquarters. First I was taken to the jail next door and locked in an empty cell for an hour before being escorted to the office of Commandant Kovalenko, a handsome Armenian.

"Do you have a fiancé in Dubno or Rowno?" he asked, shuffling through the papers and documents taken from my home.

I replied "No," not suspecting the question. (Later I found out my father claimed I had a fiancé there, in order to mask my underground missions). I asked Kowalenko why I was under arrest. He told me not to worry--I'd find out soon enough.

I was taken back to the adjoining jail composed of five cells housing men and women undergoing nightly interrogations which were very often brutal. I curled up alone amid the smell of human urine and feces, and could hear female voices through a vent, but I was afraid to make contact.

This was the NKVD jail, while the main prison in town, designed for 150 people, was now jammed with 500 prisoners whose diet consisted of cow ears, tails and intestines. Hundreds would be tortured and executed here.

In the middle of the night I heard a roll-call of prisoners with familiar names: Galkiewicz, Basinski, Jagodzinski--but one of them sent a jolt through me. It belonged to my father. I could hear them coughing in the hall when suddenly the peephole in my door, the so-called "Judas," quickly opened and three fingers squeezed in and waved at me. I recognized my father's long slender fingers!

And then he was gone as the prisoners were taken to the main prison. That was the last sight I had of my father for over two years. Next morning a horse-drawn sleigh with two NKVD guards took me away. I assumed they were taking me to the main prison, but when we turned onto the main road, I realized we were bound for Dubno. It took us the whole day to cover the 25 miles.

That evening on the outskirts of Dubno, a car with a driver and guard were waiting to take me to NKVD headquarters. I believed I could convince the Soviets to release me, but I also knew that the Soviets had mowed down countless people with machine guns on these very streets. At NKVD headquarters, I was taken to Major Vinokur, the Nachalnik [commandant] for Dubno region, who was dressed in a black leather jacket. His office was crammed with looted items: mirrors, an old-fashioned sofa, tapestries, a glass-case with jams and conserves.

Major Vinokur was seated behind a large desk and asked me to sit down as if I were an old friend who'd just dropped in for some tea from his samovar. Vinokur spoke in Ukrainian (he was a Jew from Kiev) and I answered in Polish. He impressed me with his knowledge of Polish literature, but it disconcerted me that he knew dates and places connected with my education and travel. Through our "conversation" a number of NKVD officers would silently enter the office, sit down, and closely observe me.

Finally Vinokur introduced one of them as my "personal" interrogator who, along with two others, had been sent from Moscow to handle my case! I felt like a mouse being toyed with by cats, and Vinokur who purred so beautifully, had the sharpest claws.

I was peppered with questions in Russian, but I just shrugged my shoulders. A dim-witted Jewish girl was called in as translator but I was able to befuddle her, and she was sent away by Vinokur who decided to demonstrate to the boys from Moscow the finer points of an interrogation.

I continued to play the part of an innocent victim, indignant at being dragged into such a misunderstanding, and amused at being surrounded by so many important men saying such terrible things! A quiet moment ensued, and Vinokur gently wheeled his chair around, and with his back to me, fiddled with the radio. Pleasant music filled the room which relaxed the tension.

My gaze was wandering over a Polish tapestry hung upside-down on the wall when abruptly Vinokur turned back, and in perfect Polish asked: "And how is Pius Zaleski's health?"

"Oh, better now, thank you," I replied--and immediately recoiled in horror. How did Vinokur know that Pius had suffered frostbite in trying to cross the border on our secret mission! "So you do know Pius!" Major Vinokur growled, and fixed me with a gaze that was black and utterly soulless.

A numbness came over me as I realized that Pius and probably many others were in Soviet custody. How easily I had fallen into Vinokur's trap. I felt like a child caught with her hand in the cookie jar and could only hang my head in confusion and fight back tears. "Take this polskaia kurva [Polish whore] out!" Vinokur waved his hand as the men from Moscow nodded their heads in awe.

The guards drove me across Dubno to the very same jail which we had observed on our trek to the railway station. Was that really just a few days ago? The middle section of the prison was three stories high with two expansive wings of two stories on either side, and guard-towers on the corners.

I could not yet conceive of what lay in store for me inside but it was a horrid feeling when the gate clanged shut behind me. I was taken into the processing section and pushed into a windowless room where a female guard ordered me to strip. She checked my pockets and possessions then began on my body.

My garter, belt, shoelaces and even my compact kit were confiscated. My garnet necklace was also taken-- but it would miraculously survive endless revisions and adventures, and is still in my possession. And then I experienced what I thought were my last moments.

Marched toward the prison office, I was suddenly thrown face-first into a recess and pressed flat by the guard: I awaited a quick shot in the back of the head! But I was pulled back and we continued. I soon realized that this painful detour (my nose was bleeding) was a precaution to prevent prisoners from coming face to face.

I was led upstairs to a room which was hot and bare except for two chairs. Sergei Titov, my "personal" interrogator, entered and sat down. He looked absurd thanks to his recent eyebrow highlighting and slicked hair--outdated movie star looks were the rage among Soviet officers.

Titov began his Soviet "song and dance" routine: "How could I be duped by that bastard Sikorski? If I confessed now the Soviet Union would forgive me and I could live in happiness and equality."

350

I just shrugged and smiled back. His interrogation was concerned with our anti-Soviet communications and leaflets, focusing on a copy of an original leaflet made by Dzunia which was found in my home. In fact the NKVD never produced a single leaflet or any other piece of evidence.

I'd later discover that Bronek was forced at gunpoint to help the NKVD in a search for the leaflets I had given him and which he buried--but without success. Still it was obvious that someone had talked--or been forced to talk.

I had not been given water or food for two days now. I lost track of time. The questioning went on into the night, or was it already morning? Titov sent for a replacement, an uneducated soldier who made sure I didn't sleep. He kept droning on about what a wonderful paradise the Soviet Union was and how factories in the USSR manufactured oranges.

He insisted that I write down my "confession" on the paper that Titov had provided. At one point I asked the soldier if I could borrow his pocket mirror--and I was transfixed by the eyes of a hunted beast in which there was almost no iris! I agreed to start writing my "confession" hoping to catch a few winks at the desk. Like a drunk on a barstool, I scribbled my name and other innocuous details.

Finally I was sent back in the care a female Ukrainian guard (many positions were filled by local Ukrainians and Jews, while higher functionaries were from the USSR and under NKVD supervision). I was pushed into my solitary cell and collapsed upon the straw mattress--but shouting and banging of keys jolted me.

Each attempt to nod off brought the same response from a guard who scrutinized me through the Judas. Whenever I slumped down, the door was flung open and screams hurled at me. A bright bulb filled my eyes with buzzing pain.

I started to pace: four steps to the door, and four back. This prison wing was made up tiny "solitary" cells, just big enough to lie down on an elegant parquet floor. A small radiator stood near the door and the tiny window, painted from the outside, could be partially flipped open from the top.

This prison was being completed by the Poles as a modern institution for criminals modeled on Sing-Sing, but now it was run by the Soviets for Polish political prisoners awaiting deportation to hard labor.

The irony was not lost on the Russians and the staff who joked that it had been constructed by Polish men so that their wives would have somewhere to languish! And we would answer: "And a wonderful job they did too!"

Under the Soviets it held 1,500 prisoners, including 250 women and 50 children, ages 12-15, both boys and girls--but at one point 3,000 would be crammed inside. Among them were pregnant women whose babies would be given to Soviet families while they would be sent to Siberia. Women being interrogated were routinely raped. In the massacres of June 24 to 25, 1941, some 550 prisoners (other estimates run as high as 1,500) perished here--my friends among them.

Suddenly I felt a sensation of being watched: a guard's eye was staring at me through the Judas! I began to pace while the eye kept watching. I thought I'd go mad and attack that disembodied eye! But I calmed myself with inner strength. I decided not to give in to the NKVD.

Slowly I fell into a trance and realized that I was blessed with an opportunity to experience something amazing, a chance to "earn" my soul, which I must not squander. I had never experienced such a state of grace and strength, and without it I might not have survived what awaited me.

That evening I was taken to my second interrogation session that lasted till morning. Titov cursed me and tore up my "confession"--but I serenely smiled back at my interrogator's contorted face. He was amazed and asked me if I'd been allowed to sleep.

The question of the leaflets was still his concern. In spite of my exhaustion, I tried to lead his investigation down a blind alley with the invention of a refugee named Mrs Dolska--it was she who had left the incriminating leaflet in my home.

After two days and nights of brutal treatment I was dragged to my "permanent" cell in the women's block of Dubno Prison. Though utterly exhausted, I was proud of defying my tormentors and not betraying our cause.

Titov had grown hoarse in shouting and I had even outlasted Vinokur! At last I would be allowed to sleep and return to my senses as the NKVD realized that other 24-hours of interrogation could undo my sanity.

I would now be allowed to recuperate--but only enough to undergo further questioning. The method of my captors was such that every night's sleep would be interrupted; prisoners were kept in a state verging on mental and physical collapse. A bright light constantly shone in my cell and any attempt to cover or turn my face from the door resulted in guards beating their keys on the door or the water pipes producing a cacophony. Constant harassment and humiliation were two tools of the NKVD interrogators--starvation, disease and torture were other ones I'd experience.

Next morning, over burnt bread masquerading as "coffee," I met my solitary cellmate. Marusia had been in prison since October, 1939, and was still wearing summer sandals and a tattered dress.

A few years older then me, she had been a factory-worker right here in Dubno. Originally Polish, she had been trapped with her family in the USSR after the Bolshevik takeover.

But she and her younger sister managed to escape from Ukraine in 1932 at the height of the "terror-famine" imposed by Stalin. They'd crossed the border, struggling over barbed wire, and at one point were sprayed by machine-guns, which miraculously missed them.

Marusia then started a new life in Dubno just a few miles from the Soviet starvation that claimed millions, even as she worked in a huge bacon works that exported to England and elsewhere.

But with the Soviet invasion of Poland in 1939 she lost her job, and then her freedom. Marusia was betrayed by a Jewish co-worker, a fervent Communist, who met her on the street and generously offered her work.

She eagerly jumped at the chance and followed him-- straight into the hands of the NKVD where he denounced her as an escapee from the USSR, a serious crime as she was still considered a Soviet citizen.

How many co-workers and friends had he betrayed, and how many more would he still send to hell? I soon discovered that most of the positions in the prison and security systems were given to the dregs of Jewish and Ukrainian society.

Marusia and I spent almost two months together, sharing our sorrows and life-stories. I described to her my university days and the night-life of Warsaw; she told me horrific stories of life in the Ukraine under Soviet collectivization and the wars against the Ukrainian people.

She would shake in rage as she described people being forced to eat grass and bark, and in some cases their own children, while soldiers guarded warehouses full of grain and food requisitioned from the victims themselves.

Emaciated corpses littered the streets of villages and towns. Millions who resisted were shot as kulaks or shipped off to camps. And this was still going on. Poor Marusia had lost most of her family in this way, and I tried to console her as best I could; and she was a tower of strength for me during this period when I was a victim of constant interrogation.

355

On May 15, 1940, Marusia was taken from our cell without explanation. I gave her a pair of nylons and some rags for she had nothing. Just before the door shut, we exchanged a final look, admitting that as a Soviet citizen she would never be allowed to leave alive.

I would spend the next two months completely alone in this cell. That night I thought about the great monster that the Soviet system was: how it consumed millions of people and still craved more. And I had no idea that I was heading into the belly of this insatiable beast....

The Glory of Soviet Work

The Poles were put to work in the brick factory. A typical day began with rising at 3 a.m. and a bowl of soup with a bit of bread.

By 4 a.m. we were standing in our work-brigades at the gate where the head-count would take place. This was a complicated affair as there were always stragglers or those who refused or were unable to go to work.

The guards would drag prisoners from their bunks, beating and kicking them mercilessly. Most of them were simply too tired or sick to work and were at the point of death.

All this activity would be accompanied by an accordionist, a fellow-prisoner, playing "uplifting" music from a platform. To some Soviet song, we'd at last march out past the forbidden zone where we'd be counted one last time before being given over to a strilok [armed guard] who'd intone: "A step to the left, a step to the right, will be seen as an escape and I'll use my weapon without a warning!" By 5 in the morning we were required to be on our hour-long march to work supervised by the convoy commandant upon his huge horse.

The work was very heavy. I was with a group carrying pieces of clay to the kiln on large pallets with tandem handles, where they'd be baked into bricks, and carried back in a similar way.

The bricks were still hot, and a huge hole was burned in my coat when my partner stumbled showering me with steaming bricks. We also transported raw clay in wheelbarrows along swaying planks.

Mornings were cool while afternoons were blisteringly hot. Just before the sun reached its zenith, we were allowed a lunch break, though there wasn't anything to eat except what one saved from breakfast--and this would be chewed slowly.

We would drink a little water, roll cigarettes, and spend lunch break resting and talking.

At 5 in the afternoon we'd be re-assembled into brigades, counted, and marched back to camp--a group of people barely able to lift their feet. For dinner in the mess hall we'd receive a bowl of soup without bread.

After our meal we could go to the sick ward, meet acquaintances, do laundry or sewing. It would be close to midnight when sleep would finally be possible, after the last head-count and when the conversations and activities stopped.

We all tried to avoid the Kawecze [propaganda officer] whose job was to spread Soviet joy among us...just as we wanted to go to sleep. This position was usually filled by a junior official who made up for his stupidity and lack of imagination by persistence.

But sleep, when it did come, was also an ordeal as we were tormented by fleas and lice as well as mosquitoes. The chronic lack of sleep and fatigue bothered most of us much more than the constant hunger, and together they spelled death for many of the older women.

Eventually the women were put into permanent work brigades: two Polish teams and several Soviet ones. Our brigade leader was Keller, a tough German who pushed us without pity.

Thanks to her we were able to meet our work-quota, and thus could feed from the best No. 1 cauldron. After several weeks of toiling under the relentless Keller, we discovered our group was featured on the bulletin board as a Stakhanovite brigade [workers who exceed quotas] that had been completing 140% of our quota, ahead of everyone else!

We felt it a useless honor that was not worth the effort, and fought with Keller who cut back her demands but maintained the discipline.

Some of the hardest work was in tending fields of potatoes and beets which involved carrying water in wooden buckets for long distances, sometimes uphill--work that left every muscle screaming.

My boots were too heavy for this summer work and I preferred bare feet. As a result the cuts and sores on my legs and feet deteriorated into a festering mess.

But we also had the chance to steal a potato and eat it secretly. Other tasks given to our brigade was in the clearing of roots and rocks after a forest stand had been cut down.

The summer heat was oppressive; lightning might flash but hardly a drop of rain ever fell. Our sunburn and blisters were treated by a balm which we smeared over our wounds, or even drank in a diluted form as a cure for diarrhea.

I covered myself head to foot with this stinking mess, as my leg and foot sores were spreading upwards while my mosquito bites were turning into chronic scabs.

On one of our foodless "lunch breaks" we heard a gunshot from the forest. We were too tired to think about it--but when we returned to camp we learned of a tragic death resulting from that single shot.

On the transport here, my group had taken a vulnerable high school student under our wing. I was impressed how Julia Kosowska had regaled us with recitations of Polish poetry in our cattle car.

But on arrival she'd fallen in with a gang of Russian criminals. We tried to convince her to join us, but she was controlled by the older women in the gang who used violence and manipulation.

These leaders, covered in obscene tattoos and self-inflicted scars, even worked out deals with guards. The last time I saw Julia, her startling blue eyes were now dull and resigned.

I learned from other prisoners that Julia had been shot. That morning she had gone around acting strangely and apologizing to members of her work brigade.

At midday break, two cries of "Halt!" came from the forest. And then a single shot. Julia was killed while trying to escape, but we knew that it was suicide.

But there were questions: the shot had come from a pistol, and the only person who carried one was the Convoy Commander. And the bullet had been fired at close range and from the front. Why had they not tried to stop her physically?

I was in my second year of captivity and at forced labour at that, but I still hadn't been charged with any crime, much less sentenced for it.

Some of the Polish women petitioned the camp commandant, who merely replied: "Don't worry--you'll get your sentence."

And in spite of the war, Moscow hadn't forgotten about us. In the middle of July we were summoned in a large group to the camp headquarters where each of us was called to a table and handed her "sentence" which we had to read and sign.

I was found guilty under article 58 - 2 - 11 of the Soviet Penal Code for participation in a "revolutionary Polish-Ukrainian organization." I didn't know what organization they were referring to, until I recalled the magazine M'oda Wie, taken from my home, which my interrogators had been obsessed with.

I received 8 years in a hard-labour camp, including forfeiture of property and denial of rights. It was in effect a death sentence as few survived the labour camps.

Only two others received 8 years, most getting sentences of 3 and 5 years in a labour camp. Yet most of us felt that the German-Soviet war would be our deliverance and that eventually freedom would come our way. If we could just hang on.

During the summer we'd sleep outside our barracks, preferring mosquitos to lice and bedbugs. One night under the stars I opened my eyes--and saw nothing.

The morning was a hazy landscape filled with vague shadows. I realized I was suffering from "chicken blindness" caused by avitaminosis, resulting in temporary blindness.

Luckily at that time, as Stachanowki, we were receiving small sardines as reward for our work, and Marzenka slipped me her portion of fish so that my sight returned to normal.

Loss of sight was merely a step to full-blown scurvy, and I met women who were losing teeth and hair, and who eventually died. We were working near the camp, where we quickly converted the overgrown gardens into a valuable source of vegetables.

We were able to nibble on beets, cucumbers and other sources of vitamins and nourishment, as well as smuggling plants in our cuffs and clothing to women and men toiling in the brick yards and the forest. Besides being tormented by lice, fleas, ticks and mosquitos, we had to contend with the black fly, which could drive a person mad with its incessant bites.

We were pretty sights indeed swollen from black fly bites, and covered in mud and preventative ointments. And what's worse, Marzenka and several us came down with an attack of the scabies. We were good workers so we received two days off, balm, and a sauna with soap.

In desperation many of us turned to an old Romanian woman called "Moses" who had powers of prophecy. I paid her with a cigarette and she lifted the blanket to her corner of the barracks. Here she foretold my future with the aid of dried bread-balls which she threw down on a cloth and "read."

Moses told me my fate: "You will be separated from everybody and will be very sick and close to death. Your life will change for the better only in February, and you'll find yourself in a place where there are many women and few men.

But then you'll travel to where there are few women and many men, and you'll be sick here once more. Along the way you'll also meet your future husband-- but only very briefly, and you'll not see each other for a long time. Eventually you'll meet and get married." It seemed totally improbable to me. Yet I made a note of it.

In a few days we were transferred to the dreaded Punishment Camp Number 6." [25]

In this example you can plainly see that when you find yourself in a Labor Camp that all of your hope will be sucked right out of you.

Granted, you may be one of the lucky few who survives the years of abuse, hard labor and torture, but to the kind of human being you once were, you will never be again.

This will also be true of all of your family members should they survive too.

"When the gods wish to punish us, they answer our prayers."
Oscar Wilde

Chapter 16: Concentration Camps

When you walk through the gates of the Concentration Camp you leave all hope of life behind.

Only to God can you turn too now, in both your silence and desperation.

Such is a human being that they will not just endure but willingly travel to the greatest depths of human barbarity and deprivation that human beings are capable of.

As you walk through these gates you will know with utter simplicity that all of the plans you should have made are those exact same reasons that you are there.

And if you don't fully understand those words, you most assuredly will as you enter what is most likely to be your last home on earth.

Since you will more than likely not be around to write your own story I feel it is only right that you read one that may be similar to the one that will be written about you.

Liberation of Buchenwald
By: Harry J. Herder, Jr.

"Over fifty years ago, I went through a set of experiences that I have never been able to shake from my mind. They subside in my mind, and, then, in the spring always, some small trigger will set them off and I will be immersed in these experiences once more.

The degree of immersion varies from year to year, but there is no gradual diminution with time. I note, but do not understand, that the events occurred in the spring, and the re-immersion seems to be always in the spring.

This year I set those memories on paper, all of them, or at least all of them I recall. I hope for the catharsis. I do not expect a complete purging -- that would be expecting too much -- but if I can get these memories to crawl deeper into my mind, to reappear less vividly, and less frequently, it will be a help.

We are as we are, we saw what we saw, and we remember as we remember. So be it. These are my memories. It is enough for me that I feel what I do feel, and I am now attempting to thin those feelings out. And I use you, the reader. I must purge these feelings on someone, and if I have readers, it is they I am using. I apologize to you, and I ask for your understanding.

This all happened to a group of us on April 11, 1945. The things we found then were grotesque enough without knowing some of the other things we did learn later. As a P.F.C. in the U. S. Army, there was no way that I could learn the origin of the orders that started it all. In fact when we started there was no way for those of us at the bottom of the ladder to have any idea at all where we were going or what we were up to.

What I do remember is that we eventually drove up some gentle valley where there were trees on either side of us, when we made a sharp left turn, so sharp that those of us on the tops of the vehicles were grabbing things to keep from falling off. By the time we had regained our balance, there it was: a great high barbed wire fence at least ten feet high.

Between us and the fence and running parallel to the fence was a dirt road, with high guard towers every fifty yards or so. Beyond the fence were two more layers of barbed wire fence not quite as tall. There seemed to be about five yards between those fences. The barbed wire in those fences was laced in a fine mesh, so finely meshed no one was going to get through it. Our tanks slowed down, but they did not stop; they blew straight at and through the barbed wire.

Those of us riding the top scurried quickly to get behind the turret, while those vehicles just continued to charge. When we broke through the first of those fences we got a clue, the first clue as to what we had come upon, but we had no real comprehension at all of what was to assault our senses for the next hours, the next days.

We hit those fences with enough speed so that it was unclear to me whether it was the first level, or the second, or the third, but at least one of those levels was hot with electricity. We hit the fences, blew through them, and shorted out whichever it was on the damp ground.

Once we were through the fences we turned left a bit and took off up a gentle cleared hill toward a concentration of buildings. Those buildings were still two hundred yards or more up the hill from us, but it didn't take long for those tanks to growl their way up toward those buildings. I recall that I was very much on the alert. The tanker on our vehicle assigned to the machine gun was on that weapon and ready to use it, and those of us riding the top were ready to bail off and hit the ground on the run and do whatever it was that we were going to have to do.

I was an assistant bazooka man, and I had a sack with ten bazooka rounds hung over my shoulder; I had an M1 Garand, and some bandoleers of ammo for that; some grenades hanging one place and another; a fully loaded cartridge belt; and I was on my toes ready to scramble off that tank at the first sign of trouble. I would follow the bazooka man: wherever he went I would go. It turned out that we didn't need any of that hardware.

I remember scouting out the area in front of us quickly with my eyes. There were no great details, but I saw that over to the left, next to, and just inside of the fence, and to our front, were some major buildings, and next to one of those buildings was a monster of a chimney, a monster both in diameter and in height. Black smoke was pouring out of it, and blowing away from us, but we could still smell it. An ugly horrible smell. A vicious smell.

The tank which we were riding, along with two other tanks in our column, wheeled to the left so that the three of them made a front. Two more columns containing the rest of our company, off to our right, made the same maneuver so that all of us presented one front. Our Company Commander and the commander of the tank destroyer outfit were riding in a jeep somewhere near the middle of all of that mess.

Once we presented that front, those of us who were on top of the tanks jumped off and spread out on the same front. I was prepared to flatten out on the deck, but it turned out we didn't have to, and none of us did. I stayed close to Stover, my bazooka man, ready to do whatever it was he was going to do.

None of us--well, none of us in the lower ranks--knew what it was we were up to or where we were, but we were fully expecting a fire fight with German troops, whose camp we had just stormed and taken, and we thought they would be angry at us. It turned out there were no German troops present.

Slowly, as we formed up, a ragged group of human beings started to creep out of and from between the buildings in front of us. As we watched these men, the number and the different types of buildings came to my attention. From them came these human beings, timidly, slowly, deliberately showing their hands, all in a sort of uniform, or bits and pieces of a uniform, made from horribly coarse cloth with stripes running vertically.

The stripes alternating a dull gray with a dark blue. Some of those human beings wore pants made of the material, some had shirt/jackets, and some had hats. Some only had one piece of the uniform, others had two, many had all three parts. They came out of the buildings and just stood there, making me feel foolish with all of that firepower hanging on me. I certainly wouldn't be needing it with these folks.

The jeeps, our company commander's and a few others, rolled forward very slowly toward these people, and, as they parted, drove slowly through them, to the brick building next to that tall chimney, and our officers disappeared inside. Our platoon sergeant had us form up some and relax, then signaled that horde of human beings to stand fast; he just held both hands up, palms out, and motioned them backwards slowly. Everything was very quiet. The tanks were all in slow idle.

Hesitatingly we inched closer to that strange group as they also started inching closer to us. Some of them spoke English, and asked, "Are you American?" We said we were, and the reaction of the whole mass was immediate: simultaneously on their faces were relaxation, ease, joy, and they all began chattering to us in a babble of tongues that we couldn't answer--but we could, and did, point the muzzles of our weapons at the ground, making it obvious these weapons were not "at the ready".

It was then that the smell of the place started to get to me. Our noses, rebelling against the surroundings they were constantly subjected to were not functioning anywhere near normally. But now there was a new odor, thick and hanging, and it assaulted the senses.

There was still space between us and the group in front of us, the people on both sides now relaxed, one side considerably more jubilant than the other, but all of the tensions were gone. We were inching closer together when our platoon sergeant was called back to one of the tanks and got on the radio.

He wasn't there but a few minutes, came back, formed up our platoon, and took us back away, toward the place where we had entered the camp, back toward the fences through which we had ripped holes. At each hole in the fence he left two of us. The sergeant left us there with instructions that we were to let no one through that hole from either direction.

He left Bill and me in the middle of the hole in the fence, and told us to hold that hole. Bill and I were vigorous young things with an immense curiosity, and it was difficult standing still in the middle of a hole through a set of three fences. We hadn't the vaguest idea what we had run into. Not yet.

Soon Sergeant Blowers came by and told us that all of the people inside of the camp had been told to stay inside of the fence, that we were down by the holes to make sure they stayed inside. Bill and I were told to go into the tower, go to the top floor, to stay there, and to keep people from coming out through the hole. We still had no idea what this place was.

Containing the prisoners was not expected to be any trouble because they understood the need, and they were being provided for in every way that we could think of: the field hospital had just arrived, a big mess unit was on the way, loads of PX rations were coming. Sergeant Blowers told us that some of the prisoners spoke English.

Then he got even quieter, looked at the ground for as moment, raised his eyes, and looking over our heads, began very softly, so softly we could barely hear him. He told us that this is what was called a "concentration camp", that we were about to see things we were in no way prepared for. He told us to look, to look as long as our stomachs lasted, and then to get out of there for a walk in the woods. I had never known Sergeant Blowers to be like this.

The man had seen everything I could imagine could be seen, and this place was having this effect on him. I didn't understand. I didn't know what a concentration camp was, or could be, but I was about to learn.

Bill, Tim, and I started off through the trees, down the hill to the front gate which was only a couple of hundred yards away. The gate was a rectangular hole through the solid face of the building over which was office space and a hallway. High up above the opening for the gate was a heavy wooden beam with words carved into it in German script, Arbeit Macht Frei. In a clumsy way I attempted to translate the inscription to Bill and Tim as, "Work will make you free".

The three of us headed through the gate, through the twenty or thirty feet to the other side of the building. We were slightly apprehensive of what we might see. Our antennae were up. We had been teased by bits of information, and we wanted to know more. The lane we were walking on bent to the right as we cleared the building. We had barely made the turn, and there it was. In front of us a good bit, but plainly visible.

The bodies of human beings were stacked like cord wood. All of them dead. All of them stripped. The inspection I made of the pile was not very close, but the corpses seemed to be all male. The bottom layer of the bodies had a north/south orientation, the next layer went east/west, and they continued alternating.

The stack was about five feet high, maybe a little more; I could see over the top. They extended down the hill, only a slight hill, for fifty to seventy-five feet. Human bodies neatly stacked, naked, ready for disposal. The arms and legs were neatly arranged, but an occasional limb dangled oddly. The bodies we could see were all face up. There was an aisle, then another stack, and

371

another aisle, and more stacks. The Lord only knows how many there were.

Just looking at these bodies made one believe they had been starved to death. They appeared to be skin covering bones and nothing more. The eyes on some were closed, on others open. Bill, Tim, and I grew very quiet. I think my only comment was, "Jesus Christ."

I have since seen the movie made about Buchenwald. The stack of bodies is vividly displayed in the movie, just as I saw it the first day, but it is not the same. In no way is it the same. The black and white film did not depict the dirty gray-green color of those bodies, and, what it could not possibly capture was the odor, the smell, the stink. Watching the movie was, in a way, a reliving of the first walk through those stacks of bodies. The three of us looked, and we walked down the edge of those stacks. I know I didn't count them--it wouldn't have mattered. We looked and said not a word. A group of guys from the company noticed us and said, "Wait till you see in there."

They pointed to a long building which was about two stories high, and butted up tightly to the chimney. It had two barn-like doors on either end of the building we were looking at, and the doors were standing open. We turned and walked back to the building where we found others from our company, along with some of the prisoners milling around in the space between the bodies and the building.

We moved gently through those people, through the doors and felt the warmth immediately. Not far from the doors, and parallel to the front of the building, there was a brick wall, solid to the top of the building. In the wall were small openings fitted with iron doors. Those doors were a little more than two feet wide and about two and a half feet high; the tops of the doors had curved shapes much like the entrances to churches.

Those iron doors were in sets, three high. There must have been more than ten of those sets, extending down that brick wall. Most of the doors were closed, but down near the middle a few stood open. Heavy metal trays had been pulled out of those openings, and on those trays were partially burned bodies.

On one tray was a skull partially burned through, with a hole in the top; other trays held partially disintegrated arms and legs. It appeared that those trays could hold three bodies at a time. And the odor, my God, the odor.

I had enough. I couldn't take it any more. I left the building with Bill and Tim close behind me. As we passed through the door someone from the company said, "the crematorium." Until then I had no idea what a crematorium was.

It dawned on me much later--the number of bodies which could be burned at one time, three bodies to a tray, at least thirty trays--and the Germans still couldn't keep up. The bodies on the stacks outside were growing at a faster rate than they could be burned. It was difficult to imagine what must have been going on.

Later that evening, sitting on the front steps of the barracks with a group of people from the company, Sergeant Blowers among us, the three of us started to pick up the parts of the story we had missed because we were on guard at the towers. All of the German guards had packed up and moved out about three hours before our arrival.

There were bits and pieces of personal gear still left around the barracks, but not much. We saw neither hide nor hair of those German guards. When the Germans left, the crematorium was still going full blast, burning up a storm, the chimney belching out that black smoke. Our First Sergeant, Sergeant Blowers, our Company Commander, and the Leader of the TD group found the source of the fuel, and played around with one thing and another until they figured out how to turn the damned thing off.

That was the start. That was just the "openers". There was more, but it was impossible to assimilate it all at once. General Patton had assigned us to this place for four days, ostensibly to keep the now-free prisoners off the roads needed to supply his troops who were racing through Germany at the end of the war.

The full explanation was given the prisoners, and there was no problem, they understood. Patton had assigned a whole field hospital to the place along with a big kitchen unit. He eventually sent in an engineering outfit with bulldozers to dig a mass grave for those bodies. We were doing everything we possibly could for the prisoners. Later on, when things became quieter, military government people arrived to help the prisoners get home--if there were homes for them to get to.

A little later in the evening the three of us walked back into the camp, passed by the crematorium and the stacks of bodies, and wandered into the camp proper. There were temporary lights strung around for the medics to do their work. The prisoners came up and surrounded us, moving with us as they jabbered, but they spoke a language we did not understand--they were probably speaking several languages we did not understand.

There was the slightest of communication. They gave way and moved along with us. We must have appeared as giants in their midst: we well-fed, healthy, strong, young men; they gaunt, shrunken, their ugly striped uniforms hanging on them.

They were jabbering, and we wanted to listen, to understand, but there seemed to be no way we could. After some moments we figured out they wanted our cigarettes. In no time we were out of them--they just disappeared. We had nothing else with us they really wanted, but they stuck with us and guided us to another set of buildings, which had the look of large barns with wide doors in the middle of the front.

Entering the first of these we found we were entering their home. There were stacks of bunks five or six high, crowded together with very little room between a bunk and the one above it. (It was my thought that one would have a rough time merely rolling over.) The bunks were much too short even for short people.

The lower bunks served as rungs of a ladder to the upper ones. How many hundreds of people slept in this one building was beyond me. Then there were all of those dead bodies outside that must have come from here. Where did the Germans get them all?

Just inside the door were people on the lower bunks so close to death they didn't have the strength to rise. They were, literally, skeletons covered with skin--nothing more than that--there appeared to be no substance to them. The next day when the press arrived, one of the photographers for LIFE magazine had one of the really bad ones propped up against the door frame in the daylight.

He took the photograph, but out of sight in the darkness of the building, behind the man, were the people propping him up. I have seen that photograph several times in the years since, and every time I see it my stomach rolls a little, my mind goes into some kind of a dance, and it takes me a little time to return to normal. There are still altogether too many things that flood my mind once a trigger is pulled.

Later we were told the medical unit was moving around searching for the most desperate cases, in order to get them to the doctor as quickly as possible. They told us the story of one prisoner who was so close to death that even thinned chicken broth was too rich for his stomach. The doctors were doing everything they could, trying mightily; but in too many cases they had no chance at all and would lose in spite of their best efforts.

We were about to do what Sergeant Blowers had told us to do--take a walk in the woods. We headed for the woods talking softly to each other, the talk full of wonderment--the hows, the whys. We had no answers. As limited as our combat experience had been, we had seen dead men, we had seen wounded men from both sides with the immediacy of battle, with no time for conjecture.

We had done what we could for the wounded and then had got on with the job that had to be done. None of us, no one in our company, even amongst those who had been the originals, was prepared for what we were now surrounded by. It was not "human". It did not seem real. But it was all too real, it was the only life that some of the prisoners had known for years. Maybe it was all too human. Maybe this is what we are.

Later that evening, a bunch of us from the company were sitting on the front steps of the barracks, talking. There were questions, far more questions than there were answers. Those of us assigned to the towers at the beginning had missed a great deal of what had gone on, and we were catching up.

Amongst other things, Sergeant Blowers was explaining our duties while we were here: we were to stand guard for four hours at a time, and then take eight hours off; there would be one of us in every other tower most of the way around the camp. We would be covering all of the holes we had ripped in the fence. The first platoon, ours, had the midnight-to-four, and the noon-to-four shifts.

Sergeant Blowers told us some things about the Commandant of Buchenwald and his wife. We could see their house down the hill through the leafless trees from our seats on the front steps. Blowers painted a picture of truly despicable human beings. The wife, Ilse Koch, favored jodhpurs, boots, and a riding crop.

He told us this story about her: Once, she ordered all of the Jewish prisoners in the camp stripped and lined up; she then marched down the rows of them, and, as she saw a tattoo she liked, she would touch that tattoo with her riding crop; the guards would take the man away immediately to the camp hospital where the doctors would remove the patch of skin with the tattoo, have it tanned, and patch it together with others to make lamp shades.

There were three of those lamp shades--the history books say there were two, but there were three. One of them disappeared shortly after we arrived. This may give you a glimmer of an idea of what Ilse Koch was like--and her husband--and the camp "doctors."

We learned that only a very few Jews remained at Buchenwald, most of them in terrible physical shape. The Jews who had been healthy, to any degree, had been marched away from the camp weeks before. No one knew why they had been taken away, or where they had been taken. Originally, in the camp, the Jews and the non-Jews were largely separated and given different food rations and different jobs to do.

Treatment of the prisoners varied also, depending on ethnic origin. There were a few women prisoners, but we wouldn't see them for a time as they had been taken immediately to the field hospital to be checked over and cleaned up. Those who were able began working with the American nurses or helping out in the kitchen.

They gave the impression they no longer felt like slave laborers; in fact, they seemed only too glad to assist. There were children prisoners, some of them born in the camp. The females had been forced into prostitution often (though not the Jews). We learned more from an American Lieutenant who had entered the camp later as an interpreter. Things that he had learned interviewing prisoners in the hospital.

378

After listening to all of this, a half dozen or so of us went down to the Camp Commandant's home, walked in, and looked around. It was a grand home, luxuriously furnished, but messy now from the many feet trudging through it all day long. We looked for the lamp shades-- we found only the lamp bases where they had been.

Then, since we were to go on guard duty from midnight to four in the morning, we thought a little sleep was in order, so we returned to the barracks, threw our blankets across our mattresses, crawled under them, and slept, or tried to sleep. My mind was full. Sleep did not come easily. Sergeant Blowers broke us out a little after eleven o'clock that night.

We gathered our equipment and piled into a truck and went around the watch towers, jumping out as we came to our assignments. I climbed the stairs to the top floor using the flashlight handed to me by the man I relieved. As I stood on the top floor looking out, I saw nothing. There was no electricity so the search lights in the tower didn't work.

I had with me my Garand rifle, the rifle belt with a full canteen hanging on it, a field jacket over my woolen shirt. The pockets of the field jacket were loaded: in the top left pocket was a toothbrush which I had quit using for its primary purpose once I started cleaning my rifle with it; there was a mess kit spoon right beside it, along with a pack of cigarettes and two or three cigars; in the top right pocket was another pack of cigarettes and some Hershey bars.

I started by stacking my rifle in the corner, took off my belt and put it on the table, and, leaning on the table, I started thinking about all of the things that had happened during the day. Strange things. Things I could not yet understand--could never understand. I thought about those things and questions entered my mind, but there were no answers. Finally I merely slumped and realized how good a cup of coffee would taste. I had my canteen cup.

There was water in my canteen. There were packets of instant coffee (horrible stuff) in my pocket along with packets of sugar. I had everything I needed for a cup of coffee except heat. With the help of a flashlight I started scrounging around, finding little wood chips all over the place. The trench knife from my belt helped me make some more of them, and I ended up with a tidy bunch of wood chips.

I built the fire right in the middle of the machine gun table, heated the water in my canteen cup and made myself a cup of coffee. After sweeping the fire from the table and stomping on the sparks, I sat on a corner of the table, lit a cigar, drank the coffee, and looked out into the darkness. Less than a half an hour later I saw a fire in Bill's tower and guessed that he had seen what I was up to and done the same thing.

The next morning while we were sipping coffee after breakfast, a great commotion broke out down at the gate. We wandered off in that direction, coffee cups in hand. A bright and shiny jeep came through the gate, with this fellow standing in front of the passenger seat, holding onto the windshield.

His helmet was gleaming and elaborately decorated, his uniform spic and span, his pistol highly polished and oddly shaped, and, by God, there he was: it was George Patton himself touring this place. From time to time the jeep would stop and he would ask questions. In front of the crematorium the jeep stopped, he alighted and walked inside.

He was out of sight for some minutes, appearing again with a very stiff back. Into the jeep and he was all over the place in just a few minutes. He passed us on the way out--and damn he looked mad--about as mad as I had ever seen anyone look. I would not have wanted to cross that man right then. The jeep sped back out the gate and on down the road and George just sat.

Now that we had gone through a tour of duty at the towers, we knew what it was we wanted to take along with us. I fully intended to load up with candy bars, instant cocoa, and a bunch of other good things to stash away in one of the tower cupboards.

Eventually Sergeant Blowers came down the hall, out the door, and onto the front steps with the rest of us. I got to my tower, crawled up the staircase, and relieved the fellow from the third platoon. I set all my things down and surveyed the scene in front of me. I stacked my rifle in the corner and threw my rifle belt on the machine gun table.

There was a tiny char mark on the table by now, the word apparently having been passed around. It was a warm afternoon so I took my jacket off, dropped it on the table and leaned on the ledge of the opening for a while. After a bit I crawled up on the table and sat on it cross-legged. I dug a cigar out of my jacket, lit it, and enjoyed it, and I studied the landscape around the camp.

There were some heavily wooded areas around the outside of the camp, and the spring weather was turning the leaf buds a fuzzy green color. I imagined it would be very beautiful there in the summer with all of the trees leafed out.

I was ruminating in this manner when I heard a tiny voice, and my attention came back to the inside of the camp. I could see nothing, but I heard the voice again, under me, down near the fence. I scrunched forward on the table to where I could see almost straight down. There, right in the middle of the hole in the fence, looking up, calling me, was this very small person.

I waved my arm at him letting him know that it was all right to come on through the fence, to come up the tower. He did so immediately. The sound of his footsteps coming up the stairs was almost instantaneous. I barely had time to get off the table and over to the stair opening before he was beside me.

He was young, very small, and he spoke no English. He was dressed in bits and pieces of everything, ragged at best, and very dirty. He chattered up a storm and I could not understand one word. First, I got him to slow down the talk, then I tried to speak to him, but he could not understand a word I said. We were at a temporary stalemate.

We started again from scratch, both of us deciding that names were the proper things with which to start, so we traded names. I no longer remember the name he taught me, and I wish so badly, so often, I could. Our conversation started with nouns, naming things, and progressed to simple verbs, actions, and we were busy with that. As we progressed I reached over into my field jacket to pull things out of the pocket to name. I came across a chocolate bar and taught him the word "candy".

He repeated it, and I corrected him. He repeated it again, and he had the pronunciation close. I tore the wrapper off the chocolate bar and showed him the candy. He was mystified. It meant nothing to him. He had no idea what it was or what he was to do with it. I broke off a corner and put it in my mouth and chewed it. I broke off another corner and handed it to him and he mimicked my actions. His eyes opened wide. It struck me that he had never tasted chocolate.

It was tough to imagine, but there it was. He took the rest of the candy bar slowly, piece by piece, chewed it, savored it. It took him a little while but he finished the candy bar, looking at me with wonderment the whole time. While he was eating the bar, I searched around for the old wrapper, found the word "chocolate " on it, pointed to the word, and pronounced the word "chocolate".

He worked on the correct pronunciation. I am sure that was the first candy the little fellow had ever had. He had no idea what candy was until then. We worked out words for those things close around us. He was learning a bit of English, but I was not learning a word of his language--I do not even know what language he spoke. This wasn't something that happened consciously, it was just something that happened.

I spent the rest of my four-hour tour with him. I pretty well ignored what happened in the rest of the camp. There was nothing much going on down in my corner, so it was easy to ignore. My whole world shrank to the inside of the fourth floor of the tower and the young boy. Toward the end of the tour, I found one of those blocks of compressed cocoa that came in the K-Rations in a pocket of my field jacket, and the two of us constructed a hot cup of cocoa for ourselves.

We used the same method I had used the night before to make a cup of coffee. A canteen cup is a rather large cup and the two of us shared it. On the first sip he looked at me with a large smile and said the word "chocolate". We were starting to communicate. I gave him other things from the K-Ration packages, among them a small can with cheese and bits of bacon, which we opened with the can opener I wore on my dog tag chain. This meant he had to study the dog tags. His curiosity was immense.

He ate the cheese mixture (which I ate only when I was very hungry), and sorted out the words "cheese" and "bacon", and he loved the stuff. It did not even begin to enter my mind that he might have been Jewish and shouldn't have been eating bacon. I made up my mind to really load up before I came to the tower the next day.

That's the way the tour went, and it was all so pleasant. The little fellow was a joy scampering around. I figured him to be somewhere between five and eight years old, but I was probably wrong, on the low side. Later, when I thought more about it, I realized whatever growing he had done had been on the rations of that camp.

No great growth could be expected from a diet like that. When we split at the end of the four hours, he pointed to my pack of cigarettes. My first thought was that I didn't want him to smoke them, but then I remembered the events yesterday in the camp when my pack of cigarettes simply disappeared. Cigarettes were for barter; they were exchange material. I had no idea how rich one was when one had a whole pack of cigarettes.

To these people cigarettes were money, and I was getting them free from PX rations. When we parted I loaded him up with candy bars and my extra pack of cigarettes. He had them all inside his shirt and went streaking back through the whole in the fence and on up the hill. After I was relieved and heading back up the hill, I saw Tim coming down the road behind me and I slowed until he caught up. When we got to Bill's tower, Bill was waiting for us, and the three of us walked up the road together.

As we approached the gate area, we noticed the place was in a kind of a mild uproar. The press people were still there, joined by a lot of big shots from the army. Buchenwald was filled with those who had to "spectate." People were walking around and through the aisles of those stacks of dead bodies. To me this was the final indignity.

It was an exhibition. God, help us. Those people in the stacks were dead, they were gone. Nothing could really hurt them further, but it hurt me that they were now an exhibition. The three of us at the gate stood there, looked, turned our backs, and walked away.

All of the way from the tower I had been telling Bill and Tim about the little kid. Bill had noticed the two of us in the tower. I'd had the kid standing on the table and had put my field jacket on him, which was much, much too large for him; then I put my steel helmet on his head, and the two of us giggled.

On the way back up the road our moods lightened a little with the stories about the little fellow, we had started to feel a little better. We got to the gate and saw the carnival atmosphere, and our good spirits vanished. Scowling, we quietly walked back to the barracks. We had to go near the Commandant's house, and all of the "tourists" were lined up to go through another "exhibit," where someone was busy telling "Ilse" stories. That was enough for me. I was glad to get back to the barracks.

We headed for the mess tent, talking about what had been going on all day long with the press and the visitors. Some of our guys had been disgusted by a bunch of nurses or WACs in their Class A uniforms taking pictures of the naked dead. It was not the display of the genitals that shook some of us up; it was that final indignity, the exhibition.

Some one mentioned, while we were eating, that the engineers would be here tomorrow to bury those poor people. That made me feel a little better; no one could hurt them anymore after their burial. The trays at the crematorium would be emptied also. It would not be the most desirable of burials, but we would be rid of part of the exhibit.

There was other talk too, and I was turning into one hell of a listener. It seemed that Patton had become so angry at what he had seen in the camp that he scooted into the nearest major town, Weimar, broke the mayor of the town out, and told him he wanted every citizen up the next morning, ready to march to through Buchenwald so as to see what the German people were responsible for. The engineers were not to bury the dead until after the grand tour by the German townspeople.

We heard stories that night from two professors who had been non-Jewish prisoners at Buchenwald for over four years. They were intelligent. They had seen and were aware of everything that had happened at the camp. We asked them questions and we were given answers. We were flooded with information.

There is no way I could present those stories as we heard them, chronologically, after this great a time. What I remember now are bits and pieces, and certain of those bits surface more rapidly than others.

We sat, that night, around the table on the second floor of Bill's tower and talked--Bill, Tim, the man from the third platoon, the two professor prisoners, and myself. In one way the talk was an interrogation: four of us with insatiable curiosities, two who could satisfy those curiosities. Four of us asking questions, two providing the answers.

There were times when we lit Sterno cans and made ourselves some instant coffee, but the talk never ceased. The four of us emptied our pockets of the little goodies we were carrying, spread them out on the table top, and made them available to everyone. We kept talking and time disappeared. The minds of the four of us grew and stretched in terms no psychoanalysts would ever be able to measure. Four hours of education happened that night which could have happened no place else.

Of the events at Buchenwald described by the two professors, I remember some. I told the two professors about the young person who had been at my tower the past afternoon, and described him as best I could. They thought they knew which of the young boys it was and believed he had been born at Buchenwald. The only life

387

he knew was that of the concentration camp. There was no way he could have known about chocolate candy before this afternoon. That flipped me.

One story: The German army had been losing men on the Russian front because they were freezing to death. Some had been still alive when brought to the field hospitals, but had died in spite of the best efforts of the German doctors. Those field hospitals had requested some research on how to revive human beings who were very nearly frozen to death, but were still alive.

The research had been done at Buchenwald. Groups of Jewish men had been taken outside on winter nights, stripped, and sprayed with a mist of water until they were nearly dead. They were then trundled into the hospital, and every effort was made to revive them. Every effort failed. The ungrateful Jewish prisoners just went ahead and died, in spite of the best efforts of German medicine at the time.

Finally, some bright medical type thought there might be a kind of animal heat that would revive them. They took one more group out, freezing them until they were nearly dead, brought them back into the hospital, and put them into bed with naked women. Their animal desires would revive them, or so the theory went. It goes without saying the experiment failed--again. The still ungrateful prisoners simply continued to die.

Another story: There had been a factory a couple of kilometers down the railroad line from Buchenwald that was manufacturing something that was in demand by the German government. It was not clear to me what the plant had been making, but, in any event, it was the place where most of the political prisoners worked.

388

Some Jewish prisoners worked there too, but they were only trusted with the menial jobs. One particular night our bombers flew over the camp to the factory, which they pulverized. They leveled it completely. Everyone working there was killed, but that didn't seem to matter to the two professors; not one bomb had missed the factory, not one bomb had fallen inside Buchenwald. The two professors thought that was remarkable--to be able to bomb with such precision. To listen to them was to get the feeling they believed it was a blessing to die in a bombing raid rather than in other circumstances at Buchenwald.

The dead were better off, and the factory was out of business also. The Germans had made no effort to rebuild it. It had all happened not too long before we arrived.

Another story (to me the most gruesome): German doctors at the camp were doing research on some human diseases. Groups of Jewish prisoners would be selected (which must have been some kind of an admission they were human beings) and inoculated with the diseases.

They would then be observed, and all of their reactions charted until death occurred. A post-mortem of the body would be done, and those organs affected by the disease would be preserved and stored. The doctors would then move onto another disease, repeating the process. A building in the camp, near the hospital, held all of those preserved specimens.

The two prisoners told us of the building and its location, how we could find it in the morning if we were so inclined. In that building were rooms devoted to each of the organs: a kidney room, a liver room, a heart room, etc. The two named some of the diseases studied, but I have forgotten (willfully?) the names.

Another story? No. About what they did with the women prisoners? No. I quit. No more. That was probably the most brutal night I have ever lived through. Enough. A major reason I need a catharsis.

The next morning we did a check on the building, and there they were. Rooms full of bottles of organs, all neatly and voluminously labeled. We turned and walked away. I had had enough. Any prisoner could tell me anything he wished from now on, and I would believe. That building was enough.

After seeing the organ building and my walk in the woods, I still had a few hours before my next tour of guard duty. I spent the time straightening my gear out and loading up the pockets of my field jacket. I expected the young boy again, and I wanted to be able to give him everything I could.

After a quickly gobbled lunch at the mess tent, we took off for our towers and relieved the third platoon men. I had barely reached the top floor when the young fellow came running up the steps. I hadn't seen him out in the field on the other side of the fence, but there he had been watching, waiting for me.

The first thing he got was another chocolate bar, and he took his time with that while we worked some more on our language. We made another cup of cocoa, this time over a Sterno can rather than a fire on the table. I tried to give him some boxes of K-Rations, but, hell, he was eating better than that at the mess tent. Maybe those K-

Rations would be used for barter--that was all right with me. I had more cigarettes to give him when we parted too.

I saw a gang of about thirty or forty of the prisoners still wearing their striped garb. They were heading back toward the camp, which mystified me, because they should not have been outside of the camp in the first place. As they passed the tower I noticed that one of them, one in the middle of the group, had his hands tied behind his back, and a rope tied around his neck.

He was being led back into the prison. The commotion was centered around that individual. The little fellow in the tower with me became all excited and tried to explain things to me. After a bit, I got the idea that the person on the end of the rope had been one of the German guards at the prison camp, and these people found him in a small village near the camp. They were bringing him back.

It was then, too, that I noticed a lot of action up in the camp. Something important was happening there. People were scurrying about, and most of the prisoners were headed toward the gate. I was too far down the hill to discern the nature of what was going on, but I was betting it was the people from Weimar touring the camp after being marched out from the city. It turned out to be a good guess.

An interpreter met them at the gate, marched them around, and, according to the word I heard later, carefully explained in great detail what had been going on in the camp. In fact all the interpreter would have needed would have been a few words and a pointed finger.

The evidence was all there; the massive pile of bodies still stacked, just as they were when we first found them; the doors in the crematorium now all open, and more of the trays pulled out with their contents visible. The German people were seeing what had been going on in that place all of those years. Now we could bury the bodies.

After the tour had been administered, the group headed back out of the gate and back down the road to Weimar. There was a large patrol of our troops marching them, some on either side of the road. As they were moving back to Weimar, not even out of sight of the camp, a number of Germans in the group found something to laugh about. The commander of the American troops heard them and became livid with anger.

He turned them around and marched them, then and there, back through the camp again. This time they went through much more slowly. By the time they returned to the camp the bodies in the stacks were already being loaded on to trucks to be carried away to the mass grave. This time, on the march home to Weimar, there was no laughter. The next day we heard that after returning to their town, the mayor of Weimar and his wife both committed suicide.

The ovens were soon cleaned out, and the bodies were almost all gone, being buried over the top of the hill where the engineers had dug a monstrous trench. The Buchenwald prisoners had found one of their German guards in a nearby village dressed in civilian clothes, and they had him now in a cell in one of the buildings and were interrogating him.

No one knew how this gang of prisoners had been able to sneak out the hole in the fence to get to the village. We walked through the gate to the door that opened to the cell area. It was crowded and the onlookers parted to let the three of us through, and we went to the door of the cell. The German was standing at attention in the middle of the room and was being peppered with questions that we did not understand. The answers were all monosyllabic.

Tears were coming down his cheeks. One of the Buchenwald prisoners seemed to be in charge, but a group of them were participating in the interrogation. The one who appeared to be in charge also appeared to be one calm individual. The three of us watched, but we couldn't understand what was being said, so we turned and left. The crowd parted again to let us through. A most welcome sight to my eyes was the absence of the stack of bodies as I came through the door from the cell area.

Back inside the cell the former Buchenwald prisoners, and their current prisoner presented a riveting scene: The hands of the German were untied, and, in them was placed a stout piece of rope. He was being given instructions, and, as we watched, it wasn't long before I and the people who had come with me realized he was being told how to tie a noose in the rope.

The German guard was corrected three or four times, and had to undo some of his work to re-do it correctly. When he was finished, he had a very proper hangman's noose, thirteen turns of the rope and all. A table was brought to the center of the room and placed under a very strong looking electrical fixture.

The guard was assisted on to the table and instructed to fix the rope to the light fixture. Finishing that he was told to put all of his weight on the rope and lift his feet. The fixture held. The guard was told to place the noose over his head, around his neck, and to draw the noose fairly snug. Then he was told to place his hands behind his back and his wrists were tied together.

The table was moved until he barely stood on its edge. He couldn't see that--his eyes were unhooded and open, but the noose kept him from looking down. He was talked to some more and then he jumped. He was caught before all of his weight was on the rope, and they set him back on the table. The next time he stepped gently off the end, and the table was quickly slid away from him and out of his reach, and he dangled there. He slowly strangled. His face went through a variety of colors before he hung still.

My stomach did not want to hold food any longer. I turned and walked away, the rest of our guys following me. The Buchenwald prisoners stayed on to view their handiwork.

I walked through the crowd, out the door, through the gate, on up to the barracks, and I didn't say a word. The others with me didn't speak either. It was murder; there can be no doubt of that. The Buchenwald prisoners never touched the rope after it was placed in the German's hands. They did not tie the noose, nor did they fix it to the ceiling.

They did not place the rope around the man's neck. They did not pull the table out from under him. In one sense, they had not committed murder; rather, the

German had committed suicide. A sophist could rationalize that one I suspect.

That was not what was bothering me, however. I had the ability and the means to stop the whole thing, and I did not. Neither did my companions. Here we were-- five or six of us--fully armed with semi-automatic rifles, and we did not make the Buchenwald prisoners stop. We let them continue.

In one way, we sanctioned the event. Ever since that day I have been convincing myself that I understood why the Buchenwald prisoners did what they did. I had witnessed their agonies. I had wondered how human beings could treat other human beings as the prisoners at Buchenwald had been treated. I felt I knew why the prisoners of Buchenwald did what they did - so I did not stop them.

I have become some kind of a sophist for myself now. I could have stopped the whole action, and I did not. I have had that under my hat for the past forty-six years. Now I have written it. I have acknowledged it. Maybe it will go away. There are so many things from that week I wish would go away, things I wish could be scrubbed from my memory. When we returned to the barracks we did not tell anyone what we had witnessed.

I was not about to sleep, however. I flopped on my bunk without a thought of my tiny bunk mates, the bugs--I merely lay there. My eyes were closed, but my mind wasn't. I tried to think of other things, but it was impossible. I reviewed in my mind the multiple things the Buchenwald prisoners had gone through, the length of time they had been living through hell, and I didn't have to rationalize their actions.

Hell, I knew why they were doing what they did. That train of thought took me further and further from my own guilt, and, in a little while, I was absolved. At least, as absolved as I was ever going to be. Absolved enough to be a little more comfortable with myself. That was enough for then.

The bunch of us walked around to our towers and some of us walked very quietly. Others were full of talk about tomorrow. The electricity had been restored in all of the towers, but I didn't bother with it as I entered mine--I knew my way around. Upstairs, I relieved the guy before me and put my rifle over in the corner, threw the rifle belt under the table, crawled on the table, lit a cigar, and my thoughts continued.

I thought of my German heritage, my Grandfather Hugo who had come from to the United States from Germany while he was still a teenager, my mother's grandparents who had come over from Germany long before that, my mother who had grown up early in this century in a small town in Minnesota, where there were two catholic churches: one for the Germans, the other for the Irish.

They were only about a block apart from each other, each having its own grade school. My mother had attended the German school, and the only language spoken through the fourth grade had been German. When I was very young she had taught me how to count in German, and how to sing the German alphabet. She also taught me a very few words in German, everyday kinds of words which I still remembered. Three quarters of me was from German background, solid German stock. Pictures of the formidable Hugo had always been around me as I was growing up.

I wondered...Suppose my ancestors had not come to the United States; suppose they had stayed in Germany, and, through some fluke, the two people who had become my mother and father had met, and I had been born a German citizen. What would I be like? Would I be like the people who had instituted and guarded a place like Buchenwald? Could I have been that?

Would I have been in the German army? The answer to the last question is obvious--certainly I would have been in the German army. But what kind of work would I have done? I hoped that I would not have been like most of the Germans I had seen. I could have accepted a likeness to some members of the German army whom we had fought, but there were many I would have been uncomfortable with. Much of what I had seen ran counter to everything my mother had brought me up believing.

This whole situation would have appalled her. I have never ever told her, or my father either, most of these stories about Buchenwald. I did not feel it necessary. They knew early on that I had been there, and they took LIFE magazine. They had been made aware, like most people in the United States, of what had gone on.
During these past forty-six years, these memories have been creeping out of my mind, leaving me with sleepless nights afterwards. Never the whole story at once. Until now. I relive that night sitting on that machine gun bench, smoking a cigar, staring at the darkness. That night I sat in the dark and went through two or three cigars, and several cigarettes.

I stared out at the darkness, and there were two reasons for not seeing anything: my eyes couldn't see anything, and my mind wouldn't see anything. My thoughts kept me too busy. They do now also.

I saw the lights up in the camp, but, at that time of night, nothing distracting was going on. My relief arrived, but I didn't notice him until he was on the way up the stairs, turning the lights on as he came. By the time he reached the top floor I had my belt back on, my rifle in my hands, and was standing by the stair opening.

Nothing had happened during my shift, and that was what I reported to him when he reached the top. I walked down, and caught up to Bill on the road. The two of us walked slowly until Tim caught up to us. As we all three walked together our only conversation was of our departure later in the morning.

I was nineteen, Bill and Tim were eighteen-- chronologically anyway. We had aged years in a few short hours." [25]

Final Thoughts

I wish I was able to tell you that the knowledge you have learned from this book will never be needed by you. I wish that I was able to wish you a long and comfortable life too. I wish more than these though that you have paid attention to what you have just read and are ready to apply these lessons to your own personal circumstances.

It is foolish to never prepare for those things that could occur in your life. It is beyond foolish to see these things approaching and ignore them. You then have to ask yourself if you are a foolish person.

When the winter time is coming, do you prepare? Do you cut down the trees before winter so that you will have firewood? Do you store up for yourself the food you will need to survive the coming cold months? Do you make sure that you will have the winter clothing and coats you will need to protect yourself against the weather?

Then likewise you prepare for war.

As I had told you in the beginning of this book, all of the information you will need to know in order to plan for war is not, and cannot, be contained in just one book. There are many books, many sources of information and many people you will have to resource in order to make your decisions and your preparations.

There are many new skills that you will have to master ahead of time too, but will also serve you well even during times of peace.

Every country, especially the United States, have very strict laws regarding the making and using of forged documents, be very aware of these laws! But the histories of war have likewise shown the value of these very things in saving many lives. Think very hard about these words and include them into your preparations.

As you close this book a new part of your life is going to begin. You are either going to heed these lessons and instructions and begin your preparations, or you are going to do nothing. But one thing you will never be able to say again is that you did not know of these things.

The War Prayer
By: Mark Twain

"It was a time of great and exalting excitement. The country was up in arms, the war was on, in every breast burned the holy fire of patriotism; the drums were beating, the bands playing, the toy pistols popping, the bunched firecrackers hissing and sputtering; on every hand and far down the receding and fading spreads of roofs and balconies a fluttering wilderness of flags flashed in the sun; daily the young volunteers marched down the wide avenue gay and fine in their new uniforms, the proud fathers and mothers and sisters and sweethearts cheering them with voices choked with happy emotion as they swung by; nightly the packed mass meetings listened, panting, to patriot oratory which stirred the deepest deeps of their hearts and which they interrupted at briefest intervals with cyclones of applause, the tears running down their cheeks the while; in the churches the pastors preached devotion to flag and country and invoked the God of Battles, beseeching His aid in our good cause in outpouring of fervid eloquence which moved every listener.

It was indeed a glad and gracious time, and the half dozen rash spirits that ventured to disapprove of the war and cast a doubt upon its righteousness straightway got such a stern and angry warning that for their personal safety's sake they quickly shrank out of sight and offended no more in that way.

Sunday morning came-next day the battalions would leave for the front; the church was filled; the volunteers were there, their faces alight with material dreams-visions of a stern advance, the gathering momentum, the rushing charge, the flashing sabers, the flight of the foe, the tumult, the enveloping smoke, the fierce pursuit, the surrender!-then home from the war, bronzed heros, welcomed, adored, submerged in golden seas of glory! With the volunteers sat their dear ones, proud, happy, and envied by the neighbors and friends who had no sons and brothers to send forth to the field of honor, there to win for the flag or, failing, die the noblest of noble deaths.

The service proceeded; a war chapter from the Old Testament was read; the first prayer was said; it was followed by an organ burst that shook the building, and with one impulse the house rose, with glowing eyes and beating hearts, and poured out that tremendous invocation – "God the all-terrible! Thou who ordainest, Thunder thy clarion and lightning thy sword!"

Then came the "long" prayer. None could remember the like of it for passionate pleading and moving and beautiful language. The burden of its supplication was that an ever--merciful and benignant Father of us all would watch over our noble young soldiers and aid, comfort, and encourage them in their patriotic work; bless them, shield them in His mighty hand, make them strong and confident, invincible in the bloody onset; help them to crush the foe, grant to them and to their flag and country imperishable honor and glory -

An aged stranger entered and moved with slow and noiseless step up the main aisle, his eyes fixed upon the minister, his long body clothed in a robe that reached to his feet, his head bare, his white hair descending in a frothy cataract to his shoulders, his seamy face unnaturally pale, pale even to ghastliness. With all eyes following him and wondering, he made his silent way;

without pausing, he ascended to the preacher's side and stood there, waiting.

With shut lids the preacher, unconscious of his presence, continued his moving prayer, and at last finished it with the words, uttered in fervent appeal, "Bless our arms, grant us the victory, O Lord our God, Father and Protector of our land and flag!"

The stranger touched his arm, motioned him to step aside -- which the startled minister did -- and took his place. During some moments he surveyed the spellbound audience with solemn eyes in which burned an uncanny light; then in a deep voice he said

"I come from the Throne-bearing a message from Almighty God!" The words smote the house with a shock; if the stranger perceived it he gave no attention. "He has heard the prayer of His servant your shepherd and grant it if such shall be your desire after I, His messenger, shall have explained to you its import-that is to say, its full import. For it is like unto many of the prayers of men, in that it asks for more than he who utters it is aware of-except he pause and think."

"God's servant and yours has prayed his prayer. Has he paused and taken thought? Is it one prayer? No, it is two- one uttered, the other not. Both have reached the ear of His Who hearth all supplications, the spoken and the unspoken. Ponder this-keep it in mind. If you beseech a blessing upon yourself, beware! lest without intent you invoke a curse upon a neighbor at the same time. If you pray for the blessing of rain upon your crop which needs it, by that act you are possibly praying for a curse upon some neighbor's crop which may not need rain and can be injured by it."

"You have heard your servant's prayer-the uttered part of it. I am commissioned by God to put into words the other part of it-that part which the pastor, and also you in your hearts, fervently prayed silently. And ignorantly and unthinkingly? God grant that it was so! You heard these words: 'Grant us the victory, O Lord our God!' That is sufficient. The whole of the uttered prayer is compact into those pregnant words. Elaborations were not necessary. When you have prayed for victory you have prayed for many unmentioned results which follow victory-must follow it, cannot help but follow it. Upon the listening spirit of God the Father fell also the unspoken part of the prayer. He commandeth me to put it into words. Listen!"

"O Lord our Father, our young patriots, idols of our hearts, go forth to battle-be Thou near them! With them, in spirit, we also go forth from the sweet peace of our beloved firesides to smite the foe. O Lord our God, help us to tear their soldiers to bloody shreds with our shells; help us to cover their smiling fields with the pale forms of their patriot dead; help us to drown the thunder of the guns with the shrieks of their wounded, writhing in pain; help us to lay waste their humble homes with a hurricane of fire; help us to wring the hearts of their unoffending widows with unavailing grief; help us to turn them out roofless with their little children to wander unfriended the wastes of their desolated land in rags and hunger and thirst, sports of the sun flames of summer and the icy winds of winter, broken in spirit, worn with travail, imploring Thee for the refuge of the grave and denied it-for our sakes who adore Thee, Lord, blast their hopes, blight their lives, protract their bitter pilgrimage, make heavy their steps, water their way with their tears, stain the white snow with the blood of their wounded feet! We ask it, in the spirit of

love, of Him Who is the Source of Love, and Who is ever-faithful refuge and friend of all that are sore beset and seek His aid with humble and contrite hearts. Amen."
(After a pause)

"Ye have prayed it; if ye still desire it, speak! The messenger of the Most High waits."

It was believed afterward that the man was a lunatic, because there was no sense in what he said." [26]

References:

[1] Brigham Young University/Harold B. Lee Library/World War I Document Archive

[2] What is Fascism? By Laura Dawn Lewis (used by permission of author)

[3] The 14 Defining Characteristics of Fascism by Dr. Lawrence Britt (used by permission of author)

[4]United States Militarism by John Roberts (used by permission of author)

[5] Diary from Baghdad

[6] Closure Diary 11 December 1996 "Settlers killed in bypass road attack" (used by permission of author)

[7] Ehrlich, Blake, Resistance France, 1940-1945, Boston, Mass.: Little Brown and Company. 1965.

Lusseyran, Jacques, And There Was Light, New York: Little Brown, 1963

Perrault, Gille & Azema, Pierre, Paris Under The Occupation New York: The Vendome Press, 1989.

Pryce-Jones, David, Paris in the Third Reich: A History of the German Occupation, 1940-1944 New York: Holt Rinehart and Winston, 1983.

Shiber, Etta with Anne and Paul Dupre, Paris Underground New York: Charles Scribner's Sons, 1943.

[8] Citizenship and Immigration statistics 1987-2001, Canadian Department of Immigration.

[9] Public Works and Government Services Canada

[10] Embassy of Paraguay

[11] American Refugee Committee

[12] Bristol Alive Presented by Team DISCOVERY Bristol Central High School Bristol, CT

[13] Holocaust Survivors Organization http://www.holocaustsurvivors.org

[14] Holocaust Survivors Organization http://www.holocaustsurvivors.org

[15] Holocaust Survivors Organization http://www.holocaustsurvivors.org

[16]http://www.snipercountry.com

[17] The Avalon Project at Yale Law School

[18] Human Rights Watch Organization

[19] World Wide Words, Michael Quinion

[20] Escape or Die , Authentic Stories of , The R.A.F. Escaping Society , By Paul Brickhill, Published by Evans Brothers Limited, London, 1952.

[21] The Underground EconomyHans F. SennholzCopyright © 1984 by the Ludwig von Mises Institute.

[22] US Government documents and open source/public domain material.

[23] Internet Armory LLC

[24] A Gulag and Holocaust Memoir of Janina Sulkowska-Gladun

[25]Liberation of Buchenwald by: Harry J. Herder, Jr.

[26] Mark Twain, "The War Prayer"

About the Authors

Sorcha Faal is a researcher and author who goes beyond the simple explanations used to explain today's issues. *"Life is meant to be more than accepting our world as separate pieces; everyone must see the interconnectedness of everything."*

Sorcha and many others believe that we are entering a Century of great change, not only for our hearts and minds, but perhaps for our very souls also. Like many others also around the world, and from many countries, Sorcha joins the effort to educate as many as possible towards these events so that they will not become surprised, or be led into despair.

David Booth is an internationally known psychic, researcher, and author who has appeared on numerous television (BBC, In Search Of, 20/20, etc.) and radio programs and whose unique life story has been featured in numerous magazine articles, books, and websites.

He also remains to this day the only person in the world to have had a pre-cognitive experience fully documented prior to the event by a government agency.

WWW.WhatDoesItMean.Com